SUNY series in Hindu Studies

Wendy Doniger, *editor*

CATHERINE BENTON

GOD of DESIRE

Tales of Kāmadeva in Sanskrit Story Literature

STATE UNIVERSITY OF NEW YORK PRESS

Published by
STATE UNIVERSITY OF NEW YORK PRESS
ALBANY

Printed in the United States of America

For information, address
State University of New York Press
194 Washington Avenue, Suite 305, Albany, NY 122010-2384

Production, Laurie Searl
Marketing, Michael Campochiaro

Library of Congress Cataloging-in-Publication Data

Benton, Catherine.
God of desire : tales of Kāmadeva in Sanskrit story literature / Catherine Benton.
p. cm. -- (SUNY series in Hindu studies)
Includes translations from Sanskrit.
Includes bibliographical references and index.
ISBN 0-7914-6565-9 (hardcover : alk. paper)
1. Kāma (Hindu deity) in literature. 2. Desire--Religious aspects--Hinduism.
3. Sanskrit literature--History and criticism. I. Title. II. Series.
BL1225.K36B46 2005
294.5′2113--dc22

2004028953

10 9 8 7 6 5 4 3 2 1

For my parents

Rosemarie and Edwin J. Benton

Contents

Illustrations

Introduction

Chapter One

Chapter Seven

Acknowledgments

This project has evolved through many forms, beginning with a graduate student's attraction to a handsome figure carrying a sticky sugarcane bow and scented flower arrows trailing with honeybees. This curiosity became a quest for unfamiliar stories in neglected Sanskrit manuscripts, and eventually the framework for a doctoral dissertation. Then as these tales and images were filtered through the questions of many undergraduate students, the narratives of Kāmadeva led to a fascination with the complexities of human nature as expressed in temple art. Throughout this process, many friends and colleagues have supported me.

After reading the very first drafts, Wendy Doniger saw enough promise to encourage me to keep researching, reading the texts, and writing. For her generosity many years ago, inviting me to read Sanskrit texts with her on Sunday afternoons and mentoring my dissertation process at another university, as well as her unwavering confidence and friendship over the years, I am deeply appreciative. From Wendy, I learned not only how to connect more deeply with Sanskrit story literature but also how to nurture talent and creativity in my own students.

Three people who edited chapters at different stages, my sister, Susan Benton, and two friends, Carol Slavin and JoAnn Crawford, helped me speak more clearly in these pages. Their careful attention to detail and artistic sensibilities allowed me to unravel the teachings of Kāmadeva and his stories without losing the poetry of the Sanskrit images. As I worked through Sanskrit manuscripts early on, Larry deVries, a meticulous Sanskritist and insightful teacher, walked me through the layers of double entendre that Indian sages had cleverly imbedded in the language of the tales. He will recognize several of the tales in this book.

Several people in India helped me think more carefully about desire through the course of this project. However, given the polarized and personal nature of current political tensions in India, I will not thank these Indian colleagues, mentors, and friends by name. Out of concern for their welfare, I thank them here without identifying home places or positions. Nonetheless, I am truly grateful for their generosity in sharing their expertise and insights. Their knowledge of the nuances imbedded in the Sanskrit tales and narrative images carved on temple walls deepened my understanding of these verbal and visual texts. Over the years, their warm friendships have given me a second home in India.

Colleagues at Lake Forest College, the Associated Colleges of the Midwest, and ASIANetwork, have been generous in providing me with opportunities not only to return to India but to engage in serious conversation in the United States about learning and teaching other views of the world. My colleagues' continued support for India studies as an integral part of the liberal arts has allowed me to continue exploring the richness of the Indian religious traditions within the context of liberal learning.

Finally, I thank my husband, Bob, for thoughtfully materializing countless dinners while I wrote, and for grounding me with his perceptive, bone-tickling humor—and steady love.

Introduction

STORIES EXTERNALIZE THE INTERNAL COMPLEXITIES OF DESIRE

In the vast flow of Indian oral and written narratives, the god of desire appears as the handsome and charming deity who arouses passion in all living beings. This god of desire is known as *Kāmadeva,* literally the god (*deva*) of desire/passion (*kāma*). Just as passion forms the backdrop for good stories everywhere, the passion evoked by Kāmadeva promises captivating and amusing drama, as well as an exploration of the myriad ethical and philosophical questions raised by desire.

This book offers a collection of stories involving Kāmadeva from the Sanskrit story tradition. Analyzing these stories individually and as a whole highlights their common patterns, as well as shared themes and perspectives. My search for Kāmadeva tales led me not only to a number of variant tales, but also to several obscure rituals in which Kāma is propitiated, varied iconographic representations, and Buddhist texts which present Kāma as the embodiment of all that lures would-be buddhas away from enlightenment. Using these tales of love-struck gods, angry curses, and passionate seekers of enlightenment to structure the book, I have focused specifically on how these stories function as vehicles for teaching about desire. Tales of Kāmadeva in some guise form the core of each chapter.

Stories effectively preserve cultural and religious worldviews and their corresponding systems of ethical behavior. Teachers and elders around the world have used narratives as pedagogical devices, allowing the tales, rather than the humble teller of the tales, to shape attitudes, curb behaviors and set social limits. Indian *kathā,* or story literature, is one of the richest and most colorful of this genre of didactic storytelling.

The stories of Kāmadeva express a myriad of Indian perspectives on the nature of desire, addressing obvious but complex questions: What is desire? What fuels its power? What "turns on" desire? Where does it reside? How does it disappear? What makes desire so pushy, so overwhelming? Is it possible to escape the clutches of desire and remain human? In English and in Sanskrit, poets and playwrights and storytellers speak of the heat of passion and its opposite, love grown cold. But what constitutes this phenomenon that engenders both human strength and frailty?

Rather than a linear approach of straightforward questions and answers, stories speak at once to many levels of human experience, offering metaphors in endless shades of color. Stories present philosophical and psychological questions in a rich complexity that invites understanding beyond logical analysis. Carefully observing and truthfully mirroring human behavior, stories follow a careful logic of their own, internally consistent and coherent though filled with paradox and irony—delighting in making the seen and unseen switch places. Although stories are told in words, they aim for the gut, evoking smiles and nods of agreement rather than analytical responses. Given this mode of communicating, storytelling is an ideal vehicle for exploring the amorphous phenomenon of desire that celebrates life even as it tyrannizes.

The Indian tale of Brahmā's creation of Kāmadeva quite literally gives the experience of desire a face, an externalized form with whom we can debate and converse. Brahmā's creation of Kāmadeva allows us to project desire outside ourselves as a separate entity, an adversary to conquer, a partner to rebuke and blame, as we shift responsibility for our actions to this external force. On a more philosophical level, the embodiment of this human element allows for discourse about the function and range of desire without being pedantic or categorical. In the genre of story, Kāmadeva can speak for himself, as he does in the "Kāmagītā," (Song of Kāma), a passage from the *Mahābhārata* in which Kāma mocks the arrogance of those who think themselves beyond his reach. Kāmadeva's song describes how easily his arrows destroy beings who do not understand and respect the depth of his power.

Such dialogues between "the human being" and "his or her desire" create a delightful literature, but more importantly offer commentary on being human. Using the externalized figure of desire, the storyteller can move easily between scenarios of wrestling with and reveling in desire, examining each from different angles. Why am I irresistibly drawn to her? Why am I incensed by his words? Why is it so difficult to turn off anger, frustration, remorse? What draws me into a burning building looking for my friend? Why do I replay the same tension-filled argument over and over? Who, or what, is really in control?

The storyteller explores all these questions, careful to describe a Kāmadeva whose behavior is consistent with the workings of ordinary human desire. Indeed, only when audience members see their own desiring reflected in the antics of Kāmadeva do the stories work. Operating within limits defined by the reaches of human behavior, Kāmadeva presents us with an often comic performance that invites us to see the excesses and limits of our own passions.

Indian stories do *not* teach that Kāma's power is uncontrollable, but rather that human beings must respect the pervasive and deep nature of his power in order to balance it with other elements. In fact, the stories emphasize that while too much desire will cause the scales to tip, no desire at all will also create an imbalance. Kāma dies in the central story involving his struggle with Śiva, but is resuscitated out of his own ashes so that life can continue. A world without Kāmadeva is shown repeatedly to be barren, dry, leafless—indeed, unbearable.

As noted earlier, each chapter of this book is focused around a particular story, and each of these stories is discussed within the textual and religious tradition which produced it. In presenting these stories about Kāmadeva, my primary intent has been to present the Indian tradition's understanding of their meaning. To this end, Indian commentaries on the stories and discussions with colleagues in India have been most helpful. Although I have lived and worked in India for various periods over the past twenty-five years, I am always aware of the need to adjust my lenses, inevitably tinted by my own experiences and cultural frames. Imbedded within every culture are assumptions about what constitutes reality, assumptions that differ significantly around the globe. Acknowledging these differences, the goal of this book is to provide access to the tales of the god of desire in translations from the Sanskrit texts and an analysis of these tales within the context of Indian themes and perspectives.

The stories of Kāmadeva offer authentic perspectives that challenge us to explore new boundaries for desire and offer new vantages from which to view ourselves.

SEXUAL DESIRE (KĀMA) AS PARADIGM FOR GENERIC DESIRE (KĀMA)

The god Kāmadeva is a minor god within the Hindu pantheon. There are no temples to Kāmadeva, no *mūrtis* (images) of Kāmadeva sold for the kitchen shrine, no devotees singing his praises or performing *pūjās* (offerings) to Kāmadeva in contemporary Indian religious practice. At the same time, the name of the god and the sensuality and sexuality he represents are familiar to most people. Indeed, the most common word for passion/lust/desire in Hindi is *kām,* the shortened form of the Sanskrit *kāma.* People know Kāmadeva through stories.

Who is this god whose name means desire? Who is he in the earliest literature of the Vedas[1] and the classical literature of the purāṇas? In other words, who is Kāmadeva in the story literature of India? What do the stories of Kāmadeva tell us about how the tradition understands desire? How do the tales admonish us to behave when we feel ourselves slipping under the spell of desire? What consequences are in store for us, and what rewards? How do the gods become entangled in the complex patterns spun out of colorful strands of unbearably intense longings woven into the fabric of dharmic responsibility and karmic consequence? How do the gods suffer and cope? How do humans?

Kāma as sexual desire in the Indian religious tradition is the paradigm for all forms of desire, all forms of wanting/longing/craving.[2] Sexual desire is used as the particular form of the more general category because sexual desire is "wanting" in its most forceful, its most powerful guise. If desire can be controlled in its sexual form as sparked by the arrows of Kāmadeva, it can be controlled in other parts of life. Within the setting of a story, sexual desire is clearly recognizable, rarely completely extinguished, and fun to exploit as characters become bumbling fools; in short, a good attention-getter, guaranteed to keep audience interest.

But presenting sexuality per se is *not* the purpose of Kāmadeva tales in Indian religious literature. The escapades of Kāmadeva are meant to take us beyond sexuality to the broader category of generic desire, a concept more like the Buddhist *tṛṣṇa* (thirst or craving) than the *śṛṅgāra rasa* ("taste" of sensual/sexual passion) of classical Sanskrit drama and poetry—though the Sanskrit word *kāma* connotes both tṛṣṇa and śṛṅgāra. Desire in its sexual form is understood to be one of the strongest kāmas human beings experience. The stories of desire are meant to guide listeners beyond the sexuality embodied in Kāmadeva to a deeper understanding of the nature of desire in its myriad human manifestations.

Kāma holds a prominent place within śāstric literature as one of the three *puruṣārthas,* or "aims of life."[3] A philosopher, B. G. Gokhale discusses kāma as a puruṣārtha, describing it as that which gives pleasure. Gokhale cites early visitors to India who remarked on the different ways that people, noble and common, enjoyed the pursuit of kāma: finery and ornaments, precious stones, ornamented clothing, cosmetics, sandalwood paste, garments smoked in incense, garlands, spiced betel leaf to perfume the mouth, rich food, liquor, and festivals.[4] The pursuit of kāma, according to Gokhale and the examples he cites, is not limited to amorous adventures, but indicates rather a wide range of objects which afford pleasure, and are thus desired.

Dipankar Chatterjee, in an article titled "Towards a Better Understanding of Indian Ethics," describes each puruṣārtha as the *way* one is interested in pursuing a goal. The "kāma way" of pursuing a goal involves taking "interest in something in an involved and passionate manner, at least partly for its own sake. . . . Objectives are called kāma (meaning passionately desired) objectives because their being objects of interest is due to their being *desired* by one (but not in a fleeting or idle manner)."[5] For example, when one desires money for its own sake, money becomes a "kāma interest."

Karl Potter, discussing the three puruṣārthas from the point of view of the Sanskrit philosophical texts, describes kāma as an "attitude of passionate concern toward anything in the world," marked by "an element of possessiveness in the concern one has for the object of one's attentions, coupled with a partial identification of oneself with that object."[6] Potter goes on to describe relationships with both things and people as proceeding from a kāma attitude. Although kāma is often understood to connote only sexual desire, Potter points out that kāma has a much broader application in the philosophical texts.

> When the Indians describe kāma in terms of sexual relations they do not mean to restrict the operation of this attitude to just those objects with which one can come into a sexual relationship, but are rather pointing to sexual relationships as typically involving instances of the taking of this kind of attitude.[7]

Reflecting this broader understanding of kāma, the stories of the purāṇas focus on sexual relationships as a clear example of the attitude Potter calls kāma operating in the world. The puranas explore kāma as sexual desire in order to understand the flash points and subtle influences of this kāma attitude.

The narratives paint a picture of a deity who embodies desire, an athletic bowman who uses his perfect marksmanship to evoke passionate longing in all creatures. We hear Kāma's arrows whiz by, fragrant with the compelling and confusing feelings of falling in love, while we observe the god himself indulging in the delights of passion with his wives and other women. Ever the ladies' man, Kāmadeva is mischievous and daring, athletic and sensuous, inspiring hope and longing in men and women, indeed in all creatures of air and land. Paradoxically, Kāmadeva is both avoided and adored. His wives worship him of course, but those seeking to kindle passion in a would-be lover also perform rituals of devotion to secure his help. Yet others run from Kāma's searing arrows. Grieving lovers know that Kāma's arrows bring only more tears of longing.

STORIES MOLD WORLDVIEW

As noted earlier, stories in all cultures act as molders of behavior, maintainers of cultural values, and preservers of societal order. We tell our own stories to one another for comfort and laughter, and to remind ourselves how to behave. We recite stories to children to transform them into the next preservers of society and culture. We sing stories to dance them into bodies and hearts. Stories reflect, form, and reinforce particular views of the world.

Well crafted structures, stories from other peoples' cultures also offer us a bridge into other ways of explaining the world. When we learn another culture's stories, we learn to understand the people who live that culture. For a moment, we see through their eyes, hear through their ears. Gradually this effort to look through the eyes of other people enriches and enlarges the image we see with our own eyes.

As a child, I grew up hearing my grandmother's tales of her mother's native Ireland and an Irish view of life she had brought with her to a midwestern city on the Mississippi. With her daughter, my mother, I became mesmerized with books as wonderful vehicles for more stories. Following my father, I learned about digging deeply, to learn as much as possible, to go beyond the familiar. As I found my own footing, I found myself reaching for worlds beyond the borders of my own history and religion and culture. The stories of biblical figures and saints had taught me the inside world of Christian and Jewish thinking.

Learning the stories of the Indian gods and goddesses introduced me to completely new subtleties of color, broader textures of nuance, seemingly infinite harmonies of sound, and new angles from which to view old questions.

In this study, the stories of the god Kāmadeva pull us into the world of Indian storytellers and pundits and their understanding of human desire. These stories are drawn almost exclusively from the Sanskritic tradition, texts produced by teachers who were primarily if not exclusively male, and most probably Brahmin. As such, they exemplify a predominantly male view of life which did form, and continues to form, the foundation of much of Hindu thought. I mention this fact not as a criticism but rather to remind us that no story exists in a vacuum and various influences have shaped these tales as they passed through the oral tradition and into written form in the cultured language of Sanskrit. Other elements of Indian society, for example non-Brahmin village women, may tell the same stories differently, in versions that highlight other characters, offer new punch lines, or surprise with alternate endings. This book focuses on tales recorded in Sanskrit story literature, mainly the purāṇas,[8] acknowledging that these stories were crafted and honed in the oral tradition for countless decades before taking shape in the written Sanskrit. Although the purāṇas are the writings of a mainly educated class who most probably borrowed plots and motifs from the oral tradition, the tales have been retold and reshaped in specific ways to reflect the views and values of the narrators.

TALE OF YAYĀTI: TELLING STORIES ABOUT DESIRE

Indian stories often comment upon their own practice of storytelling by including a character who explains a particular point by telling another story within the framework of the original story. Of course this motif is not unique to Indian story literature, as readers of the *One Thousand and One Arabian Nights* and Chaucer's *Canterbury Tales* know. But the Indian storytelling tradition has made great use of this technique in numerous well known texts such as the *Kathāsaritsāgara* (The Oceans of Rivers of Stories); the *Pancatantra* (The Five Books), a source of fables told in Persian, Arabic, and Greek collections, notably Aesop; the *Vetālapañcaviṃśati* (The Twenty-five Tales of the Vampire), the *Yogāvasiṣṭha* (The Discipline of the Sage Vasiṣṭha); and the two Indian epics, the *Rāmāyana* and the *Mahābhārata.*

The story of Yayāti introduces us to the discussion of desire, but also comments on this technique of using a story to communicate the kind of insight that combines intuition, experience, reason, and a kind of emotional knowing. Stories communicate with a matter-of-fact quality that encourages the listener to think more deeply, but invites no debate. Here, when the husband, Yayāti, tells his wife a story in order to explain his intention to become an ascetic, he precludes further discussion about the merits of his decision. By using the story to communicate on several levels, Yayāti lets his wife know why, ultimately, only one action makes sense to him. In this way, storytelling is the perfect literary genre for commenting on desire, inviting listeners to rethink their own perspectives, to view desire in new ways but provoking no argument, no either-or positions.

The characters in the story resonate with human qualities: jealousy, anger, misunderstanding, revenge, fear, sexual attraction, lying, hurt, vulnerability, altruism. All the ingredients that allow human beings to feel at home. So when the story ends, we take Yayāti's analysis of his misery to heart. Perhaps we can learn something from him.

The protagonist of the tale is a king named Yayāti whose desire for women brought him pleasure, premature old age, more pleasure, and then the impetus to pursue religious knowledge. This well-known story and its commentary on the phenomenon of desire was told in the epic, the *Mahābhārata* as well as in numerous purāṇas.[9] One translator of the *Bhāgavata Purāṇa* notes that a Marāthi novel, based on this legend and titled *Yayāti,* received a Bhāratīya Jñānapītha Award in 1978, reminding us that the legend is still very popular today.[10] This is the story as recounted in the *Bhāgavata Purāṇa.*

Tale of Yayāti

Once upon a time the daughter of the king's advisor Śukra, Devayānī, and Śarmiṣṭhā, the daughter of the king, were out walking with their retinue and decided to go for a swim in a pool of water. When they emerged from the water, Śarmiṣṭhā mistakenly took Devayānī's garment for her own. Devayānī, being enraged, derided Śarmiṣṭhā, accusing her of being a lowly Kṣatriya needing to steal a Brahmin's garment. Śarmiṣṭhā, angry in return, took all of Devayānī 's clothes and pushed her down a well. (IX.18.6–17)

Yayāti happened to be out hunting and went to the well for some water. When he saw the naked girl in the well, he gave her his upper garment and pulled her out of the well. Devayānī offered him her hand in marriage and Yayāti, feeling that his heart was now attached to her, accepted her hand. (IX.18.18–23)

Devayānī went to her father, Śukra, and while crying, complained about the actions of Śarmiṣṭhā. Śukra spoke to his disciple, the king, asking him to let Devayānī have whatever she wished. Because the king was afraid of losing his preceptor, he agreed, and Devayānī asked that whenever she married, Śarmiṣṭhā be allowed to go with her as her attendant, along with all of her attendants. Because Śarmiṣṭhā, too, realized the peril involved for the kingdom if Śukra were lost, she agreed and followed Devayānī. (IX.18.24–29)

Śukra [knowing the potential problems here] warned Yayāti never to share his bed with Śarmiṣṭhā. Yayāti had two sons with Devayānī, and, in spite of the warning, slept with Śarmiṣṭhā, having three sons by her. When

Devayānī learned of the duplicity, she left Yayāti in a rage and returned to her father. (IX.18.30–34)

Yayāti followed his beloved to Śukra's house, trying to reconcile her but she would not be appeased. In a rage, Śukra cursed him with the decrepitude of old age. When Yayāti pleaded that he was not yet sated with the enjoyment of the pleasure of his [Śukra's] daughter, Śukra told him that he might exchange his old age for the youth of anyone willing to accept this switch. (IX.18.35–37)

Having secured this mitigation of his curse, Yayāti asked each of his sons, beginning with the eldest, to exchange his own youth for the old age of his father. All refused except the youngest, Puru, who said he must obey his father. In this way, Yayāti continued to rule as a young man and to gratify his desires with Devayānī. (IX.18.38–46)

After many years, Yayāti began to become disenchanted with the life of the senses, and told a story to his beloved Devayānī about a goat. This goat, though married to a she-goat whom he had rescued from a well, was possessed by the demon of sexual passion. The goat had been castrated for his womanizing but had continued to enjoy himself with his she-goat after his testicles had been reattached. Yet even then, his desires were not satiated. (IX.19.1–11)

Yayāti said to Devayānī: "Desire is never satisfied by the enjoyment of the [objects of] desire: like fire fed with sacrificial oil, it only increases in intensity." (IX.19.14) All the food-grains, gold, animals, and women cannot satisfy one whose mind is subject to desire. (IX.19.13) Therefore, concentrating on Brahman and freeing my mind from the pairs of opposites [pleasure-pain etc.], I will live in the forest. (IX.19.19)

The story of Yayāti provides a fitting introduction to the study of Kāma/kāma in Sanskrit story literature. An Indian paradigm for the human struggle with desire, Yayāti loses his passion but sees that it is an unwinnable game, and so shifts his focus to gaining religious insight. Though the god Kāmadeva makes no appearance in this story, Yayāti's strong yearnings can be attributed to the god's flower arrows that have aroused in him, as they do in all creatures, intense and insatiable desire.

Yayāti's curse, losing his wife and his virility while his desire remains strong, is the curse of human existence, to desire with intensity that which we are powerless to have. Yayāti realizes *for us* that in spite of its promise of euphoria, desire is ultimately insatiable, no matter how much time is devoted to its pursuit. He acknowledges the futility and emptiness of a life driven by desire.

In this tale, Yayāti's behavior exemplifies a dominant Indian teaching that because desire can never be fully satisfied for more than a few moments, the only way to be truly free in a spiritual sense is to move outside the magnetic pull of desire. Yayāti's decision to withdraw to a cave reflects the familiar dichotomy between passion and asceticism. But considered within the larger context of the many stories that explore the ramifications of desire, Yayāti's asceticism, although a course of action well known in Hindu texts, represents only one way to resolve his dilemma. Holding desire to the light, stories examine this component of human nature from different angles. In this process, traditional answers begin to unravel and complexities emerge.

Speaking to the gut, heart, and mind, stories communicate on many levels. Just as Yayāti expressed to Devayānī the complexity of his internal conflict in the form of a story, the Indian tradition presents its conflicting perspectives on desire through stories. The Sanskrit tales of Kāmadeva explore the ambiguities of this paradoxical human emotion, gently displaying a myriad of contradictory elements like a prism refracting sunlight into rainbows.

A FLOW OF STORIES WITH NO RELIABLE DATES

My first plan was to organize the Kāmadeva material to reflect a loose chronological development of the god within the limitations posed by dating the texts, and more particularly, the stories within those texts. Although we can safely say that references to the god in Vedic, Brahamanic, and Upanishadic texts predate references to Kāmadeva in the *Mahābhārata* and the purāṇas, after that, the chronological progression breaks down. Wendy Doniger referred to this problem of dating the purāṇas in her work with stories of Śiva.

> The general chronology seems to hold true: Vedas, Brāhmaṇas, Upanisads, *Mahābhārata, Rāmāyaṇa,* early Purāṇas, and late Purāṇas; and within this framework it is usually possible and sometimes profitable to argue chronologically. But scholars disagree to an astonishing extent even on the relatively simple question of the date of the Purāṇas as a group, let alone their relative chronology within that group.[11]

Ludo Rocher comes to the same conclusion after reviewing the printed texts and numerous handwritten manuscripts of puranic works: "I submit that it is not possible to set a specific date for any purana as a whole. . . . even for the better established and more coherent puranas—*Bhāgavata, Viṣṇu,* etc.—opinions, inevitably, continue to vary widely and endlessly."[12]

Rocher proposes that we should think in terms of the individual stories and legends themselves as purāṇas, or "mini-purāṇas." He points out that the distinctions among the terms "*ākhyāna* (tale, legend), *upākhyāna* (episode within a story), *gāthā* (song, verse), *kalpajokti,* (sūtra lore) and even *itihāsa* (legend, history)" and *purāṇa* have become blurred even in the literature itself.[13] Further, he encourages the comparison of several versions of a *mini-purāṇa* in order to correct details which might have been poorly transmitted in the written texts, but he cautions against using this system as a way to produce a definitive chronological order even for these individual stories because the texts draw from such a vast oral tradition, as well as other written works.[14]

Equally unpromising, warns Rocher, is the system of presenting either the simplest or the most complex form of a story as proof of its earlier or later composition. Referring to an argument put forth by R. N. Mehta, Rocher says: "I agree with the more cautious and open-minded approach ... [that] when a series from simple to complex is considered providing the chronological framework, a counter argument that with the passage of time, the same complex situation would get simplified also requires to be carefully considered."[15]

Working with the stories of Kāmadeva, I have come to the same conclusion, that while it is possible to see the god's development from personifying an abstract concept in the Vedas to becoming a robust, skilled, fun-loving character in the later epics and puranas, it is difficult to provide an accurate chronology beyond that. Although I have located tales within historical periods when possible, I have organized the book around particular characteristics represented by Kāmadeva in the story literature. This approach allows the reader to see how stories comment on one another by what they repeat, omit, add, and change, without establishing an original or most significant version. Drawn from a common tradition, the variants are examined together to understand not only their specific messages but how, together, they illuminate what is significant. Noting what motifs or patterns are repeated in most versions, or by contrast highlighted in only one, viewing the collection as a whole allows the reader to see the primary teachings of the narrative. Influenced by structural analyses of myth and folklore, this approach assumes all variants of a story to be significant and mutually illuminating.

For example, the five variants of the story of the burning of Kāmadeva, along with several stories that parallel the structure of this story, allow us to analyze themes that, on the one hand, emerge as important for all five and, on the other hand, become significant by virtue of being unusual, or found in only one text. Reading the variants as a group highlights the fundamental structure of the tale, which in turn highlights the most significant teachings.

This methodology for working with the stories as didactic literature emerges naturally from the stories themselves. As much as various tales merge with, blend into, and build on one another regardless of contradictory details, the narratives also maintain their integrity as individual units constructed to convey specific teachings. To present both aspects of each story, I first present the tale as a discrete unit with its own coherent structure, and then set it within the larger framework of other tales. Moving between the individual tale and the group of variants of which it is a part allows the reader to appreciate how the multiple contexts resonating within a single story influence the messages it conveys.

VISUAL REPRESENTATIONS OF KĀMADEVA

Although Kāmadeva is a colorful figure in the tales, few sculpted and painted depictions of the god have survived. Images of Kāmadeva accompanied by one or two of his wives were sculpted on the outer walls of major Indian temples. The Bhuvaneshvar temple complex in Orissa and the Kailash cave temple in Ellora preserve such sculpted depictions of the god of desire and his wives. Free-standing sculptures and paintings can also be found, but Kāma does not appear to have been a common subject for commissioned artists.

Beautifully carved wooden sculptures of Kāma and Rati stand just inside the entrance to the Salar Jung Museum in Hyderabad.[16] Two colorfully painted six-foot wooden carvings of a robust Kāmadeva with sugarcane bow and bright green parrot *vāhaṇa* along with a seductive-looking Rati greet all entrants to the museum. Graciously given permission by the museum's director of education to photograph these statues, I have included them here to show how one artist envisioned the god of desire and his consort. Both deities are portrayed as large-eyed, slim figures, full of energy and personality.

Stella Kramrisch discusses the erotic sculptures on the walls of the Bhuvaneshvar temple, explaining that they were meant to draw the devotee toward the deity enshrined within.[17] However, a somewhat different perspective was explained to me by a former director-general of the Archaeological Survey of India, Dr. C. M. Joshi, during a visit to his home in Ellora in January of 2003.[18] He explained that placing amorous couples and scenes outside a temple was the artist's way of making the entrance an auspicious place. Like rangoli designs drawn on the steps leading into a home to ensure good fortune within, the amorous scenes depicted around the doorways of Buddhist caves and Hindu temples are auspicious designs that mark the entrance as a place of blessing and good fortune. Certainly the Hindu and Buddhist caves of Ellora and Ajanta, which display numerous beautifully carved amorous couples and heavenly deities, have long been considered highly auspicious places, known originally as centers for religious mendicants and teachers, and then as important pilgrimage sites.

Vidya Dehejia, in discussing early Buddhist caves near Ellora and Ajanta, the Karle Caves, describes similar images on the front walls of the monastery there, connecting the auspicious nature of these images to the good fortune of fertility.

> Six sets of over life-sized images of loving couples, known as *mithunas,* adorn the front wall of the veranda, while two more occupy its facing wall. Men stand relaxed, with one arm around the shoulder of their partners who are carved with high, rounded breasts, narrow waist and broad hips. . . . [the] sensuous nature of the carving . . . represents an acknowledgement of the widespread veneration of fertility that was already in evidence in the sculpted bracket figures adorning the gateways of the Sanchi stupa.[19]

Further clarifying the use of these amorous couples and seductive women to adorn temples and stupas, Dehejia explains that although their appearance on the walls of a Buddhist cave or Hindu temple may seem incongruous to modern minds, these images were clearly considered auspicious figures.

0.1 Wood carving of Kāmadeva, Salar Jung Museum, Hyderabad. *(Photo by Cathy Benton, 2003)*

0.2 Wood carving of Rati, Salar Jung Museum, Hyderabad.
(Photo by Cathy Benton, 2003)

0.3 Amorous couple 1, Kailash rock-cut temple, Ellora.
(Photo by Cathy Benton, 2003)

0.4 Amorous couple 2, Kailash rock-cut temple, Ellora.
(Photo by Cathy Benton, 2003)

> . . . artists, patrons and monastic authorities display their faith in the widely held pan-Indian belief that the figure of woman is auspicious. Woman was associated with fertility and thus, in turn, with growth, abundance and prosperity. What might seem a paradox to modern minds was not so to the ancient Indians. After all, in the Buddhist and Hindu context woman was not associated with sin; there was no Eve responsible for the fall of humanity. Beyond auspiciousness, however, the woman-and-tree motif carried an added dimension of meaning due to a widely prevalent ancient belief that by her very touch, woman could cause a tree to blossom or bear fruit.[20]

The connection between amorous couples and seductive apsarases and gandharvas is discussed in more detail in chapter seven, but images of Kāmadeva on temple walls in various parts of India indicate that he was also viewed as one who bestowed fertility.

The Indian art historian T. A. Gopinatha Rao, in his two-volume work on the iconography of Indian deities, describes how Kāma, as part of the Kāmāntaka representation of the destruction of Kāma by Śiva, should be depicted. The iconographic texts stipulate that in this image:

> the figure of Manmatha or Kāma should be sculptured as having fallen down at the mere glance of Śiva. The height of the figure of Manmatha may range from one to seven-tenths of that of Śiva; he should be shown as decorated with golden ornaments; his complexion should also be golden yellow. He is required to be represented as carrying in his hands the five different flowery arrows and the bow made of sugar-cane and being in the company of his dear Rati. . . . The arrows should be held by Manmatha in the right hand and the bow in his left. The figures of the companions of Manmatha may or may not be represented; also instead of five arrows, he may be shown as carrying only one.[21]

This text detailing rules and standards for classic iconography indicates the importance of portraying Kāmadeva with the sugarcane bow and five flower arrows, as well as with his consort, Rati, and the personification of the spring season, Vasanta. In line with these instructions, surviving depictions of the god of desire do indeed show him with Rati, a sugarcane bow, and at least one flower-tipped arrow, though not with Vasanta.

A sixth-century sculpture identified as the god of desire and his consort on a Bijapur temple wall displays an embracing Kāma and Rati under a canopy of leaves that may be growing from either a tree or a blooming sugarcane.[22] A sculpture of an embracing couple in an almost identical pose stands in the Metropolitan Museum of Art in New York. In this beautifully sculpted large stone image, the sculptor has added an interesting detail. The shaft of a lotus flower ending in a sharp bud looking very much like one of Kāma's flower-tipped arrows has been placed in the leaves just above the head of the male figure. Although the museum has labeled this sculpture an

0.5 Amorous couple 3, Kailash rock-cut temple, Ellora.
(Photo by Cathy Benton, 2003)

0.6 Voluptuous tree goddess in the tribunga pose on entranceway pillar, Buddhist cave, Ajanta. *(Photo by Cathy Benton, 2003)*

0.7 Sandstone sculpture of Kāmadeva and Rati, entrance pillar, Cave III Mukhamandapa, Badami, Bijapur, Karnataka, fourth to seventh century CE, Digital South Asia Library, American Institute of Indian Studies Collection (AIIS). Used by permission of the American Institute of Indian Studies.

0.8 Loving Couple (mithuna), thirteenth century, Orissa. Used by permission of the Metropolitan Museum of Art, Purchase, Florence Waterbury Bequest, 1970. (1970.44)

amorous couple, the artist might indeed have modeled this couple on iconographic depictions of Kāma and Rati, like that from Bijapur. (See figures 0.7 and 0.8.)

In addition to sculptures, some evidence suggests that images of Kāma and Rati, may have been painted in palaces. Devangana Desai notes that poets such as Bana in the *Harsacarita* and Harsa in the *Naisadhacarita* described the "inner apartments" and "love chambers" of royal couples as being decorated with paintings or idols of Kāmadeva, Rati, and Prīti.[23] But unfortunately these paintings have long since deteriorated and replicas of these paintings are rare.

STRUCTURE OF THIS STUDY

Chapter 1 tells of the origin of the deity in the mind of the god Brahmā, who assigns specific duties to Kāmadeva that become his unique dharma. Assisting him in fulfilling his dharma, Brahmā also bestows upon the handsome god a beautiful wife, delightful companion, and effective, if flowery, weapons. The narratives in chapter 2 describe Kāmadeva's skirmishes with other deities, including the ascetic, Śiva, and Devī the Great Goddess. These tales ask who wins when a god or goddess is pitted against Kāmadeva in a battle of wills. Who is ultimately stronger and more powerful? Who more clever? But on a deeper level, the tales explore how desire functions in ordinary human lives. The outcome is never certain as power seesaws back and forth between the god of desire and others.

The third chapter presents another character, Pradyumna, son of Kṛṣṇa, who is understood to be a manifestation of the god of desire and husband to Māyāvatī, goddess of illusion. Because the Indian story tradition considers both desire and illusion to be aspects of mind, as well as weapons wielded by the gods, this story explores the interaction between desire and illusion through the adventures of these characters. In chapter 4, Kāmadeva is again centerstage as he pricks himself with his own arrow and falls in love with a sage's wife, suffering painful consequences. Though Kāmadeva is cursed with leprosy and his lover turned to stone, the narrative provides rituals to undo these curses and those of other angry husbands.

The texts presented in chapter 5 describe rituals to Kāmadeva for men and women hoping to acquire the god's magnetic charm to woo prospective lovers, inattentive wives, or wandering husbands. Some of the oldest references to kāma and Kāmadeva are discussed in chapter 6, in the context of the most ancient Sanskrit texts: Vedas, Brāhmaṇas, Upaniṣads, and the voluminous epic the *Mahābhārata,* as well as a Tantric text describing devotion to the headless goddess Chinnamastā. Chapter 7 examines Kāma as he is depicted in visual representations with his assistants: the heavenly apsarases and gandharvas, his bright green parrot mount, and the water dwelling makara displayed on his banner.

Shifting to Buddhist Sanskrit texts in chapter 8, Kāmadeva appears in two apparently opposite forms, that of demonic tempter and bodhisattva. This chapter explores how desire is characterized and re-imaged by Indian Buddhist teachers, as they use the familiar Kāmadeva to explore Buddhist perspectives on desire. Over the centuries, Buddhist tales transformed this tempter into a follower of the dharma.

The concluding chapter examines what these many tales of Kāmadeva teach about human desiring, both within the context of the Indian religious tradition and in any culture that knows the heartache and euphoria of desire.

In the course of my research, one finding particularly surprised me. I had expected to find many expositions on the vicious tendencies produced by desire, such as those listed by Manu in writing about right living. (VII.45–50):

> . . . hunting, gambling, sleep by day, finding fault [with others], women, drunkenness, [excessive indulgence in] dancing, singing and instrumental music, and aimless wandering; of which, drinking wine, gambling, women and hunting are the most harmful, each preceding vice worse than the next.[24]

But on the contrary, I found that most stories and rituals involving Kāmadeva reflect an acceptance of desire as a natural part of human existence, if not an indirect route to spiritual practices and goals. Recognizing the importance of desire as an essential and even celebrated aspect of existence, most stories acknowledge the paradox of desire as a source of frustration and of joy. Kāmadeva and his arrows act as enemies in tales of asceticism and as renewers of life in tales that teach the comforting cycle of life. Ultimately, tales of Kāmadeva illustrate that the Indian tradition integrates this insatiable force in many different ways.

Nevertheless the following verse from the story of Yayāti is quoted in every variant of this tale as well as in numerous unrelated stories and texts.

> Desire is never satisfied by the enjoyment of the [objects of] desire:
> Like fire fed with sacrificial oil, it only increases in intensity.[25]

CHAPTER ONE

Stories of Beginnings: Kāmadeva and His Wives

THE BIRTH OF KĀMADEVA

The story of the birth of Kāmadeva is told in several purāṇas, but most prominently in the *Śiva Purāṇa*[1] and the *Kālikā Purāṇa*.[2] The frame narrative for the description of the birth of Kāma is, appropriately enough, a story about the creator god, Brahmā, doing his work of creating. Brahmā's particular technique is to think beings into existence. Brahmā conceives of a particular nature and appearance, and, in that thought-instant, Brahmā's conception begins functioning in the world as a separate being. In this way, the mind of Brahmā mentally churns all of existence into being.

An obvious commentary on the power of the mind to create its own idiosyncratic universe, the story of Kāma's emergence, within Brahmā's creation story, narrates how the mind of Brahmā quite literally gives life and form to his own desires. One thought-filled instant produces a beautiful woman, his own body in a state of arousal, and desire embodied in a young man. In the *Śiva Purāṇa,* Brahmā himself tells us what happened.

Creation of Kāmadeva

> After creating the guardians of creatures, the Prajāpatis, as well as Dakṣa and other gods, I considered myself higher than others and was delighted.
>
> [But] O sage, as I created Marīci, Atri, Pulaha, Pulastya, Angiras, Kratu, Vasiṣṭha, Nārada, Dakṣa, and Bhṛgu—my mental sons of lordly stature—a beautiful woman with handsome features was born of my mind.
>
> She was variously called Sandhyā,[3] Divakṣantā, Śayam Sandhyā, and Jayāntikā. She was very beautiful with well-shaped eyebrows capable of captivating even the minds of sages.

1.1 Kāmadeva and Rati with sugarcane bow, Kailash rock-cut temple, Ellora. *(Photo by Cathy Benton, 2003)*

Neither in the human world nor among the gods was there such a woman of complete perfection in all ways. Nor was there such a woman in the nether worlds, or in the three times [past, present, future].

Just as I was thinking like this, another amazingly beautiful being appeared out of my mind.

He had a golden complexion. His chest was stout and firm. His nose was fine. His thighs, hips, and calves were round and plump. He had blue [blue-black] waves of hair. His eyebrows were thickset and tremulous. His face shone like the full moon. His hairy chest was broad like a door. He was as huge as the celestial elephant Airāvata. He was wearing a blue cloth. His hands, eyes, face, legs and fingers were red in color. He had a slender waist and fine teeth. He smelled like an elephant in rut. His eyes were like the petals of a full-blown lotus. He was fragrant like the filaments [of a flower]. His neck was like the conch. He had the emblem of a fish. He was tall. He had the makara[4] for his vehicle. He was armed with a bow and five flowers for arrows. His glance was very seductive, as he rolled his eyes here and there. O dear one, his very breath was a fragrant wind. He was accompanied by the sentiment of love [śṛṅgāra rasa].

On seeing that being, my sons were struck with curiosity, fascination, and eagerness.

Their minds immediately became crooked [perverted] and confused. Smitten with love, they lost their mental resolve.

On seeing me, the creator and lord of the worlds, this person bowed down, his shoulders bent in humility, and said:

"O Brahmā, what is the work I am to do? Please assign me an honorable task. Please tell me. What is my honorable and suitable place? Who will be my wife?"

The poet added:
On hearing these words of the noble-souled Kāma, the creator did not say anything for a short while, surprised at his predicament. Then, steadying his mind and abandoning his surprised demeanor, Brahmā, who was already a victim of Kāma, spoke the following:

In this form and with your five flower-arrows,[5] you can enamour and captivate men and women, carrying on the eternal task of creation.

In this universe, consisting of the three worlds and both mobile and immobile beings, no living beings, not even the gods, will be able to defy you.

O best of beings, even I, Brahmā, Vāsudeva, and Śiva will be in your control, not to speak of ordinary living beings.

> Invisibly you will enter the hearts of living beings, excite thrilling feelings of pleasure and carry on the activities of creation that are to last forever.
>
> The minds of all living beings will become an easy target for your five flower arrows. You will be the cause of elation.
>
> So have I assigned you the task of facilitating creation.[6]

The storyteller places a confession in the mouth of the creator god Brahmā, an admission that the god of desire slipped fully formed out of his own passion-filled mind. According to Brahmā, in the moment that male and female beheld one another, desire simply happened. Overwhelmed with the beauty of Sandhyā, Brahmā looked up to see Kāma, fully formed and well armed, with his own beauty, five flower arrows, and a seductive gaze.

Significantly, even the creator god whose powerful mind is the source of all creation cannot control the coming and going of desire. In this story, Brahmā conceptualizes beauty, projects it onto his creation, and then falls in love with this beautiful creation of his mind. Using this same logic, the story may be explaining that we, too, project our ideal attractive qualities onto another person, with whom we proceed to fall in love. Convinced that this person embodies our ideal, we fall in love, like Brahmā, with our own creation. But unlike Brahmā, who knows that Sandhyā is the fabrication of his mind, over which he ultimately has control, we are permanently confused about who our lovers are. How much of my lover have I created and how much is truly a separate being? Caught between our mental image of our ideal lover and the real person standing before us, we find ourselves untangling infinite emotional knots trying to make sense of someone who is and is not the reflection of ourselves. And, again like Brahmā, we look up to find Kāma witnessing all.

The story pushes us to understand this desire that broke Brahmā's mental concentration and continues to break our own. How is it that we are pulled so quickly and completely into chasing and longing and sighing? In the Indian religious tradition, understanding the fundamental principles of cosmic order gives the knower control over some aspects of existence. The Vedas prescribed rituals in which priests reeneacted creation in order to preserve the cosmic order. Contemporary religious rituals, from daily pūjās to pilgrimages, are performed to maintain individual and societal harmony, with the understanding that the rituals reflect deeper cosmic realities. Similarly, the stories of Kāmadeva offer insight into the nature of desire, empowering those who hear them to keep this element of the cosmos in balance.

The story of Brahmā and Kāma teaches that desire originates in the mind, and that human beings often desire those who reflect elements of themselves. However, in the next episode, the relationship between knowledge and power becomes more complicated. Brahmā learns that even his knowledge as creator of the universe does not empower him to easily resolve his predicament with Sandhyā. Simply understanding the nature and origin of desire does not reduce its power over us. Although Brahmā understands every dimension of this being created by his mind, he cannot escape the power this creature wields. No one is exempt from Kāma's power, not even his creator. And Brahmā's lack of control mirrors the human condition. Examples abound of situations in which the knowledge of destructive consequences has no effect on controlling the act that precipitates the damage. Smoking a cigarette or agreeing to meet an abusive lover just one more time are self-destructive acts repeated over and over because the desire for even elusive satisfaction has greater motivational power than the knowledge of negative consequences.

In the next episode, the mesmerized Brahmā, his senses tingling with arousal in Sandhyā's presence, longs to draw her to him. Ostensibly, Kāmadeva is responsible, but who created Kāma?

> Deciding to test the power given to him by the creator, Kāmadeva stood in the archer's position [*ālidha*] with the right knee advanced and the left leg retracted, and shot his arrows into all those assembled: Brahmā, his mind-born sons, the Prajāpatis, and the woman, Sandhyā. (15–19)

Brahmā continues his narration:

> The sages [his sons] and I were enamoured, feeling great changes in our mental states.
>
> We began to stare at Sandhyā frequently, passion depraving our minds. Our lust was heightened. . . .
>
> Making us feel thoroughly enchanted, Kāmadeva did not stop till all of us had lost control over our senses. . . .
>
> She [Sandhyā] too began to manifest the instinctive gestures of side-glances and the pretences of concealing her feelings, the result of being hit by Kāma's arrows as she was being stared at. . . .

[While all the sages are in this state of sensual excitement, Brahma's son, Dakṣa, begins to meditate on the god Śiva to protect himself. This petition draws Śiva into the scene.]

Brahmā continues:

> When Śiva saw me and the others in such a mental state, he laughed, mocking us.
>
> In the midst of his laughter, making all of us blush with shame, the great god spoke these consoling words:
>
> Alas, O Brahmā, how is it that you were overwhelmed with lustful feelings on seeing your own daughter? This is highly improper for those who follow the Vedas.

Sister, brother's wife, and daughter are like one's mother. A sensible man never looks at them with such reprehensible vision.

The entire path of the Vedas is present in your mouth, O Brahmā. How could you forget [the Vedas] under the influence of this momentary passion?

O god with four faces, O Brahmā, your mind should always remain strong and alert. How did you undo your mind for this dalliance in passion?

How is it that your mental sons, Dakṣa, Marīci, and others who forever practice yoga in isolation and meditation, have become enamoured of a woman?

This Kāma is a fool. How is it that he has begun to torment all of them with his excessive power? (verses 39–45)

Brahmā continues:

On hearing Śiva's words, I, lord of the world, perspired profusely in shame.

Although the desire to seize Sandhyā of such attractive features still lingered, fearing Śiva, I curbed my aroused senses.

From the drops of sweat that fell from my body rose the *manes*, beings who had not performed sacrifices while living on earth. They shone like split collyrium and had eyes resembling full-blown lotuses. They were meritorious ascetics who had given up worldly activities.

The *manes* were sixty-four thousand in number, and those called *Barhishads*, seated on the grass, were eighty-four thousand.

From the drops of sweat that fell from Dakṣa's body, a splendid woman endowed with good qualities was born.

She had a slender body with symmetrical hips. Her waist was well-shaped, small curly hairs embellished it. She was soft in body with fine teeth and a shining golden complexion. Along with her perfect body, her face shone like the full moon and the full-blown lotus. Her name was Rati, Delight, and she was capable of captivating even the sages. (verses 46–53)

Brahmā's story allows us to sigh with relief, to put our own desires into perspective. Sweating in his intense struggle to resist lust, and producing hundreds of thousands of new beings out of this struggle, Brahmā assures us that resisting desire is inherently difficult, if not impossible. Seeing Brahmā and his meditating sons succumb so completely to desire allows the audience to smile at Brahmā and at themselves.

Brahmā mirrors too the embarrassment we feel when caught. We reach into cookie jars filled with desires that we know should be curbed. Yet we watch our arms reach again and again, and hope that no one is looking. Śiva tells

Brahmā that Kāmadeva is a fool, but even more poignantly, Kāma turns others into fools, as they attempt to satisfy inherently insatiable desires. But the Indian audience also know the irony of Śiva's remarks as they forshadow his own fall to Kāma's arrows in a few more verses.

Clearly the odds are in Kāma's favor whenever he takes aim. When Kāma arouses the passions within us, internal battles ensue: caution versus adventure, good sense versus indulgence. Brahmā models such an internal struggle. Through a strenuous effort of will, Brahmā does counteract the effect of Kāma's arrow, but his internal conflict produces new creatures who must be reckoned with. Though satisfying one's desire always promises gratification, or even happiness, this process often requires compromise or produces conflict in other areas of one's life. For Brahmā, as for us, the hope to simply gratify desire with no eventual consequences is naïve. Kāma's presence in Brahmā's universe brings inevitable internal struggle.

By contrast, for the god of desire, practicing his newly bestowed archery skill with Brahmā and his sons brought him a beautiful wife. One of these sons, Dakṣa, produced an abundance of sweat as he struggled to restrain his own desires. Appropriately enough, from the droplets of his sweat emerged another enticing woman called Rati, meaning delight or sexual pleasure. But this woman was immediately handed off to Kāmadeva to be his wife. Formed by droplets of desire literally sweated out of the pores of Dakṣa's body, Rati embodies carnal desire and sexuality, a perfect marriage partner for Kāma. Born of desire-ridden sweat, Rati also carries the obvious association with the bodily fluids produced during sexual activity. But her association with bodily secretions implies a certain irony in the context of Indian standards of purity and pollution. As all bodily fluids are considered polluted and polluting substance, Rati necessarily embodies this pollution. However, being joined with the auspicious god of desire, Rati was transformed from polluted substance into auspicious goddess. Indeed, both Kāma and Rati are welcome sculptures on temple walls throughout India, along with other figures representing good fortune and prosperity.

As the scene ends with the wedding of Kāma and his bride, the storyteller again reminds us that desire has a dark side with the foreshadowing that Kāma will soon die, leaving his beautiful wife a widow. The cycle of desire will repeat itself in a constant round of passion and grief.

KĀMADEVA'S WIFE: RATI

As discussed earlier, Kāma's wife, Rati, whose name connotes sexual delight or pleasure, is his constant companion, almost always depicted with him. The *Śiva Purāṇa* story continues with a description of Rati and her interaction with Kāma as his wife, as seen through Brahmā's eyes.

Brahmā describes what happened next:

After marrying the beautiful daughter of Dakṣa who could enchant even sages, Kāma rejoiced greatly.

On seeing Rati, his auspicious wife, Kāma was pierced by his own arrow and overpowered by the pleasure of dalliance.

His wife of fair complexion, tremulous side-glances, and fawn eyes was admirably suited to his love of pleasure. She offered him ample sport.

[But] on seeing her eyebrows, doubt arose in Kāma's mind: "[Perhaps] Brahmā has given her these two [perfectly arched eyebrows] in order to excel my bow and undo its power!"

Watching her rapid-roving glances, he no longer thought his arrows swift.

Inhaling the naturally sweet fragrance of her steady breath, Kāma lost faith in his Malaya breeze.

Seeing her face resembling the full moon with all its [auspicious] marks, Kāma was sure there was no difference between her face and the [perfect] moon.

Her pair of breasts resembled the buds of golden lotuses with nipples shining like bees hovering round them.

Certainly Kāma had set aside and forgotten the bees that formed the string of his own [sugarcane] bow that buzzed with their tumultuous hum. He had forgotten because his eyes were riveted to the auspicious necklace made of the wide-eyed feathers of a peacock's tail. This necklace was resting on her firm protruding plump breasts and suspended over them to her umbilical cord.

His eyes were covering her skin with their gazing. The skin around her deep orifice[7] shone like red plums.

Her thighs were lovely like the cut off trunks of plaintain trees, and Kāma looked at them as though they were his javelins.

Her heels, along with the tips and sides of her feet, were tinged with red. With these hennaed feet, she truly looked like the companion of Kāmadeva.[8]

Her hennaed hands with nails like [red] Kumsuka flowers were very beautiful with well-rounded tapering fingers.

Her arms were perfectly shaped, like lotus-stalks, glossy and soft. They resembled corals putting forth beams of splendour.[9]

Her glossy hair was blue like a rain cloud and fluffy like the tail of a Camarī deer. The wife of Kāmadeva glowed with beauty.

> Just as Lord Śiva accepted Gangā,[10] flowing from the snowy mountain, Kāmadeva married Rati. She carried a discus and a lotus in her hands, with arms as fine as lotus-stalks. Her eyebrows formed small waves, and her side-glances moved up and down like gentle tides. Her eyes resembled blue lotuses, and her curly body hair was like the mossy growth in the river. With mind expanded like a tree, Rati glowed. The depth of her orifice was like a deep eddy. Rati's body glowed with beauty. In fact, she appeared as the abode of beauty itself, like the beautiful goddess Lakṣmī.
>
> She had twelve varieties of ornaments, and was expert in the sixteen types of amorous gestures. Capable of charming the whole world, she illuminated the ten quarters, the universe.
>
> Seeing Rati like this, Kāmadeva eagerly accepted her, just as Viṣṇu accepted Lakṣmī when she approached him with passion. (verses 7–29) . . .
>
> Having reached the epitome of happiness, Kāmadeva thought all miseries were at an end. Dakṣa's daughter, Rati, also was extremely delighted to receive Kāmadeva as her husband. Like a cloud at sunset mingled with sparkling lightning, the sweet-voiced Kāma rejoiced with Rati.
>
> Kāmadeva took Rati to his chest in happy delusion, like a yogi with his knowledge. Having secured this fine husband, Rati's face shone like the full moon, just as Lakṣmī's face had shone when she secured Hari [Viṣṇu]. (verses 32–34)

The goddess Rati is both the wife of the god of desire and his assistant as he engenders desire in creatures large and small. Indeed, Rati enchants the god of love himself. But she also helps him ensnare others, using her sensuous appearance to arouse sexual feelings in those around her. In this *Śiva Purāṇa* narrative and that recounted in the *Kālikā Purāṇa,* the text dwells on the details of Rati's body, beginning with the shape and movement of her head and face, moving down her body to her genital area, and further down to the decorated sides of her feet. Aside from her seductive appearance as Kāma's consort, Rati is significant in the story of Kāmadeva for her role in pleading for his resuscitation after he has lost his body, a series of actions discussed more fully in the following chapter.

For Indian storytellers, sexual desire functions as a paradigm for all forms of desire. This paradigm offers a clear way to discuss how desire works, in this case highlighting the senses as the primary vehicle for arousing and attempting to satisfy the urges of desire. The detailed description of Rati allows the storyteller to spend lots of time reveling in desire's sensuality. The Indian epistemological tradition explains that we gather information through six, not five, senses: sight, hearing, taste, smell, touch, and the mind. So in meeting Rati, we see her feet dyed red with henna like a bride, hear the jangling of her ankle bells (in some versions), feel the softness of her hair, smell the fragrance of her breath, and can almost taste her presence as it might fill a room like the light of a full moon. The poet wants us to experience our own "sensuous delight" as we learn about Kāma's consort. He wants us to know her through our senses so that later we will grieve with her when she loses the desire that motivates her, her Kāmadeva.

A minor character in any drama involving Kāmadeva, Rati in some ways represents an attribute of the god of desire. Rati personifies sexual delight, but only this aspect of the sexual encounter. She has no connection with other typical wifely duties such as childbearing and childrearing. Rati remains only the delight that accompanies the arousal and satisfying of desire. Because the existence of this delight is so fundamentally rooted in the presence of desire, when Kāma is burned to ashes, Rati's existence also is curtailed.

KĀMADEVA'S COMPANIONS: VASANTA AND THE MĀRAS

In order to persuade the great ascetic god Śiva to marry the beautiful Pārvatī, Brahmā commands Kāmadeva to fill Śiva with passion. Although not in a position to refuse the creator's command, Kāma is nervous about attacking the great yogi. Worried that his arrows will incur the great god's wrath, even as they are deflected by his internal discipline, Kāma asks Brahmā for a stronger weapon. Brahmā, knowing that Kāma's fear is well-founded, ponders what weapon might be strong enough to penetrate Śiva's asceticism. But with a sense of despair, Brahma sighs.

Out of this sigh steps Vasanta, Spring, covered head to toe in clusters of flowers. The narrative continues in Brahmā's voice.

> While I was agitated with this thought [of whether Kāma could excite the passions of Śiva], I heaved a deep sigh. Out of this sigh, Spring [Vasanta] appeared, fully clothed in clusters of flowers.
>
> He was [aglow] like a red lotus with eyes resembling full-blown lotuses. His face shone like the full moon rising at dusk, and his nose was well shaped.
>
> His feet were arched like a bow, while his hair was dark and curly. Wearing two earrings, he looked as bright as the morning sun.
>
> His gait was majestic like that of an elephant in rut. His arms were long and stout, with raised shoulders. His neck resembled the conch-shell, and his chest was broad. He had a full and finely shaped face.
>
> Vasanta was beautiful in appearance, dark-complexioned and endowed with all the characteristic marks of beauty. He was very handsome to look at, capable of heightening feelings of desire [kāma] and enchanting everyone.
>
> When the Spring season, endowed with all these features and storehouse of flowers, arose, a very fragrant wind blew. All the trees began to blossom. . . . (verses 37–42)

Just as wind is the friend of fire, helping it everywhere, so Spring will always help you.[11] (verse 46)

The Spring with all its characteristics—brightly colored flowers blooming, fragrant breezes blowing, birds calling to their mates—creates a readiness to receive Kāma's arrows. Like Rati, Vasanta accompanies the god Kāmadeva to make him more effective. But unlike Rati whose very essence is desire, Vasanta emerges from a sigh of frustration, anxiety over how to make Kāma more effective in the face of the great ascetic's power. In a quandry about how to make a more powerful weapon for Kāmadeva, Brahmā's agitated sigh produces Spring: full-blown and fully formed like Kāmadeva, a young man clothed in the flower petals of his season. Because Brahmā creates unconsciously, the beings who spring from his mind surprise him, and the audience of the story. Like a creative thought that appears fully formed, Vasanta emerges from the mind of Brahmā as he ponders how to penetrate Śiva's ascetic discipline, how to soften his yogic concentration. In the powerfully fragrant and gentle breezes of Spring, perhaps Śiva will weaken for a moment, long enough for Kāma's arrows to enter.

As the story continues, Vasanta prepares the way for Kāma, causing flowers to bloom on trees and gentle scented breezes to blow through Śiva's hair as they tickle the glassy surfaces of spring-fed lakes in his mountain retreat. Spring, with his flowers and breezes and mating calls, now runs ahead of the god of desire, who hangs back to approach his target more slowly, armed with beautiful but sharp arrows. However, Vasanta is not Kāma's only assistant. Kāma receives less charming attendants later in the narrative, beings who are violent and loud and ugly, types more difficult to reconcile with charm and seduction.

As the story resumes, Kāmadeva has reported to Brahmā that he has been unsuccessful in his attempt to pierce Śiva with an arrow. Even with the help of Rati and Vasanta, Kāma has not been able to stir the great ascetic. Now Brahmā sighs again, but this time more intensely and in sadness, despair producing beings very different from Vasanta. These sigh-beings shout, "Kill! Kill!"

Brahmā tells us:

The gusts of wind generated by my deep sighs were variously formed and very violent. They were terrifying and appeared to have shaking fiery tongues.

They played on different musical instruments such as drums, with terrible natures and loud sounds.

Groups of beings issued forth from my deep breaths and stood in front of me [Brahmā] shouting, "Kill! Cut!" . . .

Kāma asked, "Who are these terrible creatures? What is their task?"
So Brahmā explained:
Even as they were born shouting "Kill" [māraya] their names will be "Māras," Killers, bringers of death.

This group of beings will hinder the activity of every other creature but you; they will be engaged in the activities of desire [kāmarata].

Their chief occupation will be to follow you, O Kāma. They will assist you always. Wherever you go to fulfill your purpose they will always follow and assist you.

They will create confusion in the minds of those who fall to your weapons. They will hinder seekers on the path of knowledge, in all possible ways.[12]

These Māras become Kāmadeva's troops, his *gaṇa*s (paralleling Śiva's gaṇas) always at his beck and call. As a warrior, Kāmadeva needs troops of soldiers for his battles. As a psychological force, Kāma's troops symbolize the force of his power, the force of desire. The name of these troops, the Māras, is derived from the causative form of the verb *mṛ* (to die), meaning "to cause to die" or "to kill." Desire works always in the shadow of death. In the language of the story, the Māras connect desire and death, a theme developed in other tales and texts.

Literature of all cultures is filled with characters who ultimately destroy themselves in a passion that becomes more important than life. In western literature, from Dickens's Miss Haversham in *Great Expectations* to Flaubert's Madame Bovary and Pasternak's Zhivago, these characters are familiar to us. Yet, when Brahmā gives the Māras to Kāma as his troops, we cringe. Does the story really mean to say that desire carries the power to kill? Though the text does not recount any episode in which the Māras take an active role, this story of their emergence from the sorrow of Brahmā clearly associates desire with death. The Māras raise the stakes of entering the ring with Kāma. They warn that passion obsessively seeking satisfaction can lead to death.

In the Indian epic, the *Rāmāyana,* the hero Rāma in his passion for truth in its purest form sends his beloved wife, Sitā, to her death. In the same epic, Rāma's father, Daśaratha, makes a promise in the heat of his passion for a woman that ultimately ends his life. The examples are endless both in literature and in life. The same beings that inspire passionate desire can also chant death knells as they accompany the god of desire.

KĀMADEVA'S OTHER WIFE: PRĪTI/KARṆOTPALĀ *(SKANDA PURĀNA)*

In contrast to the somber tone of the Māras, other aspects of Kāma evoke the well-known feeling of being elated in love. Aside from his seductive wife, Rati, Kāma is often portrayed with a second wife, Prīti, whose name connotes images of pleasurable sensation, gratification, and affection. More a figure noted in visual representations of the god of desire than in story literature, this second wife is presented in one story, the tale of a maiden called Karṇotpalā. The name *Karṇotpalā* means one who wears a lotus flower fastened to her ear as an ornament.

As the tale begins, we find Karṇotpalā praying and performing penance to the goddess Gaurī, beseeching her for a husband. However, Karṇotpalā is praying not for her own happiness but for the welfare of her father. In despair over not finding a husband for his daughter, who is growing old, Karṇotpalā's father himself has taken up ascetic practices. Engaged in severe penance, her father has given up the ruling of his kingdom and is wasting away without his family to care for him. For the sake of her father's well-being, Karṇotpalā begins her own ascetic practice in devotion to the goddess. After some time, the goddess appears to Karṇotpalā and prescribes a ritual whereby she will have her youthfulness restored and gain a husband. As Karṇotpalā is performing the ritual in the specified manner, the goddess inspires Kāmadeva to go to see the newly youthful Karṇotpalā. As soon as he sees her, Kāma is completely smitten and proposes to her on the spot. But she does not immediately agree to become his wife. As the story closes, Karṇotpalā gives the god of desire a nuanced response to his plea that she become his wife. "If you go to my father and [hear that] this marriage is his will, then what choice does a maiden have?"[13]

Full of admonitions for daughters and their fathers, the tale assures the fathers of "old" daughters that if they and their daughters are virtuous, they may indeed still find a husband for them, even a husband as handsome as Kāmadeva. Speaking to unmarried women "past their prime," the story tells them to persevere, specifically for the welfare of their fathers. If an unmarried woman performs these rituals to Gaurī, goddess of the golden form, the goddess will restore her youthful beauty and attractiveness so that a man will desire her as his wife. Finally, by this devotion to Gaurī, such a woman will protect the well-being of her father and be filled with affection for a husband.

In the cycle of stories in which desire is personified, Karṇotpalā is easily joined to Kāmadeva as his second wife, Prīti. Kāma tells Karṇotpalā, "Because I have come to you out of affectionate pleasure (prīti), O Beauty, you will be called Prīti." Because the text makes it clear that Kāma is attracted to Karṇotpalā's attractive youthful body, the connection between physical attractiveness and desire allows the audience to immediately accept Prīti as Kāma's second wife. In other texts, this wife is referred to only as Prīti.

WHO IS KĀMADEVA?

A deity with two wives, Rati (Sensual Delight) and Prīti (Affectionate Pleasure), a companion, Vasanta (Spring), a troop called Māras (Killers), and a quiver of arrows that heat, intoxicate, and madden, the god of desire is presented in the story tradition as a handsome young man whose beauty and dashing manner knock people off their feet. While the great gods, Brahmā and Śiva, are not immune to his charm, human beings are lost immediately.

However, the story of desire is never so simple or straightforward. Brahmā does manage to exert yogic control over his senses, though only with intense effort. Śiva, the divine yogi, who appears to have no problem with desire, easily disposes of the nuisance known as Kāma in one story. Yet, in another tale, Kāma's arrows do find that chink in his armor, and even the great god is overwhelmed by the elation and grief that inevitably accompany passion.

In the story literature, Kāmadeva arises from the mind of the creator god, dies in the fire of the god who is an ascetic, and is resuscitated without body by various deities including the great goddess. Each of these stories instructs us further about the nature of human desire. Where does it come from? Why does it appear out of nowhere? Does desire really have such power over us? Why are we compelled to pamper ourselves, feel more powerful, want more comfort, more success? How do we release ourselves from the desires that destroy us? How do we enjoy those that pleasure us? When should we walk away? When should we stay and indulge? These are the questions that give rise to the telling of these stories. We may like, or not like, the descriptions of ourselves that we find in them, but at the very least the stories allow us to smile as we recognize the fundamental components of human nature, of ourselves, within these narratives.

In the following chapter, in the most well-known story of the god of desire, we see Kāmadeva in action as he proceeds to do his part in Brahmā's great drama of continuing creation.

The Tale of Karṇotpalā and the Karṇotpalā Tīrtha

1. The ṛṣis spoke: Tell everything about the woman who is standing in tapas [ascetic practice], the woman you mentioned by the name of Karṇotpalā. Tell us why she is doing tapas in the water.

2. The poet responded: She stood at the foot of Gaurī,[14] with the highest devotion. The Goddess [Devī], Girijā, beloved of Śaṇkara [Śiva], was so pleased [with her devotion] that . . .

3. She spoke [to her]: Child, I am pleased. Tell me your wish. Tell me what is clouding your peacefulness, even if it is something difficult to resolve.

4. Karṇotpalā spoke: O Goddess, for the sake of [finding] a husband for me, my father is distressed. He has given up his kingdom and comfort, depriving himself of the care of a family.

5. Indeed, he is performing tapas and become completely passionless [because] I have entered old age while still remaining a maiden.

6. For this reason, let there be a husband for me. O Lady of the Heavens, through your kindness, let him be someone known among gods and men as richly endowed with beauty.

7. Through your kindness, let him have the most beautiful youthful form. Let him come so that my ascetic father may be happy again.

8. The Goddess spoke: On the third of the month of Magha, on the auspicious day of Saturn, in the nakṣatra of Vāsudeva, you should concentrate on a youthful form.

Skanda Purāṇa, Bombay: Veṇkaṭeśvara Steam Press, 1867, 1910. Nāgarakhaṇḍa (VI).127.1–19.

9. You should take a bath here in the water of great merit. Imagine a beautiful divine form in this way, and without a doubt you will become youthful.[15] This is the truth.

10. O Fortunate One, other women too who bathe on this day, in this place, will receive such beauty.

11. The poet spoke: Having spoken these words, the goddess disappeared. [Following these instructions] on the third day, Karṇotpalā

12. In the nakṣatra of Vāsudeva,[16] concentrated with great effort on Devī, the goddess who grants all desires [Gaurī-Devī].

13. On the third day, she performed the ritual as it had been described by the goddess.

14. Then, concentrating on her desire for a young and handsome husband of good fortune, she entered the water at this place [to do an ascetic practice] at midnight.

15. When she emerged from this place [in the water] with a divine form glowing with youthfulness, people were astonished.

16. Purposely aroused by the voice of Gaurī, Bhagavan Kāma then came to this place yearning with affectionate desire [prīti] for a wife. He spoke [to Karṇotpalā]: O Fortunate One, I am Kāma himself who has come.

17. Pārvatī has directed me to [you as my] wife. So be mine always.

18. O Beauty, because I came to meet you through affectionate desire [prīti], as my wife you will be called Prīti.

19. Karṇotpalā spoke: O Smara, if I go to my father [to tell him about your proposal] and if [this marriage to you] is his will, how can a maiden not follow?

CHAPTER TWO

Kāmadeva, Skilled Marksman

ŚIVA WINS: KĀMA TURNED TO ASH (*MATSYA, PADMA,* AND *ŚIVA PURĀṆAS*)

The best known story of Kāmadeva is that in which he is sent by the gods to arouse desire for a woman in the ascetic Śiva, so that Śiva will beget a son to defeat the demon Tāraka. In the course of this undertaking, however, Kāmadeva himself is burned to ashes in the fire of Śiva's wrath.

A very popular tale, this story is told in the *Śiva Purāṇa,* the *Liṅga Purāṇa,* the *Matsya Purāṇa,* the *Padma Purāṇa,* the *Skanda Purāṇa,* the *Brahmāṇḍa Purāṇa,* the *Vāmana Purāṇa,* the *Saura Purāṇa,* the *Kālikā Purāṇa,* the *Brahmavaivarta Purāṇa,* and the *Brahma Purāṇa.*[1]

Although in each narration Kāma ultimately dies in the wrathful fire of Śiva's third eye, each variant uses the basic structure of the tale to present a slightly different, or even vastly different, perspective or message. For someone reading or listening to these variants, placing them side by side is like looking at pictures or videos of one subject, but shot with different camera lenses positioned at different angles.

In this chapter, the fundamental framework of the story is examined as it is recounted in two of the oldest purāṇas, the *Matsya Purāṇa* and the *Padma Purāṇa.* Using the same basic structure, authors of the variant narratives explore the issues addressed in the tale, while adding new issues and messages of their own. This chapter highlights four of these variants, but outlines first the structure common to all as it is presented in the *Matsya* and *Padma Purāṇa*s.[2] At each telling, details and parameters are altered to offer deeper insights into the human struggle with desire. One account raises the stakes of the battle by making both Śiva and Kāmadeva more powerful, another reverses the roles of Śiva and Kāmadeva, and a third presents the goddess as the most powerful deity involved.

Many of the authors, storytellers and listeners build on alternate versions of the tale in their construction of a new telling, purposefully using variant narratives as an assumed backdrop for their new twists and new insights. The message of the story becomes both clearer and more complex as each telling incorporates the nuances of others.

This discussion of the tale of Śiva burning Kāmadeva to ashes will focus specifically on those aspects which elucidate the workings of kāma, or desire, as expressed within the Indian tradition. Incorporating the variant perspectives, each story is analyzed to see what it reveals about the character and nature of Kāma/kāma. What do these allegorical stories of human desire say about the uncontrollable nature and power of our desires?

The burning of Kāma (*Matsya* and *Padma Purāṇas*)

To set up the basic structure of the myth, the version recounted in the *Matsya* and *Padma Purāṇas*[3] is summarized here. Although the purāṇas are almost impossible to date, either in their original forms or in the recensions now available, the *Matsya* is thought to be one of the earlier purāṇas,[4] possibly providing one of the earliest versions of the story. Virtually identical to that found in the *Padma Purāṇa,* the tale told in the *Matsya Purāṇa* provides the basic narrative. Because the *Matsya/Padma* variant offers the familiar outline of the story referred to in other texts, much like a child's first version of "Cinderella" or "The Three Little Pigs," it can be used as a guide for the basic structure of the narrative. Other variants then bend this basic structure to further penetrate and elucidate the nature of desire.

When the tale begins, the world is, of course, in crisis. The gods have been overrun completely by an *asura* (demon), Tāraka, who is making their lives miserable. Having petitioned Brahmā for his help, they learn that only one being has the ability to defeat this demon. In an earlier time, Tāraka had practiced an intense asceticism which had earned him an invincibility to all opponents save one. Because no one can receive the boon of absolute invincibility, Tāraka had carefully chosen the one opponent who, he gambled, would never come into existence: a son of Śiva. The likelihood that the most powerful divine ascetic would break his disciplined practice and become subject to his body's desire was remote at best. Clearly, Tāraka's shrewd choice had put the gods in a difficult situation. But they had begun to craft a plan which would move the powerful Śiva from control to arousal. Their scheme would draw Śiva out of his highly disciplined practice and entice him to desire a woman powerful enough to bear his fiery seed.

As we begin, the messenger of Indra, king of the gods, has just returned from a visit to the god of the mountains, Himācala. This messenger, Nārada, is bringing news to the gods that Himācala's daughter, Pārvatī, is the wife destined for the great god, Śiva.

*Kāma Battles Śiva (*Matsya *and* Padma Purāṇas*).*

After Nārada had informed Himācala that Pārvatī would be the wife of Śiva, he returned to Indra, saying that Kāma would now be needed to draw Śiva out of his asceticism. (207)

At that moment, Indra *remembered* [*sasmāra*] the god Kāma [who wields] the mango shoot arrow. (208) Indra told Kāma to go with Madhu [Spring], the king of seasons, to join Śaṇkara [Śiva] to the daughter of the mountain [Pārvatī]. (211)

Kāma was quite afraid, saying that Śaṇkara was unconquerable [*duḥ-sādhya*] (213); and that such schemes result only in one's own destruction.

Indra replied: We are your authority here. A blacksmith has no power without a pair of tongs. (218)[5] So Kāma left for Himācala with his wife Rati [Sexual Delight] and Madhu.

Strategizing, Kāma thought it would be better to first agitate the mind of Śiva [with the following emotions], thus ensuring victory. (220–221) He thought: Anger [*krodha*] follows hatred [dveṣa]. Envy [īrṣya], powerful friend [of desire], puts non-attachment to flight and destroys firm resolve [*dhairya*].(222–223)[6] [After agitating his mind] I will place pleasures before Śiva's senses [*indriya*]. (226)

Seeing Śaṅkara seated among the trees with black bees buzzing all around, Kāma entered his mind through an opening in his ear. (235–236) [Immediately] Śiva began thinking about the daughter of Dakṣa and his *samādhi* [deep state of meditation] vanished. (237–238) Knowing he had been betrayed, Śiva plunged himself back into his *Yogamāyā* [state of deep concentration]. (240) [Suffering with] Śiva's heat, Kāma left his heart. (241)

Outside with his friend Madhu, Kāma with the makara[7] banner sent a mango blossom arrow called Mohana [Delusion, Infatuation] to strike the heart of Śiva. Feeling passion rising, Śiva knew that emotions were taking control. Filled with anger, he opened his third eye. From the sparks of this third eye, Madana [Kāma] was instantly reduced to ashes. (249–250)

To prevent the world from being burned up, Śiva distributed the fire of Kāma [Smara] part by part: in the mango tree, in madhu [honey, wine, the spring month of Caitra], in the moon, in flowers, in black bees, and in cuckoos. (251–252)

Rati, seeing her husband, Madana, reduced to ashes, wept and wept, along with Madhu [Spring]. (256) Smearing herself with the ashes of Smara [Memory, another epithet of Kāma], Rati went to petition Śiva. (259) After many salutations to the great god, Rati begged him to restore Kāma to life. (268) Śaṅkara [Śiva] told her that in time [kale], Kāma would again be alive, famous in the worlds as "Anaṅga" [the One Without Limbs, i.e. invisible]. (272)

The story continues with a description of the subsequent asceticism of Pārvatī, daughter of Himācala, to attract the attention of Śiva, the sages petitioning Śiva to marry her, and the gods' celebration of the wedding of Śiva and Pārvatī. But our central focus remains the nature of kāma/desire as presented in the basic structure of the tale through the character of Kāma.

Nature of Kāma/kāma in the burning narratives

The basic story can be broken down into six major parts which describe the character and function of Kāma. These components of the story establish a framework for analyzing the variant retellings, focused specifically on what the story communicates about Kāma/kāma, Desire/desire. Defining the character and function of Kāmadeva in the tale provides some insight into what is being communicated about the nature of kāma, desire. And, as in life, the many facets of this character, which are highlighted by the story, necessarily overlap and redefine each other.

Focusing specifically on Kāmadeva, eight primary actions take place:

1. Kāma is *remembered* into, or in some versions *thought* into, the presence of Indra, king of the gods.
2. Indra's slave, Kāma, is told he has no choice but to carry out Indra's wishes.
3. Attacking his target subject on several fronts, Kāma enters through Śiva's mind, heart, and senses. Kāma uses specifically Śiva's senses of hearing (bees), smell (flowers), touch (breeze), and sight (woman).
4. More directly, Kāma shoots a flower arrow and pierces the heart of Śiva.
5. Angered by the stirring of his emotions rooted in still active desire, Śiva burns Kāma to ashes.
6. Kāma's burning produces a fire which is distributed among specific parts of nature.
7. Rati smears her body with the ash of Kāma and petitions Śiva to restore his life.
8. Śiva promises that Kāma will be revived in the future as Anaṅga (the Bodiless One, invisible), thus restoring harmony/balance in the world.

Carefully structured into the tale, each of these components offers insight into the nature of desire.

Kāma as Smara: Interconnectedness of memory and desire. The episode begins with Indra summoning Kāma simply by *remembering* him. This effective call to Desire reminds the audience of one of Kāma's oldest epithets, *Smara,* meaning Memory or Remembering. In the Indian tradition, desire and memory are integrally linked. Without some memory of pleasure, desire for an object does not exist. Identifying desire with memory, passages from ancient texts such as the *Atharva Veda*[8] refer to Kāma as Smara, and contemporary literature continues to use this epithet for the god of desire. Indeed, connections between desire and remembering are found throughout Sanskrit literary and philosophical texts.

The master Sanskrit playwright Kālidāsa bases the entire plot of his drama *Śākuntalā and the Ring of Recollection (Abhijñānaśākuntala)* around the nuances of remembering and forgetting. Kālidāsa weaves a masterful plot in which remembering and forgetting create the central tension that keeps desire alive but continuously thwarted. When the cloud of forgetting is finally lifted, the two lovers, separated for nine years because one has "forgotten" the other, are reunited. Passion is poignantly portrayed throughout the play in the lovers' memories of each other, which excite more emotional intensity than their time together. In the essay accompanying her translation of *Śākuntalā,* Barbara S. Miller explains this often-used Sanskrit literary technique of desiring-forgetting-remembering:

> Memory is crucial to the production of romantic sentiment throughout Sanskrit literature. Forgetfulness and memory function prominently in several works: the epic *Rāmāyaṇa,* the play *Avimāraka* attributed to Bhāsa; Bhavabhūti's drama the *Uttararāmacarita;* the collection of love-thief poems called the *Caurapañcāṣikā,* attributed to Bilhaṇa; and Jayadeva's dramatic lyrical poem, the *Gītagovinda.*
>
> In this Sanskrit literature, an act of remembering is a conventional technique for relating the antithetical modes of love-in-separation (*vipralambha-śṛṅgāra*) and love-in-union (*saṃbhoga-śṛṅgāra*). . . .[9]

In her own poetic style, Miller continues to connect memory with kāma as sensual or sexual desire:

> Even as a literary convention of intense love, memory has the power to break through the logic of everyday experience—it makes visible what is invisible, obliterates distances, reverses chronologies, and fuses what is ordinarily separate.

This integral connection between intense love, sensual desire, and memory is dramatized frequently in Sanskrit literature, evoking empathy in the audience as they remember their own passionate liaisons.

Indian philosophers also connect kāma and smara. In the philosophical tradition, the understanding is that what is perceived through the sense organs (seeing, hearing, smelling, and so on) creates an impression on the mind. Subsequently, memory occurs when one of these latent impressions is awakened.[10] Because it is impossible to desire something not previously experienced, desire depends completely on memory, on the sensory impressions stored by the mind.

As memory draws these mental impressions into the present, desire materializes. Thus, Indra can easily remember Kāmadeva into his presence, and Smara (Memory) works well as an epithet of Kāmadeva. Manoja (Born in/of the Mind), Manobhava (Existing in the Mind), and Manmatha (Mind-Agitating), other common epithets of Kāma, emphasize that desire is rooted in the mind. But focusing even more specifically within the mind, the epithet, Smara, reflects the essential function of memory in evoking desire.

Kāma and the king of the gods. In the story, Kāmadeva is portrayed as being completely at the service of Indra. However, this interaction between Kāma and Indra reflects a certain irony. Indra is well known for several character traits, including his inability to resist an attractive woman even when she refuses him. Willing to deceive women about his identity in order to get into their beds, Indra is well known as a god who is enslaved by his own desires.[11] The other trait that often characterizes Kāma is his need to maintain power.

Many puranic stories begin with Indra's anxiety over the growing power of a serious ascetic. Afraid of losing power to a usurper,[12] Indra often plays a Kāmadeva-like role by sending apsarases[13] to seduce the ascetic. As lust overtakes the ascetic, dissipating his yogic power, Indra is once again unchallenged. In theses stories, Indra performs Kāma's role, ordering seductive women to distract ascetic men. Indra in these stories is associated not only with his own undisciplined libido, but with evoking the same unbridled lust in others.

A classic example of unbounded sexual desire, Indra also exemplifies a classic desire to gain and maintain power. In a story from the *Brahmavaivarta Purāṇa*,[14] Indra causes havoc among the gods when he attempts to demonstrate his power by building the most magnificent palace ever known, endlessly adding rooms and gardens and adornments. In this tale, the great gods join forces to show him the futility of a life ruled by desire. If he continues to build palaces while neglecting his inner life, he may earn a future life for himself as an ant building bigger and bigger anthills. Because Indian audiences know well the laughable Indra who runs in circles chasing his own lustful desires, they take careful note of an Indra who is mastering Kāma/kāma. A story in which Kāmadeva jumps to respond to Indra's command is a meaningful turning of the tables.

This new role for Indra posits an interesting reversal in which Indra controls Kāma. Portraying Kāma as Indra's servant immediately focuses attention on mastering desire as the focal point of the narrative. Yet, ultimately, the complexity of desire makes questions of its control difficult to assess completely. When Kāmadeva is burnt to ashes, has Śiva fully mastered desire? When Kāma is ultimately revived in an invisible form with power over all beings, does he/desire retain ultimate power in the universe? Is there a subtle balance between discipline and desire, with neither retaining full control for long?

As no one answer satisfies all perspectives, the variant narrations of the episode offer a more complete and nuanced picture in their differences. When the variants are laid out side by side as a way to see the larger picture, they present a wide-angle view of desire's complex and subtle functioning in human nature.

Kāma enters through mind, heart, and senses. In the *Matsya* and *Padma* narratives, Kāma knows that Śiva's mind must be agitated first, before he can begin to shake the yogi's disciplined focus. So Kāmadeva introduces into this mind: hatred (*dveṣa*), anger (*krodha*), and envy (*īrṣya*), mental states understood to be the antithesis of spiritual equilibrium. In contemporary India, for example, when one begins a religious pilgrimage vows are taken to abstain from kāma (desire), *krodha* (anger), *lobha* (greed/covetousness), and *moha* (delusion, infatuation)—elements that disturb the calm focus (*dhairya*) needed for religious practice. This undistracted calm focus is often described in the texts as a desireless or passionless (*vairāgya*) state.

Desire, anger, and greed (kāma, krodha, and lobha) are specifically addressed by *Kṛṣṇa* in the sixteenth chapter of the *Bhagavad Gītā,* when he describes a person with the character of an *asura,* a person with demonic traits.

> Bound by a hundred fetters of hope,
> obsessed by desire [kāma] and anger [krodha],
> they hoard wealth in stealthy ways
> to satisfy their desires [kāma]. (XVI.12)[15]
>
> The three gates of hell
> that destroy the self
> are desire [kāma], anger [krodha], and greed [lobha];
> one must relinquish all three. (XVI.21)

In line with the teachings of the Gītā, which refers to hatred[16] as a particular manifestation of desire, the poet tells us that hatred, anger, and greed will break the ascetic focus of even the great god Śiva.

Indian Buddhism places two of these three elements at the center of the Buddhist wheel of life, as mental states that trap people in the self-absorbed dramas of existence. Also called the three fires, they propel people through endless cycles of existence and are represented in the wheel by a cock (kāma), snake (dveṣa), and pig (moha), holding one another's tails in their mouths as they run in a continuous circle. Buddhist texts explain that the karmic retribution one generates as a result of desire, hatred, or delusion determines one's subsequent rebirth.

Kāma disturbs Śiva's mind by engendering anger, envy, hatred, and later the delusion of infatuation, images that are rooted in long-held teachings about the functioning of desire. Both anger and hatred are seen as flipside opposites of desire: when desire is thwarted, this desire-energy can easily become anger or hatred. Because an Indian audience knows that desire is integral to the manifestation of anger, hatred, and envy, when Kāmadeva penetrates Śiva's mind with these elements, his actions make perfect sense.

With perhaps less subtlety, these *Matsya* and *Padma* narratives continue by illustrating the connection of Kāma with the senses (*indriya*). Kāma first enters the mind of Śiva through the sense of hearing, through the buzzing of black bees which are symbols of sexual activity in the classical literature. "Resorting to the humming of the bees on the tops of the trees, Madana entered Śiva's mind through the cavity of his ear."[17] All the variants make a point of describing flowers—blooming, fragrant, and sometimes out of season. Birds sing sweetly and black bees hum in the background, while the spring month, Madhu, blows gentle breezes. Poor Śiva's senses are being bombarded, quite literally, with delightful sensations flowing directly into the mind.

Kāma's movements and Śiva's reactions reflect the overlapping and tangled mass of physical sensations, emotions, and mental states long recognized in Indian philosophical literature as manifestations of desire.[18] The story reflects this complex interrelatedness of mind, emotions, and senses in vivid images, knowing these images will more effectively evoke the audience's own experiences of longing. Just as marketers stimulate pleasurable memories from the past to evoke irresistible desires in the present, the storyteller's images awaken memories that stir up old desires. Such visual imagery creates an experiential understanding of desire which resonates to the human experience, while neatly sidestepping the cerebral question of *how* desire works.

Kāma pierces the heart of Śiva with a flower arrow. Kāma is a warrior who wields a sugar cane bow and flower arrows, a warrior who pierces the heart of Śiva. With wonderful irony, Kāma appears as a dangerous warrior but one who does not serve the god of death. His arrows are flower shafts, often sweet-smelling mango blossoms soon to be delicious fruit. Yet, the story warns of their insidious power.

Known by a plethora of epithets such as flower-weaponed (*puṣpāyudha*), flower-arrowed (*kusumeṣu*), one with a flower bow (*puṣpabāṇa*), five-arrowed (*pañcaṣara*) and flower-bannered (*puṣpadvaja*), Kāma combines the image of a warrior with that of a pleasant rogue, an enjoyer of beauty and sensuality. But the metaphor of bow and arrows insists that desire is dangerous. The story cautions its listeners to remember that Kāma's flower arrows do destroy. In the language of battle, Kāma's weapons assault the senses of his victims leaving them blinded by emotion and burning with desire.

In the *Matsya* and *Padma* narratives, as in most of the variants, Kāma's arrow, called here "Mohana," meaning *infatuating* or *deluding,* pierces Śiva in the heart. Though ultimately the catalyst for Śiva's destruction of Kāma, this arrow that infatuates also transforms Śiva. The steadfast yogi becomes a lover burning with passion.

Although the *Matsya* and *Padma* do not describe this transformation in detail, other variants[19] paint a sensuous picture of the great god completely mesmerized with Pārvatī, enjoying the vibrant spring with which Madhu has surrounded them. In these variants, when struck with Kāma's arrow, Śiva sees only his lover and can't bear to be separated from her. Indeed, after destroying Kāma, Śiva becomes totally absorbed in Kāma's domain, where all attention is focused on gratifying the senses.[20] In spite of destroying the god of desire, Śiva becomes a slave to his own desire, absorbed for eons in making love to his goddess-consort. The flower arrow that cannot kill the physical body does transform the mind and heart. According to these variant tellings, the power of the god of desire equals that of the great yogi.

However, in the version told in the *Matsya, Padma,* and *Śiva Purāṇa*s, Śiva does not succumb immediately to the power of Kāma's arrows. Rather, after being struck and burning Kāma, Śiva returns to the steadfast depth of his meditation. The message of these narratives is that asceticism is stronger than desire. The serious ascetic will defeat even the most powerful form of desire, in this case the god of desire himself. These purāṇas continue to describe the long ascetic practice of Pārvatī to win Śiva, and finally his consent to marry her but not for himself, only for the benefit of others who need his son to defeat the demon Tāraka.

These two accounts of the myth reflect quite divergent messages: the first, that focused asceticism can dismiss the lure of desire, barely losing a moment's equilibrium, and the second, that the power of desire may overwhelm even the most serious ascetic, as it did the supreme god Śiva. Although these conflicting variants indicate different perspectives within the tradition, the variants as a group indicate that ultimately each person must find the balance between desire and discipline anew. Even for the most experienced ascetic, when passion arises, the outcome is never certain.

Kāma incites anger in Śiva. The message in this part of the story is the most readily apparent to the audience. Ascetic practice, *tapas*, is understood to generate a heat that burns away the longing of desires. The first meaning of the word *tapas* in the Sanskrit-English dictionary is "warmth, heat," from the verbal root *tap,* which means to "give out heat, be hot, shine (as the sun)." Tapas is intense heat like that of the sun, but also the intense heat generated by ascetic practice.

The great yogi, Śiva, possesses the ability to obliterate any opponent with his intense heat, but the allegorical importance of desire as his opponent reflects the essential tension experienced in ascetic practice, desire versus discipline. The goal of ascetic practice is to gain knowledge and power by disciplining the desires rooted in body, mind, and emotions. Reducing the god of desire to a heap of ashes is a graphic depiction of an ascetic's victory over his desires.

However, this process of cultivating and maintaining ascetic discipline in the face of desire is endlessly complex. The god Śiva is a wonderful study of the coming together of asceticism and eroticism in one character, with the fiery intensity of both. Wendy Doniger has written extensively about how these issues are explored in the purāṇas and other Sanskrit texts in her work *Śiva, the Erotic Ascetic.*

> Indeed, it is almost impossible to find a myth in which Śiva *remains* chaste throughout, though many myths are based upon the initial premise of his chastity [as a yogi]. Even in the *Mahābhārata* passage which describes Śiva as the chaste *brahmacārin,* Śiva is praised as the god who 'sports with the daughters and the wives of the sages, with erect hair, a great phallus, naked, with an

excited look. . . . The universe was created from the seed that poured out of the liṅga of Śiva during the sexual act, and the gods worship that liṅga.'[21]

Given the allegorical frame of the story, what does Kāma as a bit of ash say about the presence of desire in the universe? Does the story suggest that desire can be eradicated by ascetic practice? Or does desire when conquered in one form merely take another, posing a new challenge to internal discipline?

Kāma's fire distributed in nature. "To prevent the world from being burned up, Śiva distributed the fire of Smara part by part in the mango tree, in madhu [wine, honey and the spring month of Caitra], in the moon, in flowers, in black bees, and in the [very amorous] cuckoo." (*Matsya* 251–252)

Acknowledging the power of Kāma's fiery passion, which ironically and poetically mirrors the fire of Śiva, the great god's act dilutes the force of Kāma's infatuating presence by spreading it more widely. Although the classical Indian tradition maintains the spiritual superiority of ascetic heat over the fire of passion, the story explains that either heat can destroy when outside its normal parameters. Just as Śiva can incinerate that which disrupts his state of *samādhi* (deep meditation), the intact force of Kāmadeva when released from the confines of his body can also enflame the world. Out of concern for the universe then, Śiva decides to release the burning passion of Kāma in small doses, into different parts of nature. The story explains the danger of attempting to eradicate the form of desire.

Unable to completely eradicate desire, Śiva pushes Kāma into the sweetness of honey, the fragrance of mangoes, the intoxication of wine, moonlight, and the brisk quality of spring air, where he will, of course, continue to incite passion. Present now in new ways, Kāma will again penetrate Śiva's ascetic defenses. The story scatters the essence of kāma through the natural world, explaining how friends become lovers while walking in the moonlight, or old lovers more amorous as they watch birds fluffed up in courtship dances, having drunk the nectar of the flowers.

Ironically then, in the instinctive act of destroying the god of desire, Śiva helps Kāma to advance his goals. No longer confined to the person and arrows of Kāmadeva, desire now appears in multiple guises. Like cutting off the head of a hydra to have two heads grow in its place, Śiva gives the world even more venues for Kāma to arouse feelings of sensuality and longing.

Finally, Kāmadeva does ultimately evoke desire within the great god. Not only does Śiva become infatuated with Pārvatī and help the gods to gain their warrior, but all beings find their own desires enhanced in the glow of the moon and the sweetness of wine.

Kāma's wife takes his ash: Delight smeared with the ashes of desire. Layers of irony and reversal are packed into the image of Rati wearing the ashes of the dead Kāma. This beautiful consort belongs to a class of beings known as *apsaras*es, seductive celestial nymphs who appear in diaphanous garments to charm even the most disciplined of beings. In this episode, however, Rati follows the behavior of a female ascetic, a yoginī, who smears herself with sacred ash before placing herself before a deity or beginning her *tapas* (ascetic practice). Covering her body with an impure or polluting substance, this yoginī's sacred ash is not the traditional burnt sandalwood paste, but the remains of her husband, which emit the still powerful energy of desire. Emphasizing the loss of Kāma's body, Rati smears her body with the ashes that are the remnants of his physical form. Although the ash of a cremated body is an extremely polluting substance within the Indian tradition, Rati wears Kāma's ash as a symbol of her intimate association with desire. Rati petitions the great god for a reversal of the death and pollution represented in his ash. Kāma, who is associated with the auspicious purity of a wedding, has now become the polluting ash of a corpse.

Rati, whose name means sexual delight, has also become her own opposite. Clothed in ash and performing tapas like a yoginī, Rati stands in prayer, grieving and petitioning the great god for a boon to restore desire in the form of her husband. A voluptuous apsaras in the role of a simply clad yoginī, Rati embodies passion, but here in the form of grief. The images burst with irony yet reflect the paradoxical reality that human grief, like anger and hatred, is deeply rooted in desire.

Kāma as invisible presence. Responding to the intensity of Rati's asceticism, Śiva tells her that after some time Kāma will again be alive and known in the three worlds, but as Anaṅga, meaning "without limbs, the invisible one." (In some variants, it is promised more specifically that Kāma will be revived only when Śiva has taken a wife.) With the revival of Kāma and the arousal of the yogi Śiva, the reversals are complete. Śiva has been transformed from yogi to lover, the sensuous Rati is now a yoginī, and Kāma has become invisible, losing his stunningly beautiful body forever. But these disruptions of the natural order also produce chaos. Paralleling the beginning of the tale when the gods needed help against the chaos-producing demon Tārakāsura, the loss of Śiva and Kāma now requires another extraordinary event to restore the order. Without Kāma, Śiva will not produce the son needed to defeat the demons, and procreation will not continue in the world. But the audience knows that the stage has been set for the great yogi to give up his life as a *brahmacārin* (celibate ascetic), to take a wife and produce the son needed to restore order in the cosmos.

In the course of time, this son of Śiva will push the demons (*daitya*s) back into their realm and place the gods again in control of heaven. The son of Śiva will restore the cosmic order. However, Kāmadeva will remain invisible, alas, without his beautiful body. Indeed, this story explains the invisibility of desire. On one level, the story acts as a grand etiological tale, explaining how all manner of creatures are subject to the intangible force of desire. Unseen and unheard, Kāma moves about freely, hidden in flowers and bees and honey.

Without announcing himself, Kāma pervades our environment and disturbs our equanimity.

On another level, the revival of Kāma as invisible establishes the dominance of Śiva over Kāma, the possibility that ascetic discipline can conquer craving. Once the god of desire has been revived as Anaṅga, he is no longer a worthy opponent of Śiva; there is no possibility of Kāma wielding power over the yogi. While Anaṅga is immensely powerful in the world and his revival reestablishes order, he is no longer a threat to Mahādeva (the Great God), not only because Śiva has defeated him with the fire of his anger but because Śiva has subsumed the essential nature of the god of desire within himself. Śiva is known by his popular epithet, Kāmeśvara, the Lord of Kāma.

The revival of the god of desire restores balance in the universe, continued procreation for all beings. The gods and Rati had pleaded for Kāma's resuscitation because they needed him for balance in their worlds. Like human beings, Rati and the gods must also have desire in their lives.

Unhindered by a body, Kāma-Anaṅga gladly resumes his proper place in the world. Once transformed in the fire of Śiva's asceticism, Kāma-Anaṅga represents the transmuting of human desire in the heat of spiritual discipline. Yet, significantly, the story makes clear that desire is not destroyed in ascetic practice but rather changed into new forms (the flowering trees, and so on), and even into forms with no form (anaṅga).

A stronger Kāma, a stronger Śiva *(Śiva Purāṇa)*

One of the wonderful elements of folklore is that each tale has a limitless number of variants. Variant narratives offer new emphases, give importance to different facets of the tale, and may even change the outcome or moral in some way. For example, the well-known folktale "Three Little Pigs" is told in two primary variants that emphasize different cultural values. In one variant, the first two pigs are eaten by the wolf because they had not disciplined themselves to do the hard work necessary to build a house that would protect them in the future. In another variant, although the pigs still had not disciplined themselves to build solid houses, the attention of the story shifts to their rescue by the farsighted, hardworking brother pig, who takes care of his family in crisis. The first variant underscores the importance of hard work and self-discipline with the consequence of a rather gruesome death if one opts for laziness and immediate gratification. In the second variant, though these pigs still have to endure a bit of drama regarding their survival, the story focuses rather on the additional virtues of kind-heartedness and caring for family in the self-disciplined third brother.

Variants of a tale can illuminate the values and teachings imbedded in prior versions or add their own messages. Variants work as teaching devices, as well as entertainment, as storytellers take a familiar image or accepted meaning and tilt it slightly to grab the audience's attention in a new way. Comedians and advertisers use the same technique, tickling the mind by tweaking commonplace images to make them say something startlingly different. For example, the Australian film "Babe" worked because the wise voice in the film belonged to a pig, commonly accepted as a lethargic farm animal without either voice or wisdom. By analyzing what has been turned inside out, we understand more fully the messages embedded in the original narration.

As we explore the significance of the variant told in the *Śiva Purāṇa,*[22] we should keep in mind that this story forms part of a collection of stories narrated primarily to extol the praises of the god for whom the text is named, Śiva. And because these stories, for the most part, maintain the primacy of the god Śiva, the Kāma story, too, should be understood within this context.

Possibly a later compendium than the texts we discussed earlier, the *Matsya* and *Padma Purāṇas,* the *Śiva Purāṇa* dates from a period not earlier than the eleventh century, and possibly later.[23] Providing another variant of the story, the *Śiva Purāṇa* offers a slightly different perspective on the interaction between Śiva and Kāmadeva. Twice the text refers to Kāma as residing within Śiva, making explicit the idea that the ascetic is battling his own inner demon rather than an external force. Though Kāma dies, he lives on as a part of the great god himself.

Kāma battles Śiva in the Śiva Purāṇa.

After hearing Brahmā's assurance to the gods that the son of Śiva would kill the demon Tāraka, Indra *remembered* Kāma who instantly appeared in his presence, along with Rati and Vasanta [Spring]. (17.2)

Indra said to Kāma: I have many good friends but no friend [mitra] who is your equal. (17.8) Even my unrivaled thunderbolt is sometimes ineffective, but you never fail. (17.9) The test of a [true] friend is in a time of adversity, (17.12) and this matter [that I have called you for] is one that concerns all the gods as well as everyone else. (17.15)

Kāma replied: O dear friend, I shall cause the downfall of your enemy [Śiva] who is performing a severe penance to usurp your position. (17.19)[24]

Indra explained further: The entire world is being harrassed by the demon Tāraka and only the son of Śiva can destroy him. (17.31, 34)

With a face shining like a full-blown lotus, Kāma agreed to perform this task. (17.41)

The arrogant [*garvī*] Kāma first spread the enchanting power of Spring all around. (18.1) So much sensuality was difficult for [all] the sages dwelling in the forest to endure. (18.10)

Though his usual position was inside the mind, Kāma took out his mango blossom arrow (18.15) and stood outside [of Śiva]. (18.18) Using the arrow called Harṣaṇa [Sexual Excitement], Kāma filled Śiva with the thrill of sexual excitement [*harṣayāmāsa*]. (18.25) Upon receiving another of Kāma's quick arrows, (18.27), Śiva became greatly infatuated with Pārvatī. (18.29–42) [But then] Śiva realized that he was just being disturbed by Kāma, and he resumed the state of detached passionlessness [vairāgya]. (18.43, 45)

However, when Śiva saw the proud Kāma getting ready to let another arrow fly, he got angry. (19.6–8) When this arrow failed, Kāma began to feel afraid. With his fear rising, Kāma remembered Indra and the other gods who came immediately to his side. (19.9–13) But before they had time to intercede, a flame of fire sprang from Śiva's third eye, reducing Kāma to ashes. (19.14–17)

When Rati became unconscious with grief (19.20), the gods told her to preserve some of the ashes of Kāma. (19.27) Because Rati was cursing the gods for sending Kāma on this mission, the gods said to her: "No one [else] gives us happiness or misery. All beings enjoy and experience the fruit of what they do [themselves]. You curse the gods in vain." (19.28)

When the gods pleaded with Mahādeva for the resuscitation of Kāma, Śiva explained that this manifestation of his anger could not be revoked. (19.37) Kāma would remain bodiless [anaṅga] until Kṛṣṇa would beget him [again] in Rukmiṇī. (19.38–39) His name at that time would be Pradyumna and he would be abducted by the demon Śambara.[25] (19.40–44)

However, the gods pleaded for Kāma's immediate return. (19.46) So Śiva said: I will resuscitate [Kāma] within, and he will be my gaṇa[26] always. (19.48) This story should not be told in the presence of anyone, O gods. (19.49)

As in the *Matsya/Padma* variant, Indra remembers Kāma into his presence. But here, Kāma also uses this mental trick when he becomes afraid and *remembers* Indra and other gods to his aid. Again, the narrative reinforces the reciprocal relationship between Kāma and Smara, desire and memory.

However, in this account, Kāma is *not* the slave of Indra. In fact, the storyteller goes to great lengths to tell us that Indra and Kāmadeva are friends. Indra professes to Kāma that he has no friend anywhere who is his equal (*tvattulyam na hi kutracit*), that is, no better friend in the world. So rather than ordering Kāma to arouse Śiva, Indra flatters him, saying that while his own weapon, the thunderbolt (*vajra*), sometimes misses, Kāma's weapons never fail. In this shift from slave to friend, Kāma's status increases. He is now a powerful and valued ally of the king of the gods who can be defeated only by a deity possessing even greater power. Viewing Kāma as a stronger opponent makes Śiva, in turn, appear more powerful when he defeats him.

Three arrows are mentioned here: the mango blossom as in the *Matsya* and *Padma* recensions, and two others, Harṣaṇa (Sexual Arousal) and the arrow that Śiva did not allow to pierce him. Kāma's arrows are especially significant here because they become his sole weapons. Unable to slip into Śiva's mind through the senses, as in other variants, Kāma must rely on an arrow to penetrate the focused attention of the yogi from the outside. But as an archer in full view, Kāma is also more vulnerable to retaliation by Śiva. Limiting Kāma to only his arrows, highlights the difficulty of arousing passion in an intense yogi whose attention is so completely focused on his internal reality.

Indeed, in this version, Śiva is so powerful that the story must be told a bit differently. In this narration, Kāma is not able to find even the smallest opening into Śiva's body/mind, like the ear or sense of hearing described as a place of vulnerability in the *Matsya/Padma* narrative. Śiva is so completely absorbed in the meditative state that nothing he hears or perceives around him arouses any response. Although he registers the arousal in his body produced by the arrow Harṣaṇa, Śiva does not allow himself to be struck a second time. In contrast to the character portrayed in the *Matsya/Padma* variant, the great god in the *Śiva Purāṇa* is more controlled, less vulnerable to Kāma, in short, the ideal yogi. A Śaivite devotional text, the *Śiva Purāṇa* praises the great god by expanding his powers beyond those delineated in other texts.

Another way that this text makes the character of Śiva more powerful is by describing how the great god finally subsumes Kāma within himself. After the gods have pleaded a second time for the resuscitation of Kāmadeva, Śiva agrees not only to make Kāma one of his gaṇas (attendants), but to resuscitate Kāma within himself.[27] In a very unusual passage, Śiva delivers an extremely *uncommon* injunction in puranic storytelling. Śiva tells the gods that this story should *not* be told. At the end of most puranic stories, the narrator describes how retelling the preceding story will bring an end to all misery, merit equal to studying the Vedas, great happiness to all who hear, salvation, and many other blessings. But here, Śiva's words sound a warning not to tell the story. As it follows the description of Śiva containing Kāma within himself, perhaps this warning indicates that while a close identity between Śiva and Kāma does exist, Śiva devotees would do well to keep these deities separate in their lives.

The identification of Śiva with Kāma is very often implicit in the structure and images of the Burning Story narrative, but it is rarely presented so explicitly. The storyteller knows he is taking a daring step to draw such a graphic connection between desire and asceticism, and yet it makes sense to an Indian audience. Śiva is famous as the god who transforms proscribed behavior into religious practice, such as meditating in the most polluted of places, the cremation ground. Here, Śiva revives the god of desire within himself while living as one who renounces all desire. Cleverly, the text takes accepted perspectives of desire and discipline and turns them upside down to emphasize the complex role of desire within human nature, for ascetic and for householder. Only those who understand the power and complexity of desire will understand that Śiva has not, by taking Kāma within himself, turned to a life of sensual pleasure. Rather, Śiva's action of subsuming Kāma within himself recognizes that desire is a powerful internal force that cannot be eliminated, regardless of how many times Kāmadeva is killed.

This *Śiva Purāṇa* variant establishes a specific power relationship between desire and discipline, as Kāma becomes Śiva's gaṇa, one of his troops, permanently attached to the great god. Making the god of desire one of Śiva's many troops recognizes Kāma as inferior to and separate from the great god, and desire inferior to ascetic discipline. Although Śiva does bring the god of desire to life within himself, the story quickly underscores the disparity between their positions as lord and gaṇa. In this clear relationship between lord and subject, Śiva remains the victor over Kāmadeva and over his own passionate nature.

Although the Indian tradition also revels in stories of Śiva and Pārvatī's love relationship, for the authors of a Śaivite purāṇa, it is important to portray Śiva as more powerful than all other deities, and in this case, more powerful than Kāmadeva.

Kāma chases Śiva into the forest *(Vāmana Purāṇa)*

In this account from the *Vāmana Purāṇa,* Kāmadeva catches Śiva at a very different point of vulnerability. Śiva is grieving inconsolably for the loss of his first wife, Satī, an earlier incarnation of Pārvatī. Seeing him already overcome with desire for his dead wife, Kāma shoots the bereft husband with a number of arrows that infuse him with even greater desire for the impossible, to feel her breath again. The text describes Śiva carrying the corpse of his wife from place to place, unwilling to accept her death.

This *Vāmana Purāṇa* variant[28] combines the burning story with two other tales, one describing Śiva's unique style of mourning Satī, and another presenting Śiva's experience in the Dāru Forest with women infatuated with his desire-ridden body and their powerful husbands.

The extant *Vāmana Purāṇa* studied by Hazra, Haraprasad Shastri, and the editors of the critical edition of the text is thought to date from the ninth to the tenth centuries.[29]

Kāma Battles Śiva in the Vāmana Purāṇa.

When Śaṅkara [Śiva] was wandering about after the death of Satī, Kandarpa [Kāma], armed with flowers, struck Śiva with the arrow Unmāda [Maddener], causing him to be mad [*unmattaḥ*]. (6.26–28) Śiva wandered around the forest madly grieving for Satī, moaning and wailing and finding no peace anywhere. (6.29–42) When Kāma pierced him with the arrow Santāpana [Heating, Inflaming], he became even more afflicted, blowing air out of his mouth again and again. (6.43) When struck again by Madana's [Kāma's] arrow Vijṛmbhaṇa [Extending, Becoming Erect], Śiva wandered about in all directions. (6.45)

Śiva then saw the yakṣa Pañcālika, son of Kubera, and asked him to take on the torment of these arrows. He said that since the death of Varadāmbikā

[Satī], he had been consumed by passion [*kāmāgni*], literally by the fire of Kāma/kāma. [Specifically] as a result of the arrows Unmāda and Vijṛmbhaṇa, he could not find contentment, pleasure, or happiness. (6.46–48)

Pañcālika agreed to take on Śiva's torment. So Śiva granted him a boon, that whoever saw, touched, or worshipped Pañcālika with devotion during the month of Caitra would become intoxicated [*unmādadhara*] with pleasure. They would sing, dance, sport, and play instruments; and in spite of talking and laughing in front of the deity, have yogic powers [*yogayutāstu*]. He would be worshipped as Pañcālikeśa, Lord Pañcālika, and through the grace of Śiva [would have the power to] grant men's wishes. (6.52–54) The yakṣa then departed to a sacred region north of Kālañjara and south of the Himālayas.

Seeing Kāma about to strike again, Hara [Śiva] fled to the Pine Forest [*Dāruvana*] where he was pursued by Madana [Kāma]. (6.57–58) [But along the way], the wives of the Pine Forest sages, seeing Śiva, became aroused themselves. They followed him everywhere like female elephants following male elephants. (6.61–64) The sages then, angry [krodha] at Śiva for captivating their wives, cursed Śiva's liṅga [penis] to fall off. When it fell, the earth split open and Śaṇkara became invisible [*antardhānam jagāma*]. (6.66)

Because the earth was quite agitated, Brahmā and Mādhava [Viṣṇu] began to investigate [where Śiva had gone]. But when they could not find the liṅga's beginning or end, they decided to propitiate the great god. (6.71–77) Hearing their words of praise, Śiva reappeared, asking them why they would propitiate him when his body was inflamed by Kāma. (6.82) [However] Brahmā and Viṣṇu requested that he withdraw his liṅga from the earth, where it was causing havoc [for others]. Śiva agreed on the condition that the gods promise to worship the liṅga. (6.83–84)

When Brahmā had departed and Śaṇkara had withdrawn his liṅga from the earth, Kāma, the god-armed-with-flowers [*kusumayudha*], attempted once more to inflame Śiva. [But] with eyes swollen in anger [krodha], Śiva stared at Smara, immediately burning him from his feet to his waist. (6.93–96)

Realizing his legs were on fire, Kāma threw down his bow, breaking it into five pieces. These fragments of the bow became the fragrant Campaka tree, the Kesar Forest [Kesarāranya], also known as Bakula Forest, the Patala, the five-petalled white Jasmine, and Mallika flowers.[30] As his body continued to burn, Smara also threw down his arrows which, by the grace of Śaṅkara, became thousands of fragrant fruit-bearing trees, like the mango.

Śiva departed to do tapas [austerities] in the Himālayas and Kāma became known as Anaṅga [the Invisible One]. (6.97–107)

In this variant, Kāmadeva holds the power through the entire episode until Śiva's anger, another manifestation of desire, incinerates the god of desire, who by this point appears to quite deserve his death.

Śiva's tumultuous internal state is reflected in the story as the great god, overwhelmed by grief and literally driven mad by his desire for the return of his dead wife, runs from place to place, in an effort to avoid Kāma'a arrows. Trying to rid himself of his painful longing, Śiva, ironically, turns a yakṣa into a multiform of Kāmadeva by giving him the power to intoxicate, in return for relieving him of his own intoxicated and maddening desire. Kāma wields the arrow, Unmāda (Maddener, Intoxicator), while Pañcālika receives from Śiva the ability to bestow the state of "unmādadhara." The text clearly connects the yakṣa with Kāma by using the same word, unmāda, to describe the state each bestows, though significantly the madness provoked by Kāma can appear as either love and pleasure or longing and grief.

Śiva runs to rid himself of both desiring and being desired. The skillful storyteller places the great ascetic under the control of the god of desire, but at the same time gives Śiva the power to act as Kāma. The ascetic is simultaneously controlled by desire, his own for Satī, while evoking desire in others, the sages' wives. Unable to escape the entanglement of desire in any form, he now evokes lust in others by virtue of his own state of arousal. His mere presence excites lust in the women living in the forest where he has run for refuge. Cursed by their angry and jealous husbands, Śiva finally separates himself from his body, the obvious manifestation of his desire. Totally at the mercy of Kāma, Śiva retreats into invisibility.

Building on images described in simpler versions of the story, this variant explores desire more directly as grief, jealousy, and anger. When Śiva becomes invisible, he can no longer evoke passion in others or exist as a target for Kāma. Only by eliminating his physical body and its out-of-control responses can Śiva find relief from the torture of desire. Of course, Śiva is not completely invisible as he leaves behind his liṅga, the physical embodiment of sexual desire, yogic discipline, and the chaos-ridden tension that exists between the two. Although Śiva cuts off that part of his body where desire is most apparent, he cannot escape the other dimensions of desire still tormenting him. Though easiest to recognize in the appetites of the body, desire is evidently not located solely in the body. Śiva explains to Brahmā and Viṣṇu that even without his liṅga, he is still being consumed by the flames of desire.

Kāma's arrows, Unmāda, Santāpana, and Vijṛmbhaṇa, need no explanation. What sets this variant apart from others is the supreme yogi's acknowledgment that he cannot bear the intensity of Kāma's arrows. Because even he is not skilled enough an ascetic to handle the pain, he must bargain with the earth spirit, Pañcālika, to suffer the torment of these arrows. Śiva grants him a nature that will please those who worship him, just as Kāmadeva pleases his devotees. In the worship of Pañcālika, Śiva describes the devoted going "mad," dancing, singing, playing musical instruments, making a lot of noise, and laughing in the spring month of Caitra. This "madness" can be associated with the arrow Unmāda, the Maddener, and also with rituals devoted to Kāmadeva.[31] Whoever receives the fire of Kāma or touches that fire *becomes* Kāma in some way. When Śiva feels the pull of desire in himself, he runs into the forest, the place traditionally associated with ascetics and the disciplining of desire within oneself. Reflecting this traditional asceticism of the forest, Śiva's sexual organ falls to the earth and is then raised up as an object of devotion. In India, the Śiva liṅga is a sacred object embodying the power of the god Śiva in an aniconic form.

Describing Śiva's inability to handle the torment of Kāma, the storyteller explores the conflict between ascetic discipline and desire. The ascetic gives away the *kāmāgni* (fire of kāma), which is burning him up inside, to an earth spirit; but because he has not yet resolved the conflict between desire and ascetic discipline, he moves on to the forest, where he immediately arouses the desires of others. Like Pañcālika when he receives the fire of Kāma, Śiva also becomes a multiform of Kāma, evoking feelings of lust in those around him. As Wendy Doniger points out in her study of the great god,[32] desire and asceticism paradoxically coexist within Śiva. This particular story demonstrates the internal struggle of the god as he attempts to resolve the tension of these conflicting forces.

The story of Śiva in the Pine Forest establishes the importance of worshipping the linga while exploring the conflict between asceticism and desire. As a story within a story, Śiva's actions in the Pine Forest parallel those of Kāma in the burning story. Śiva evokes lust in the wives of the forest sages just as Kāma evokes lust in Śiva. In the forest, Śiva loses part of his body, disappears, and is transformed into an object of devotion, a clear parallel to Kāma's burning and transformation.

As a reflection of the burning of Kāma story, the episode of Śiva in the Pine Forest is discussed in the next section as an explicit commentary on the nature of desire.

KĀMA WINS: KĀMA'S POWER WITHIN ŚIVA (*VĀMANA PURĀṆA*)

As discussed above, the Pine Forest episode in the *Vāmana Purāṇa* begins with a grieving Śiva, tortured by the overwhelming memories of his dead wife, Satī. Whether dreaming or awake, he cannot run far enough or hard enough to escape the memories of his own mind. The story portrays this internal struggle as Śiva physically runs from Kāma, yet finds nowhere to hide from Smara's (Memory's) arrows. In these opening scenes, Śiva is clearly caught in the web of desire, completely at the mercy of the flower arrows.

When Śiva's presence evokes lust in the wives of the sages and arouses anger in their ascetic husbands, his actions mirror the actions of Kāma in the Burning Story when his presence in Śiva's hermitage evokes lust and anger within the great god. Kāma is burned to death, his sexual power destroyed, while Śiva is literally castrated. Without body, Kāma disappears from the world, causing the gods and Rati grief, fear, and confusion. When Śiva disappears, his boundless sexual organ leaves the gods and sages confused and afraid. When Śiva is supplicated in the Burning Story, Kāma is reborn in a new and unusual form-without-form, Anaṅga; and when the great god is propitiated in the Pine Forest, he restores his own body while leaving a form of his liṅga on earth. In both narratives, Kāma's invisibility makes him ultimately more powerful, while Śiva's victory over Kāma/kāma restores balance to the world and himself.

Each story uses the other as a backdrop to refocus attention on the tension between desire and discipline, but in different ways. Both tales examine the conflict faced not only by ascetics seeking to attain a state of vairāgya, desirelessness, but also by householders trying to balance their own desires within the many internal and external constraints imposed by society, tradition, and even the opposing desires of others. Each tale examines the torment of unfulfilled desire in grief, jealousy, anger, madness, and confusion.

Neither narrative pretends to resolve the conflict neatly within one person. In both cases, others are needed to restore balance. Order returns only when the great god is propitiated. In the language of the story, only the worship of a powerful god can bring balance to the conflict between desire and discipline. Kāma, or desire, is never totally restricted or controlled, just as Śiva's asceticism is never completely invulnerable to the lure of desire. The more interesting episodes, however, occur when either desire or ascetic discipline moves to an extreme. Ultimately balance is the goal in all the variants, despite the fact that Śiva's asceticism most often receives prominence in the Indian religious tradition.

Yet this balance is complicated in that it rarely remains in a perfect state for long. In both the Pine Forest episode and the Burning Story, Śiva the yogi is ultimately victorious and does finally restore balance between desire and discipline. But the stories draw us through many episodes in which the tension is stretched in a multitude of ways before we get to this balance, which is then always short-lived. For example, in the cycle of stories of which the burning of Kāma is one part, after Śiva has been shot by Kāma and has reduced him to ashes, he always goes on to marry Pārvatī while retaining his identity as a yogi. Hardly describing an ascetic lifestyle, the stories portray Śiva and Pārvatī engaged in sexual love play for eons and eons. Both the core story and the variants consciously blend desire and discipline in different degrees at different times. In the resolution of the Pine Forest episode, Śiva's sexual organ is established as the primary form for his worship by brahmins, kṣatriyas, vaiśyas, and śūdras.[33] The stories maintain credibility by truthfully reflecting the wonderfully tangled knot of human desire and discipline.

Cleverly juxtaposing a series of opposites in the mutally mirroring stories, the *Vāmana* variant warns us that both Kāma and Śiva are gods who can destroy. In the beginning of the tale, Kāma destroys Śiva's self-control and balance, and in the end Śiva burns up Kāma's beautiful body. While acknowledging the danger, we are told to look for Kāma's weapons in the fragrant flowers and fruit-bearing trees that are disciplined by the earth's seasons. Finally, we are counseled to propitiate Śiva in the form of his upraised liṅga, the fertility symbol that speaks mightily of the power of desire.

DEVĪ WINS: KĀMA AS DEVOTEE OF THE GODDESS (*BRAHMĀṆḌA PURĀṆA*)

The *Brahmāṇḍa Purāṇa,*[34] which may originally have been identical to the *Vāyu Purāṇa,* is dated in its original form to a period between 400 and 600 CE and in its present form to around 1000 CE.[35] The last chapters of the text are called Lalitāmāhātmya or Lalitopākhyāna[36] and describe an incarnation of the goddess Devī, known as Lalitā, whose raison d'être is to destroy the demon Bhaṇḍāsura.

The following tale is another variant of the Burning Story in which the gods are once again motivated to arouse Śiva from his ascetic state, so that he will father a son to defeat the demon Tāraka. But as this variant begins, Kāma has already been reduced to ash by Śiva and is being revived as a demon. Kāma, as the demon Bhaṇḍa, must then be released by the goddess before he can again take up his task of arousing Śiva.

This tale of Devī and Bhaṇḍāsura is relevant to the study of Kāma because the depiction of Kāma as a demon and devotee of the great goddess allows the storyteller to explore the nature of desire from still other angles.

Kāma and the Goddess

At a time when the gods were being harassed by the demon Tāraka, they called Kāma and praised him greatly. The gods asked Kāma to evoke sexual desire in Śiva [causing him to be attracted] to the goddess Gaurī [Pārvatī], so that he would produce a son to destroy the demon Tāraka. (11.7–20)

Smara, invisible to all living beings[37] [*atdṛṣyaḥ sarvabhūtānām*], pierced Maheśvara with a flower-arrow while he was being served by Girijā [Pārvatī], daughter of the mountain. (11.24–25) Struck by this arrow, Śiva's consciousness became completely permeated by the god of desire [*manmathaviṣṭacetanaḥ*]. (11.26)

Regaining his mental steadiness [*dhṛtimālambya*], Śiva opened his third eye and burned the makara-bannered god.[38] (11.27–8)

The lord of the gaṇas, Citrakarmā [Magician, Maker of Pictures/Illusions], upon seeing these ashes [of Kāma], made an image of a man out of them [*puruṣam citrakāram*]. When Śiva looked at this image-body [*vicitratanum*], it instantly came to life, as if it were Manmatha [Kāma]. (11.30–31)

After Citrakarmā had taught him how to praise Śiva, he was offered a boon by the delighted Mahādeva [Śiva]. The man requested, "Let half the power of my antagonist be united with my strength, and let my arrows make his futile." Śiva granted this boon, telling him that he would rule the kingdom for sixty thousand years. Then Śiva said, "Bhaṇḍ, bhaṇḍ."[39] So this man was called Bhaṇḍa in the worlds. (11.32–37)

Since he was born from the fire of Rudra's [Śiva's] anger [*rudrakopānalāj-jātaḥ*], Bhaṇḍa became a demon [dānava][40] with Rudra's[41] dreadful nature [*raudrasvabhāvaḥ*]. (12.1) Bhaṇḍa gloried in power and pleasures, and sixty thousand years passed like half a moment. (12.19)

Seeing the demons [daitya] increase in ascetic power [tapas] and physical strength [*balam*] while the gods were losing power, Viṣṇu created a lovely goddess, Māyā [Illusory Being, *kāncinmāyām*] to enchant the worlds. Viṣṇu told her to enchant the demon Bhaṇḍa. (12.20–23) Deluded and deriving great pleasure from this Māyā lady, the demons forgot the sacred texts [Vedas], their sacrificial rituals [*yajñas*], and other auspicious rites. [In this way], the gods were then delivered of their torment. (12.32–34)

However, Nārada informed Indra [King of the Gods] that this respite would be short-lived. "When Bhaṇḍa realizes that he has been deluded [*sammohitaḥ*] by Viṣṇu's Māyā, he will burn the three worlds[42] with another fire. The only way to defeat this demon is to propitiate the Goddess, Parāśakti." (12.39–41). So the gods performed the worship of Parāśakti on the bank of the Bhāgirathī [river] for ten thousand years and ten days. (12.44–46)

Bhaṇḍa learned that Indra and the gods were doing penance to the Goddess, Supporter of the Universe [*jagaddhātrī*],[43] so he went to do penance to Śiva. (12.48–58) [But] the Mother of the Universe [*jagadambikā*] placed obstacles in his path, so he returned to his city. (12.59–62)

Śakra [Indra] then realized that it would be impossible to defeat Bhaṇḍa without a meat sacrifice [*mahāmāmsa*][44] to the Great Goddess. (12.65–66) When the sacrifice was almost completed, Mahādevī, the Great Goddess, rose up in a radiant circle in front of them. She was the essence of beauty, embodying Brahmā, Viṣṇu, and Śiva. In her hands were the noose, goad, and sugarcane-bow with five arrows. (12.68–73)

When Brahmā, Viṣṇu, and Śiva [Maheśvara] had given her great praise, the goddess married Śiva [Maheśvara-Kāmeśvara],[45] who looked just like Smara with a renewed physical body. (14.23–25)

After many battles, including one in which his brother was killed by the Goddess [Śrīdevī], Bhaṇḍa decided he must kill Lalitā [the Great Goddess] by any means possible. When Bhaṇḍa roared like a lion, the oceans dried up, the moon and sun fled, stars fell down from the sky, and the earth began to shake. (29.28–29)

When all had been destroyed except Bhaṇḍāsura, Lalitā killed him with an arrow called the Great Desire or Great Kāma/kāma arrow [*Mahākāmeśara*], which also set his city on fire. (29.142–43) Then, the Goddess, Ruler of Desire [Kāmeśvarī], shone brilliantly. (29.145)

Brahmā, praising the Goddess for ridding the earth of the demon Bhaṇḍa, explained to her that the gods had previously been trying to join Śiva with Pārvatī [Umā], but unfortunately Madana had been reduced to ashes, the same ashes out of which Bhaṇḍa had been formed. (30.11–35) With Bhaṇḍa dead, Kāma was once again bodiless [*atanuḥ*], [leaving] Rati still grieving and Śiva still not joined to Pārvatī. (30.36–38) Brahmā said, "The grieving Rati takes refuge in you. Please direct a small part of your compassionate glance [*kāruṇyakalā vidhehi*] toward her." (30.42)

As a result of her compassion for Rati, Manmatha was reborn from the goddess's side-glance [*kaṭākṣa*], more handsome than in his previous body. (30.45–47) Kāma spoke in devotion to the Goddess, Lalitāmbikā, "I am your son. I am your slave [*dāsa*]. Employ me anywhere in any task." (30.55)

The goddess then narrated the events that would follow concerning the marriage of Śiva and Gaurī. But, she said, this time Śiva's anger would not be powerful enough to burn Kāma's body. (30.58–60)

Kāma then proceeded to the hermitage of Śiva desiring to conquer him. (30.68–70) Pārvatī performed a severe penance standing in water[46] through the winter to secure her husband. (30.92) Finally, Pārvatī [Umā] and Śiva married, engaging in amorous dalliance for a long time. (30.96)

A Śākta purāṇa, the *Brahmāṇḍa* presents a different understanding of Kāma by assigning the core elements of the story to different characters and combining them in new ways. In this text, Bhaṇḍāsura, a brought-to-life image molded out of Kāma's ashes, is himself burned to ashes but by the Goddess rather than Śiva. The Goddess then revives Kāmadeva as himself, receives him as her servant, and takes the name *Kāmeśvarī,* the feminine form of Śiva's epithet *Kāmeśvara.* The Goddess kills Kāma-Bhaṇḍāsura, the devotee of Śiva, with the weapon called arrow of great kāma or desire (mahākāmeśara) and finally revives him as her own devotee. Because Śākta purāṇas are written to glorify the Goddess, she is the most powerful deity in the story, just as in the *Śiva Purāṇa* the most powerful deity is Śiva.

Clearly the Goddess takes the place of the great god Śiva and even surpasses him. Taking over Śiva's epithet to become Kāmeśvarī, ruler of Kāma/kāma, and destroying the god of desire turned demon with the weapon of great desire, the Goddess becomes an even more powerful tamer and wielder of desire than either Kāmadeva or Śiva. Devī demonstrates this superiority when she explains to Kāmadeva that after he has shot Śiva and evoked anger in him, the great god will no longer have the power to burn Kāma to ashes. Resuscitated by the Goddess, Kāmadeva will be at her command, under her rulership, and safe from destruction by Śiva.

This goddess is the focus of Tantric worship, a particular practice which transforms the energy of sexual interaction into a disciplined ritual for achieving religious awakening. Within the context of Tantric practice, the revival of Kāmadeva is essential, and the goddess is certainly Kāmeśwarī, ruler of desire.

One of the most characteristic elements of Tantric practice is that it consciously turns ordinary religious practice on its head by transforming behavior normally considered polluting into accepted religious practice. For instance, sexual intercourse, eating red meat, and drinking wine become powerful sacred rituals. In keeping with Tantric reversals, Devī's side-glance, normally understood as a seductive look, brings Manmatha (Kāma) back to life, in pointed contrast to the gaze of Śiva's third eye, which is powerful by virtue of his asceticism. In classical Sanskrit literature, the side-glance indicates coy, flirtatious behavior, making it a truly appropriate means of Kāma's revival. Tantric practice integrates desire into religious practice, using it as a fire that can be transformed and rechannelled into the pursuit of religious awakening. As a guide in this process, the Goddess truly is Kāmeśvarī.

Like Śiva in the other variants, the Goddess here becomes a multiform of Kāma. When she appears to her worshippers, she carries the weapons of Kāma, the noose, goad, and sugarcane-bow with five arrows. She is the essence of beauty and the abode of the sentiment of love (sṛṅgāra rasa)[47] found wherever Kāma is present. A powerful force, the Goddess combines supreme female power (parāśakti) and desire within her being.

Śākta texts diverge from the traditional Hindu view that the spiritually motivated ascetic will finally overcome all desire. "Annihilation of the sexual impulses in particular is considered by Tantrics as unnatural and impossible; the wise approach, the easy way, is to transform them by ritual means and use them to gain release."[48] The Tantric tradition teaches that the way to spiritual goals is not through asceticism, but rather through Tantra, which uses the fire of desire to transform and transcend. Thus a goddess who embodies desire, who is another Kāma, and even more powerful than Śiva the ascetic, aptly reflects this understanding.

Human desire may rage and create havoc like the demon, Bhaṇḍāsura, or it may further higher ends like the docile servant of the goddess. For a person attempting to control the urgency of desire, the goddess's ability to transform Desire with her glance makes her an important ally. In Bhaṇḍāsura, desire is a demon who has conquered the universe, who can be defeated only by the supreme goddess. The goddess restores order to this universe, however, not by returning Bhaṇḍāsura to ash but by reviving him in his beautiful form to do her bidding. Reminiscent of the account in the *Śiva Purāṇa* that describes Śiva reviving Kāma as his gaṇa, this variant emphasizes that ultimately desire cannot be destroyed but only given a different role in one's life or made subject to higher dictates.

Lest anyone feel beyond the pull of desire, the story describes how even Kāma-Bhaṇḍāsura, Desire, was not exempt from falling into the deluding trap of his own passionate desire. Indeed, so deluded that he released his hold on power for a time, Bhaṇḍāsura was aroused by the charming female form of Viṣṇu's Māyā, the one whose very name means illusion. Aiming for the shock of reversals, the Śākta text unfolds a story in which the greatest power resides in the only two female figures in the tale, Māyā and Parāśakti-Devī. As most purāṇas were written by men, this part of the *Brahmāṇḍa Purāṇa* might well express a male fear of sexual feelings aroused in the presence of a woman. But the story may also reflect the perspective of female storytellers who have contributed to this body of literature through their strong participation in the oral tradition. This tale of Kāmadeva's subjugation by the Goddess expresses the power of female deities to subdue even the demonic god of desire.

CHAPTER THREE

Kāmadeva Reborn as Pradyumna, Son of Kṛṣṇa

Several purāṇas tell the tale of Pradyumna, son of Kṛṣṇa and Rukmiṇī, born to battle Śambara, a demon terrorizing the gods. The birth of Pradyumna, son of Kṛṣṇa, mirrors the story of Skanda-Kārttikeya, son of Śiva, born to defeat the demon Tāraka. Because each demon is vulnerable only to the son of a great god, these sons are essential for the continued welfare of the gods. However, Pradyumna is not only the son of Kṛṣṇa and a killer of demons. Pradyumna is also the incarnation of the god of desire, in fulfillment of a promise made by Śiva after burning Kāma to ashes.

The Pradyumna episode consists of familiar folktale motifs: the prophesy that a demon will be killed by a child not yet born, the demon's attempt to kill this infant, a divine child raised by demons, a father who is not a father, a son not a son, and a mother who marries her son. The narrative stands squarely within the genre of well-structured folktales and reflects the familiar Indian pattern of borrowing and reshaping characters from one story cycle and integrating them into new tales, nuancing the richness of the original by placing its characters and motifs in new settings. In this Pradyumna tale, Vaiṣṇavas recast Kāma and Rati, traditional Śaiva characters, as the son and his wife of the Vaiṣṇava hero Kṛṣṇa.

This story of Kṛṣṇa's son battling his demon surrogate-father explores the effect of desire and power on the ability to perceive a situation with clarity. Kāmadeva potrayed as Pradyumna, slayer of demons and son-husband of the goddess of illusion as well as the son of Kṛṣṇa, offers another perspective on the nature of desire.

THE STORY OF PRADYUMNA

As promised to Rati after Kāma was incinerated by Śiva, Kāma is reborn in this tale[1] as Pradyumna, son of Kṛṣṇa and Rukmiṇī. The narrator of the *Liṅga*

Purāṇa reports that Śiva said to the weeping Rati: "When Viṣṇu of great renown returns to earth under the curse of Bhṛgu, the son born to him will be your husband."[2]

The *Śiva Purāṇa* describes Śiva offering the following words of consolation to the gods pleading for the resuscitation of Kāma:

> Kāma, the husband of Rati, will remain bodiless [anaṅga] until Kṛṣṇa becomes an avatar on earth as the husband of Rukmiṇī. While in Dvāraka, he will decide to have children, and will beget Kāma in Rukmiṇī. The child's name will be Pradyumna; and at the time of his birth, a demon called Śambara will abduct the boy [in order to kill him]. (II.3.19.38–40) After seizing him and throwing him into the sea, Śambara will return to his city, thinking the boy dead.
>
> [Now speaking to Rati, Śiva says:]
>
> [But] while staying in Śambara's city, O Rati, you will regain your own husband who will be [known as] Pradyumna. (II.3.19.41–42)
>
> After killing Śambara in battle and joining with his original wife, Kāma called Pradyumna will be happy. Pradyumna will return to the city with her, bringing Śambara's wealth. (11.3.19.43–44)[3]

Like the *Śiva Purāṇa,* the *Bhāgavata Purāṇa* describes Śiva making the same promise but this time in response to Rati's penance and pleas, rather than to the gods. In addition to explaining that Kāma will be reborn as Pradyumna, son of Kṛṣṇa and Rukmiṇī, Kāma tells Rati that to accompany her husband into this rebirth, she should abandon her present body to be reborn as Māyādevī, wife of the demon Śambara. In this next life, Pradyumna will ultimately kill Śambara and receive her as his wife. Once again, Śiva promises, Rati will be united with Kāmadeva.[4]

The following passage from the critical edition of the *Harivamśa* provides the clearest narrative structure of Kāma's incarnation as Pradyumna. The same tale with varying details is also found in the *Viṣṇu Purāṇa, Bhāgavata Purāṇa, Brahma Purāṇa,* and *Brahmavaivarta Purāṇa,* as well as in *Harivamśa* passages that were rejected by the critical edition.

As the episode begins, the audience learns that the demon king Śambara can be killed only by a son of Kṛṣṇa. Quite logically then, to protect himself, Śambara decides to kill the newborn son of Kṛṣṇa.

Janamejaya said to Vaisampāyana, "Describe how Pradyumna killed Śambara." (99.1)

That steadfast Kāma, begotten of Vasudeva [Kṛṣṇa] in Rukmiṇī, that one who was known as the destroyer of Śambara, was the handsome Pradyumna who looked like Kāma. [*Kāmadarśana*]. On the seventh night, at exactly midnight, Kālaśambara took the infant son of Kṛṣṇa from the lying-in room. Through divine insight, Kṛṣṇa knew this was happening, but did not seize that demon [dānava] who was so bold in battle. With his life encircled by death, the great demon seized the infant by means of an illusion [māyā]. Throwing him in his arms, Śambara returned to his own city. (99.2–5)

The demon's accomplished and beautiful wife was childless. Called Māyāvatī, she was beautiful like her name. The demon, as if summoned to Death by his wife's power, gave her the infant son of Vāsudeva as if he were his own. As she raised this boy who was the son of Kṛṣṇa and had eyes like lotus petals, Māyā gave him everything. That Dānava lady was confused by desire [or by Kāma] [*kāmamohitā*]. As he grew into a youth, Pradyumna looked very handsome; he looked like Kāmadeva [*kāmadarśana*]. He understood the designs of women and was an expert with all sorts of weapons. Filled with passion for this charming boy, Māyāvatī attempted to seduce him with gestures, glances, and smiles. (99.6–10)

So he said to this sweetly smiling goddess who was in love with him, "What are you doing, abandoning your motherhood? You are behaving badly, like a woman whose mind is unsteady. You who gave birth to me as a son are acting with desire for me. I am your son, O gentle lady, this behavior is some kind of transgression. I want you to say what the cause of this behavior is, O goddess. The nature of women is constantly changing like lightning; they are addictively attached to men, like the clouds on the top of a mountain. If I am your son, O gentle one, or if I was not born from you, O beautiful one, I want you to tell me what you are doing here." (99.11–15)

Responding to his words, though timid and with her senses agitated by desire, Māyāvatī spoke loving words to the son of Kesava. "You are not my son, O gentle one, and Śambara is not your father. You are a handsome warrior born as the son of Viṣṇu. You are the son of Vāsudeva, and the joy of Rukmiṇī. When seven days old, you were carried off from the lying-in chamber. As an infant, you were abducted by my husband. A very bold and strong man, he seized you by force, and took you from your father Vāsudeva, the killer of demons. You were stolen by Śambara." (99.16–19)

"Your mother grieved for love of you, and is still overcome with anxiety, like a cow separated from its calf. Indeed, the great Garuda-bannered one [Viṣṇu] is your father. You were not born here. You were carried here as a child. O charming one, you are a Vṛṣṇi prince, not the son of Śambara [that is, not of the demon class]. O hero, in no way can the Danavas conquer such a son as you. Given this reality, I do desire you. I did not give birth to you. Now, seeing your beauty, my heart becomes weak and despondent. O charming one, may the resolve of my heart force my mind to remember. My words to you are true, O gentle one. You are not my son, and not the son of Śambara." (99.20–25)

Hearing and understanding everything said by Māyāvatī, the son of the one armed with a cakra [Viṣṇu] became angry, and he challenged Śambara. Even knowing all the tricks of māyā [the weapons of illusion], Kālaśambara, a warrior imperishable in battle, was killed by Pradyumna's eighth weapon. (99.26–27)

Having killed the greatest of the asuras in the city Ṛkṣavanta, Pradyumna took Māyāvatī Devī and went to the place of his father. Moving through the space between heaven and earth, the quick-footed one came to a pleasant place protected by his father's power. Along with Māyāvatī, he descended from this place between heaven and earth at the palace of Keśava where he had been as an infant. He appeared like Manmatha [Kāma]. (99.28–30)

Praduymna and Māyāvatī entered the palace, producing great confusion about their identities. Kṛṣṇa, who had already heard the entire story from Nārada, assured Rukmiṇī that Pradyumna was indeed her son and had just killed the asura Śambara by means of māyā [weapons of illusion]. However, one problem remained. What was the proper relationship of Māyāvatī to Pradyumna? Addressing this question, Kṛṣṇa spoke to Rukmiṇī: (99.31–44)

"This virtuous wife and good woman, O beautiful one, is the [true] wife of your son. When she was seized by Śambara, she was called Māyāvatī. Thus, she became known as the wife of Śambara only through this misfortune." (99.45)

"When, in former times, Manmatha was destroyed and became bodiless [anaṅga], the wife of Kāma, that young woman Rati, the desire of Kāma [Kāmakāmā], that beautiful one who never ceased being beautiful, enchanted the demon with an illusory form. Because she was unhappy being under his power in her maidenhood, this beautiful woman created an illusory form of herself [ātmamāyām] to send to [sleep with] Śambara." (99.46–47)

"This woman of beautiful limbs is truly my son's wife, and your daughter-in-law. Māyāvatī will help him who is loved by the whole world, the one who is created out of the illusion of mind [manomāyam], Pradyumna/Kāma." (99.48)

A number of issues are encountered in this narrative that some have called an oedipal tale, as Pradyumna kills the man who raised him and marries the woman who acted as a mother to him. However, the Indian tale is sufficiently different from Sophocles' drama that this parallel is more misleading than helpful. Unlike Oedipus, Pradyumna learns the truth of his origins before killing his foster father and marrying his foster mother. Indeed, it is only in learning the truth of the situation that he takes these actions. Though the tale does highlight issues of intimate feelings existing between a mother and her grown son, the tale is structured more as an allegory than a presentation of human interactions. However, before examining this allegorical structure, we should first broaden the narrative to include the variants that help illuminate the subtleties and meanings of the text.

VARIANT PRADYUMNAS AND ŚAMBARAS

This tale of the incarnation of Kāma as Pradyumna is retold with interesting variants in four puranic narratives, the *Viṣṇu,*[5] *Bhāgavata,* and *Brahmavaivarta Purāṇas,* and in a section of the *Harivaṃśa* rejected for the critical edition, referred to here as *Harivaṃśa 2.*[6] These texts do not represent five different tellings, but do include new symbols and motifs that offer further insight into the role of the god of desire as demon slayer and consort of Illusion.

In two of these versions (*Viṣṇu* and *Bhāgavata*), when Śambara steals Pradyumna from the lying-in room under the cover of maya, he throws him into the sea with vicious makaras, probably crocodiles,[7] in order to kill him. However, a large fish swallows Pradyumna, allowing him to live. The fish is subsequently caught by fishermen, who bring it as part of their large catch as an offering to the demon king, Śambara, who in turn gives the fish to his wife, Māyāvatī. As she begins to prepare the fish for dinner, Māyāvatī finds the child.

In a wonderful poetic twist, the storyteller describes Śambara throwing the child who is Kāma into a sea of makaras, the water creature associated with Kāmadeva, indeed the creature on his banner. Ordinarily vicious creatures not likely to refuse an easy lunch, these predator makara-crocodiles become the child's protectors. As noted earlier, the animal depicted on a deity's banner communicates some aspect of the owner's character, as well as the god's mastery over this creature. For example, Śambara's standard displays the lion, indicating that the demon king is capable of ruling and fighting like the lion; and Śiva is known as the bull-bannered one (vṛṣa-dhvaja), signifying that he possesses the virility and power of a bull. Kāmadeva is known as the makara-bannered (makara-dhvaja), reflecting that some aspect of the makara is present in Kāma's character. In the chapter on Kāma's iconography, the identity of the mythical makara is explored further, but in terms of understanding this episode, we can be assured that the Kāmadeva babe will be protected rather than eaten by the makaras.

The Pradyumna storyteller uses this sea of makaras to provide an ironic twist to the intrigue of the plot. Because Indian audiences know that Kāma is makara-dhvaja, they also know that Śambara's attempt to kill Pradyumna-Kāma by throwing him into a sea of makaras can only fail. Like Br'er Fox[8] throwing Br'er Rabbit into the briar patch, Śambara's tossing Kāma into a sea of makaras can have only the opposite effect. Rather than being eaten, the child is protected and returned to Śambara's world. The episode also offers the audience further insight into the demon, Śambara. Although he knows Pradyumna's identity on one level as son of Kṛṣṇa, he is completely ignorant of Pradyumna's deeper identity.

When Pradyumna and Śambara finally begin their battle, some of the variants emphasize their individual powers by describing in great detail how each fights with weapons he has constructed out of the illusory nature of reality. Of course this element is a stock characteristic of Indian storytelling. Gods and heroes are so powerful that they fight not with ordinary weapons but with magical devices that take whatever shape is most advantageous for the fight. The epics and purāṇas are filled with battles featuring illusory serpents sent through the air to strike an opponent only to be countered by flocks of illusory birds of prey that swoop down to devour the serpents and then find themselves in the clutches of illusory lions that tear the birds to pieces. Visualizing a battle fought with magical māyā weapons sweeps us into that aspect of the classical Indian worldview, which cautions that reality is never quite what our senses (including the mind) perceive it to be.

Although the word *māyā* is translated as "illusion" or "illusory," the principle of māyā more accurately conveys that, on a fundamental level, the physical reality of a perceived object may be quite different from the description of that object communicated by the simple partnership of eyes and mind.[9] In other words, a solid wooden door appears to be an unchanging solid mass that our senses relay to our minds, but it is also a mass of atomic elements packed together with verifiable space between and among its molecular elements. When we walk up to a wooden door, we don't usually process the door as an object made up of space and atoms that is shedding parts of itself each time the door is slammed or even touched. But from the perspective of chemistry or physics, a door might indeed be explained as such a configuration of atoms and molecules. The principle of māyā reminds us that what we perceive with our senses and construct into a reality with our minds is only that, a constructed reality based on incomplete data. Just as we have only a partial understanding of the wooden door, we must infer that we have only a partial, or even skewed picture, of our universe.

According to the principle of māyā, human beings perceive illusions which they misinterpret as reality and then use to guide their behavior. The principle of māyā explains that we are mistaken, but not in the sense that the door does not exist. Of course the door that we can touch exists, and of course we cannot walk through it. Yet, the door as we perceive it is only part of the story. In this same way, according to Indian epistemological thinking, similar everyday perceptions of our selves only partially reflect the reality of human existence.

When Pradyumna and Śambara fight with weapons of māyā, their fighting is as real as any battle, but the physical battle represents also the battle of wills and desires that takes place between the two.

> Seeing his illusion [an illusory display of lions, tigers, bears, monkeys, horses, camels, asses and cloudlike elephants attacking his enemy's vehicle] destroyed by Pradyumna, Śambara, swollen with rage, released another illusion. He showered fresh, youthful, sounding elephants with sixty heads, ready for battle with elephant drivers mounted on them. Seeing those illusory creatures ready to fall on him, the lotus-eyed one created illusory lions. Just as the twilight is destroyed in the sun, the illusory elephant was destroyed in the illusory lion created by the son of Rukmiṇī.[10]

As the demon attempts to kill with these weapons of illusion, the audience knows that the demon's own perception is flawed by his inability to see beyond appearances. Śambara believes that his wife is simply his wife, that the person destined to murder him has been destroyed, and that he himself is invincible. Using the weapons of his mind, the demon fights by creating even more illusions. But because his opponent, Pradyumna, sees through these deceptive realities, Śambara's world no longer stands. Pradyumna knows how to dispel each of Śambara's illusions by creating a predator to devour that very illusion, leaving the demon denuded and vulnerable.

The stronger mind always wins this war of mental images, and Pradyumna as son of Viṣṇu and embodiment of Kāmadeva is more knowledgeable and powerful than the demon Śambara. Pradyumna's creation of reality becomes the final word, though perhaps no less illusory. Śambara is ultimately defeated by his desire to be invincible and his arrogance in believing that he holds total power. The combination of desire and illusion in Śambara's life is fatal, just as it is for all of us. We cling to the illusion that we are invincible, powerful, secure, and in control, but when our desires are thwarted, when we lose what we desire, our invincibility crumbles as we recognize it as another illusion created by our minds.

On the level of allegory, Pradyumna as Desire leaves the battleground unharmed with a youthful body, and once again married to the beautiful Māyādevī, goddess of illusion.

Though the battle emphasizes the element of illusion in the interaction between Śambara and Pradyumna, most of the narrative text is devoted to the conversation between the adolescent Pradyumna and his foster mother, Māyāvatī. Although Pradyumna is touted as a warrior, very few verses (only one in the critical edition of the epic) are devoted to the battle and killing of the demon. The storyteller is much more concerned about the relationship between Pradyumna and Māyāvatī, or Kāma and Rati, than with the deed Pradyumna was born to carry out, the killing of Śambara.

KĀMA MARRIES MĀYĀVATĪ: DESIRE EMBEDDED IN ILLUSION

In the conversation between Kāma/Pradyumna and Rati/Māyāvatī, the longest speech belongs to Māyāvatī, whose name means the essence of illusion or mistress of illusion (māyā). Māyāvatī must convince Pradyumna that she is not his mother, but rather more appropriately his lover. Pradyumna, on the other hand, listens intently to find that he has been completely ignorant of the real situation, living a life built on illusory identities. For the audience, Pradyumna's predicament is wonderfully ironic. Should he allow himself to be persuaded by this Essence of Illusion that her present form and his, as mother and son, are really illusory, and that they possess other forms which are less illusory, or even real? Because the audience knows them in their former incarnations as Kāma and Rati, they know (as Pradyumna does not) which identity is illusory and which real. The storyteller artfully weaves overlapping images of desire and illusion through their conversation, and throughout the episode.

Māyāvatī, mistress of illusion, must make Pradyumna see that he is really the god of desire, and she his consort, while the audience listens in suspense. The *Brahmavaivarta Purāṇa,* a much later work[11] than the *Harivaṃśa* texts, removes this suspense by having the goddess Sarasvatī explain to Pradyumna and Māyāvatī in the fourth verse of the story that they are actually Kāma and Rati. Knowing their true identities, the two carry on continuously until Śambara catches them in bed together. In this telling of the story, Rati is called Māyāvatī, but her son-lover, though described as the son of Kṛṣṇa, is referred to exclusively as Kāma. The name Pradyumna is never used. By revealing their identities early on and removing the element of illusion, the writer of this purāṇa underscores the importance of desire as victor, but loses the core tension between desire and illusion that is so central in the other versions.

Desire and illusion are purposefully intertwined in the structure and fabric of the story as it is told in the earlier variants, so that this mingling becomes the core element. In one variant, out of her own desire to be reunited with Kāma (Desire), Māyāvatī (Illusion) manipulates the demon's desire for her and deludes him into marrying her illusory form. In another, Śambara, desiring to prevent his own murder, steals the infant by taking on the form of Kṛṣṇa by means of illusion. Māyāvatī, in her desire for Pradyumna, reveals the secrets of her illusion, māyā, to him, both by teaching him the art of fighting with the weapons of māyā to counteract Śambara's weapons[12] and by revealing her true identity (or at least part of her true identity) to him. Pradyumna himself bears one illusory identity as the son of Śambara and another as the son of Vasudeva/Kṛṣṇa, while the audience recognizes him as the god of desire. In all variants of the tale, desire is properly united with illusion in the end.

Desire and illusion are most prominently intermingled within the character of Māyāvatī. The writers of the variants make it very clear that Rati uses her power to manipulate illusion to create the image of Māyāvatī; Rati never uses her own body to act as wife to Śambara. In the *Harivaṃśa* and *Viṣṇu Purāṇa,* she is described as having taken an illusory body to enchant the demon. The *Bhāgavata Purāṇa* separates Rati from any possibility of being tainted by Śambara's touch, by giving her only the role of Śambara's head cook.[13] The *Brahmavaivarta Purāṇa* underscores Rati's purity by explaining that she does not actually sleep with Śambara. Rather, she gives him only her shadow called "Māyāvatī."[14] All these texts make it very clear that if Kāma/Pradyumna is to receive Rati as his wife at the end of the episode, she must never have been touched, or polluted, by another man.[15] However, the story also gives Māyāvatī/Rati the center-stage position, explaining that it is she who wields the power of māyā to seduce both Śambara and Pradyumna.

The adolescent Pradyumna/Kāma plays a very different role here as the victim of māyā. Only when he learns the magical secrets from Māyāvatī does he outmaneuver the demon known to be "proficient in battles of illusion" (māyāyuddhaviṣārada)[16] and take the demon's wife as his own. Although the frame story is a well-known Indo-European folklore motif, that of the powerful ruler who attempts to kill the child phrophesied to be his murderer, this Indian variant uses the story to highlight the role of desire (kāma) and illusion (māyā). Within this story, desire becomes powerful only when joined with the intricacies of illusion.

Connecting desire and illusion, this Vaiṣnava narrative presents the phenomenon of desire in a clearly positive light, unlike the more ambivalent Śaiva attitude in the story of the burning of Kāma. In his guise as Pradyumna, Kāma is a lauded hero: son of the beloved god and king Kṛṣṇa, princely warrior and defeater of an evil demon, handsome lover who regains his lost wife, and darling son of the loving queen mother, Rukmiṇī. Parallelling the story of Kṛṣṇa, this tale associates the god of desire with the passion of Kṛṣṇa bhakti, devotion. In the parallel tales, both babes are separated from their mothers at birth, both threatened by the demons they will ultimately kill. Both are charming adolescents, irresistible to the opposite sex, and valiant warriors. Describing the son born to Kṛṣṇa as Kāmadeva may reflect both the popularity of the adolescent god Kṛṣṇa as divine lover, and the importance of passionate desire in the bhakti (devotional) tradition.[17]

In some versions, Kāmadeva son of Kṛṣṇa is mistaken by the women of the palace for Kṛṣṇa himself, underscoring the link between the two deities. Devotion to Kṛṣṇa inspires the same passionate feelings evoked by Kāma, but reformed as love of a mortal for the divine. The passion of Kāma is rechanneled in Kṛṣṇa bhakti to become desire for the presence of the divine. Though this text represents Kṛṣṇa in his mature form, settled with his wife Rukmiṇī, and not the adolescent, amorous and playful Kṛṣṇa, the story connects the god who evokes mundane passion and the deity who inspires ecstatic devotion.

THE PRADYUMNA STORY AS ALLEGORY

The primary allegorical statement of the tale is made at the end when Desire marries Illusion. On the level of Sanskrit grammar, māyā is feminine and kāma is masculine, facilitating this marriage of gendered nouns. But even the daily news offers examples of desire creating illusions, impairing the ability of individuals to assess a situation with clarity. Abused lovers protect their violent partners, executives lured by money ignore ethical boundaries, leaders intoxicated with power fail to recognize the frustration of the disenfranchised. Indeed, the very nature of desire is to confuse, to dissolve the ground of common sense and good judgment. As an allegory, the tale reflects this reality that desire is intimately linked with illusion.

Much has been written about the god Kṛṣṇa as divine lover. Rituals, devotional songs, and stories are built around the sensual image of the god who satisfies each of the women who long for him by manifesting himself to her alone. The image of intimate love between a man and a woman with all its intensity and passion and longing is used to provide a glimpse of the intense love that Kṛṣṇa feels for his devotees and they for him. Within the context of devotion to Kṛṣṇa that forms a bridge between human and divine love, it makes good sense in the language of storytelling to resuscitate the desire destroyed by asceticism as son of the deity whose devotees believe that ecstatic passion for the divine is the foremost path to spiritual awakening.

In this association with Kṛṣṇa, Kāmadeva is elevated from his position as exciter of mundane desire to the god who also engenders passion for the divine. Although the story does not directly pursue this connection, the family resemblance between Kṛṣṇa and Kāma reminds us that human passion is passion, desire is desire. The focus of these passionate feelings determines whether one moves closer to the divine or becomes more deeply enmeshed in the cycle of attachment and rebirth. As the various stories featuring the character of Kāmadeva demonstrate, desire is simply a human force that may be directed in a myriad of ways. It is our human task to position this archer and direct his arrows.

CHAPTER FOUR

Kāmadeva and Khaṇḍaśilā: Rituals and Metaphors

In the following story,[1] Kāmadeva pricks himself with his own arrow, immediately falling in love with a woman bathing, a woman who happens to be the wife of a powerful sage who is not amused by this behavior. As in the Greek tale of the god Eros falling in love with the woman intended to be his prisoner, Kāmadeva becomes helpless under the spell of his own powerful weapon and suffers painful scars. In a wonderfully poetic image of Desire desiring, the tale describes the consequences for the god, as well as for the rest of the universe, of lust outside the social bonds of marriage. But, taking care not to leave him (or others) stranded in passion, the tale also presents an antidote for surviving this state, both for Kāma and for the human being who happens to fall for the "wrong" person.

THE STORY OF KHAṆḌAŚILĀ

This rather obscure tale of Khaṇḍaśilā as told in the *Skanda Purāṇa*[2] offers another view of Kāmadeva, as a deity to be worshipped. In this story, Kāma becomes the victim of his own arrows and seduces a young woman, a phenomenon that does not exist in other references, but that evokes the poetic image of "Desire desiring." As the tale ends, we are encouraged to worship the god and the object of the god's desire, the beautiful Pūrṇakalā,[3] who becomes Khaṇḍaśilā,[4] to attain whatever we desire. In particular, Kāma and Khaṇḍaśilā bestow physical beauty, cure deforming skin diseases (primarily leprosy), remove sin from the act of adultery, and engender renewed attraction from an inattentive husband. This is the tale as narrated in the *Skanda Purāṇa*.[5]

There once was a well-known brahmin named Hārīta who lived in a forest āśrama practicing austerities. With him lived his extremely beautiful wife, Pūrnakalā, whom even Brahmā desired when he saw her.

One day Kāmadeva and his two wives decided to visit the holy site of the Kāmeśvara liṅgam near the edge of the water. As it happened, when they arrived the beautiful Pūrṇakalā was just taking off her clothes to enter the water for a bath. While looking at her, Kāmadeva pricked his heart with his own flower arrow and was unable to take his eyes off her.

Leaving his wives, Rati and Prīti, Kāma fell into a reverie which made his hair stand on end, his breaths fiery, and his eyes tear up. Gazing at Pūrnakalā, Kāma was like a yogi in deep samādhi, meditating on Brahmā.

Pūrṇakalā too had been pierced by one of Kāma's arrows, which evoked a tremendous longing [*abhilāṣa*] to be with him. As the two gazed at one another, Kāma began describing the power of his position in the world. Rudra, Brahmā, and Indra, to say nothing of even small insects, are subject to the confusing dictates of his arrows; so she might as well forget any thought of resisting him. Giving him pleasure would be like offering guru dakṣiṇā[6] to him; and besides, he would simply die without her.

Having grown up with ascetics, Pūrṇakalā was completely innocent in these matters. She could do nothing but look down, writing on the earth with her toe.

About this same time, Hārīta, looking for his evening meal, began to miss Pūrṇakalā. When he found her with Kāma, he concealed himself in a clump of trees long enough to hear Kāma wooing Pūrṇakalā and then burst into a rage. Hārīta cursed Kāma with leprosy, so he would no longer be beautiful to look at. Pūrṇakalā was cursed to become a stone [śilā], as she was already *vicetana,* [without consciousness], i.e., a stone.[7]

Kāma pleaded first on behalf of Pūrṇakalā. [He argued that] she had been pierced by his arrows and so was not really guilty. If the gods cannot endure the arrows of Kāma, how could Pūrṇakalā have resisted them? Although impassioned, Pūrṇakalā had neither said nor done anything sinful. Kāma continued: There are three kinds of sin, of mind, speech, and action. Sins of the mind are atoned for through austerities, sins of speech through gifts of apology, and sins of action through the rituals prescribed in the dharmaśāstras. In this situation only the mental type of sin had been committed. Therefore, she should not be punished at all, or at least not so severely. Kāma concluded by asking that the curse be limited to himself, who was the only one truly at fault.

Hārīta responded that all words and actions are first conceived in the mind. And because the mind is behind all actions, sins of the mind certainly deserve consequences. Declaring that both curses would remain as spoken, he returned to his āśrama.

As a result of Kāma's severe case of leprosy, all procreation [*sṛṣṭi*] was blocked and the world began moving quickly toward total destruction.

Worried about this situation, the gods went to see Kāma at the Kāmeśvara liṅgam where he had taken refuge.

The gods explained to Kāma that if he propitiated Pūrṇakalā—now [literally] a broken [*khaṇḍa*] rock [*śilā*] called Khaṇḍaśilā—his sin would be expiated and his leprosy cured.

Indeed, anyone who bathes here should touch this "rock" that has been liberated from sin. This well is called the Well of Good Fortune [Saubhāgya Kūpa] and all who bathe in it will be cured of skin disease.

So Kāma did perform a pūjā to Khaṇḍaśilā and again became Smara (Memory), ready for the work of procreation. Khaṇḍaśilā remained the broken rock.

The passage continues to explain that if one performs pūjā to Khaṇḍaśilā on the thirteenth day of the month before engaging in adultery, no sin is generated by either the man or his lover. Indeed, when pūjā is performed to Kāma and Kāmeśvara [Śiva] on the thirteenth day, all desires are granted.

A man should offer the blossoms of the kumkum [saffron] to gain a beautiful form. A woman neglected by her husband should offer the filaments[8] of the kumkum in order to become fertile, wise, and free from sin and suffering.

In addition to being a wonderful twist on the usual paradigm in which Kāma's arrows incapacitate others, the tale of Khaṇḍaśilā uses the motifs of other stories to refocus listeners' attention on the power of desire to evoke pleasurable as well as destructive consequences. As in the burning story, Kāma's body is destroyed and healed, his arrows precipitate infatuation and anger in turns, and his resulting form is more powerful than his original. In a series of reversals, Kāma turns his weapon against himself, worships the woman he had tried to seduce, and loses his body only to regain it in a more powerful form.

In order to place this tale within a larger context, we turn now to the more familiar story of Indra and Ahalyā, which provides another framework for the story of Kāma and Khaṇḍaśilā. This tale too examines the role of desire in relation to ascetics, curses, stones, and the mitigation of curses.

THE PARALLEL TALE OF INDRA AND AHALYĀ

The story of Khaṇḍaśilā is clearly a variant of the famous story of Ahalyā and Indra. The sad tale of Ahalyā is most familiar to those who know the episode in Valmiki's *Rāmāyaṇa,* in which the touch of Rāma releases Ahalyā from her penance. But the Ahalyā story is told in a number of variants,[9] with the Tamil version told by Kamban in the eleventh century and recounted by R. K. Narayan[10] providing the closest parallel to the Khaṇḍaśilā story.

According to Kamban, the story goes back to the time when Brahmā created a woman of absolute beauty, called Ahalyā. Completely smitten with Ahalyā, Indra felt he was the only god worthy of her, but Brahmā ignored his arrogant boasting and placed Ahalyā in the care of the sage Gautama, pure in mind and spirit. Ahalyā grew up in the care of Gautama, who returned her to Brahmā when she was fully grown. Impressed by Gautama's purity, Brahmā gave Ahalyā to him in marriage and they were quite happy.

Unfortunately, however, Indra had never gotten over his infatuation with Ahalyā and often came to the āśrama to gaze at her. Finally unable to resist any longer, he magically took the form of Gautama while Gautama was away praying, and tricked Ahalyā into making love with him. At some point she realized the trick but was unable to free herself from the situation.[11] When Gautama returned, surprising the two in bed, Indra assumed the form of a cat in order to flee. But the sage was not deceived and cursed Indra to be covered with a thousand yonis.[12] Because Ahalyā had sinned with her body, Gautama cursed her body to become a shapeless piece of granite.

As she was hardening, Ahalyā pleaded for the forgiveness of lesser beings by greater beings. So Gautama declared that she would be freed when the son of Dasaratha, Rāma, passed near her.

Both Indra and Kāma, quite proud of their physical appearances and abilities to charm women, are cursed to lose these attributes as a result of transgressing the accepted boundaries of sexual desire. There is another story from the *Sāmba Purāṇa,*[13] which is discusssed in more detail in chapter five, about a son of Vāsudeva called Sāmba, who is also quite proud of his youthful appearance and sexual charm. Though it is not clear that Sāmba actually seduces a woman, his narcissistic pride results in offending a sage, the irascible Nārada, who arranges for Sāmba to become a leper and learn a little humility.

In each of these stories, the male character becomes so absorbed in his own sexual prowess and the object of his conquest that he becomes oblivious to responsible behavior or potential consequences. Wrapped up in the narcissism of desire, each finds himself punished with the loss of his beautiful appearance, the source of his pride and means of satisfying desire. In Valmiki's version of the story of Indra and Ahalyā, the story is even more specific in making this point: Gautama curses Indra's testicles to fall off. Rather than gaining satisfaction, Indra's pursuit of desire backfires by destroying his mechanism for gaining the longed for pleasure.

Both Khaṇḍaśilā and Ahalyā are exceedingly beautiful. Having grown up in the world of the ascetic's āśrama, they are innocent of the world of desire and unable to resist the power of sexual passion. Finally, both women are cursed to become stones,[14] which in turn become places of pilgrimage where the women are worshipped by men hoping to attract the sexual favors of other women.

At the Ahalyātīrtha,[15] according to accounts in the *Matsya Purāṇa* and the *Kūrma Purāṇa,*[16] one should worship Ahalyā on Kāmadeva's day, designated as the bright[17] thirteenth or fourteenth day of the month of Caitra, in order to become as handsome as the god of love and just as dear to women. The *Kūrma Purāṇa* says that bathing at the Ahalyātīrtha will bring endless enjoyment with the apsarases.[18]

Khaṇḍaśilā and Ahalyā have transgressed the boundaries of what is religiously and socially acceptable for a married woman. Hārīta explains that Pūrṇakalā has behaved without *cetas,* thoughtlessly, as a stone. Indeed the Sanskrit word śilā (long a) means rock while śila (short a) means moral conduct. Pūrṇakalā is a woman whose broken wifely conduct has resulted in her becoming a broken rock. Gautama says Ahalyā must do penance with her body because she has sinned with her body. These stories describe the penance for married women who have violated their dharmas,[19] but nevertheless instruct pilgrims to worship these turned-to-stone women. No longer dangerous to husbands or other men as they were in their sexually (and physically) active state, the stone Ahalyā and Pūrṇakalā now have the power to free others from such consequences.

If a man worships Khaṇḍaśilā at the Saubhāgyakūpikā, he can have adulterous relationships while avoiding blame (apavāda) and gossip. If he worships Ahalyā on Kāmadevadina at her tīrtha, he can enjoy the pleasure of the apsarases. Social and religious boundaries determine where one may act on desire, but these boundaries do have crossing points at the tīrthas associated with Kāmadeva. At these tīrthas, men and women can express their taboo desires as part of a religious ritual, and gain the blessing of the woman-stone who does penance under the protection of the god of desire. In addition, devotion to the women and Kāmadeva at these tīrthas bestows a beautiful appearance, even curing a skin disease such as leprosy.

Both stories describe transformations for the women: from innocence to passion to penance with these internal transformations visible in the characters' bodily changes. Paradoxically in this process, the woman cursed to perform penance as a stone gains the power to save others from undergoing this painful process. By contrast, Kāmadeva/Indra never portrayed as innocent, moves only from passion to penance, his body from beautiful to ugly. Yet Kāma too, transformed through penance as a leper, acquires the power to heal others of their ugliness. This series of transformations implies a special role for Kāma/kāma. Desire transforms as it leads to suffering, austerities, and the power to transform others. On a psychological level, experiencing the intensity of love and its loss offers the potential to effect deep changes within an individual.

Addressing socially unacceptable liaisons, this particular story of Kāmadeva and Khaṇḍaśilā demonstrates the suffering that ensues when desire moves outside the bounds of social norms. However, the ritual to Khaṇḍaśilā and Kāma is particularly interesting in that it provides a way to include forbidden behavior within the spectrum of religious practice. The Christian ritual of Penance provides a similar mechanism for keeping even the most grievous sinners within the framework of a religious life. But the ritual performed at the Saubhāgya Kūpikā allows the petitioner to transgress sexual boundaries without suffering negative consequences. Indeed, for those considering an adulterous liaison, this bathing ritual offers a form of religious indulgence to protect them from suffering the fate Khaṇḍaśilā.

On a more mundane level, the rituals at the Saubhāgya Kūpikā offer a way to violate these societal norms and stay within the accepted boundaries of a religious society. In most textual references to Kāma, he is described as blissfully happy with one or two wives, Rati and Prīti. Yet this story takes Kāma outside marriage for a lusty fling with an innocent maid. Kāma does suffer for his transgression, but the tale also establishes a ritual that facilitates moving back and forth between wives and others, without consequence.

From the perspective of day-to-day life, we smile at the naivete, the adolescent fantasy of such a possibility. But if the story is understood as an exploration of the phenomenon of desire, this scenario accurately reflects the desirous thoughts that often stray beyond socially or religiously constructed boundaries. Even further, the rituals to Khaṇḍaśilā and Kāma actively integrate this desire that allows individuals to sweep past boundaries.

Before leaving the story of Kāmadeva and Khaṇḍaśilā, we should recognize that this analysis examines the story from a primarily male perspective. As mentioned earlier, the *Skanda Purāṇa,* like most of the purāṇas, was written most probably by Brahmin men, reflecting a predominantly male view of reality. However, the story begs for a female retelling. How might a female storyteller describe the curses borne by Khaṇḍaśilā and her mirror image, Ahalyā, for actions described in some variants as a conscious choice and in others not? Revered as embodiments of purity and auspiciousness, Khaṇḍaśilā and Ahalyā are women become stones whose experiences of desire and suffering give them saintly status and power. But how do women storytellers present these women of stone? Are there other nuances? Other endings?

WHY WOMEN BECOME STONES

The women begin as unintentional temptresses, women who are unconscious of their power to evoke desire, and end up as unconscious rocks with the power to confer beauty and sexual freedom on others. Why the image of stones? First, there is the long Indian tradition of recognizing, seeing power in, and respecting sacred stones, such as the Vaiṣṇava śālagrāma stone and the Śaiva naturally formed stone linga. But the symbolism also recognizes that the stone is truly *vicetana,* meaning "without the ability to think."[20] It follows that transforming those consumed by the arrows of Kāmadeva into unthinking stones aptly reflects the unthinking quality of sexual desire. Of course stones, too, are incapable of desire, making them a perfect curse for those whose powerful desires have led them astray.

The story of Khaṇḍaśilā explores the unconscious, or without-mind, aspect of desire more explicitly in the discussion between Kāmadeva and Hārīta. Kāmadeva argues that Pūrṇakalā is not really guilty because her feelings have arisen because of his arrows. Her feelings originated in a part of her not consciously controllable by the mind, and not focused on dharma. Hārīta makes the same point when he accuses Kāma of luring her from upholding her dharma. However, Hārīta goes on to state that all actions are born first in the mind and so mind *is* ultimately responsible regardless of the circumstances. Stepping into the morass of the workings of desire, the story of Khaṇḍaśilā and some versions of the Ahalyā story (in which she is genuinely fooled by Indra's disguise as her husband) differentiate between conscious and unconscious mental processes, or between holding one's dharma in mind and having it pushed out by some other uncontrollable mental process. Kāma/kāma, in the story, moves through fluid but still delineated boundaries, understood to be conscious and not, controllable but not, mind-born yet produced by external forces. The story explores the boundaries separating that which is conscious and therefore controllable from that which is unconscious (perhaps as a result of Kāma's arrows) and therefore not controllable. But like other human emotions, Kāma stands with a foot on either side.

The image of women turned into stones calls to mind another story, the tale of the woman who lived inside a stone. In this narrative from the Yogavāsiṣṭha,[21] a sage, through yoga, imagination, and trance, meets a woman who has been created by her Brahmin husband out of his imagination to satisfy the Vedic requirements for a man to have a wife. This celibate husband and his wife live inside a stone on a mountain at the edge of the world. The woman is very beautiful, never grows old and never experiences the "pleasures or comforts of life." She exists simply as the wife required by the Vedas. Imagined by a man intent on living as an ascetic, but still following the Vedic injunction to marry, the woman remains a beautiful object of his mind, never causing him jealousy or uncertainty. Perfect from the ascetic's perspective, but not so for the woman. She is disappointed in this passionless life inside the stone, and seeks the sage's help in gaining release.

Though the initial elements of this story are very different from the story of Khaṇḍaśilā, each tale tells of a woman imprisoned in stone by a disciplined ascetic who has also encased his own sexuality in this stone, the dry and immobile antithesis of passionate male and female bodies. For both Hārīta and this Brahmin in the stone, their marriages to stone-women help them become more accomplished ascetics, their desires contained and confined, their Vedic duty to marry fulfilled, and their religious discipline and authority unchallenged.

Unlike flesh and blood wives, these beautiful stones remain exactly where they have been placed.

REFLECTING ON KHAṆḌAŚILĀ: ŚIVA IN THE PINE FOREST

In the stories of Śiva's adventures in the Pine Forest [Dāruvana], the actions of Śiva parallel almost exactly the actions of Kāmadeva in the Khaṇḍaśilā story, although Śiva remains the great god in these stories and, in some versions acts from motives much loftier than those of Kāma. As discussed in an earlier chapter, there are a number of variants of this well-known episode of Śiva in the Pine Forest, but I will summarize only that told in the *Brahmāṇḍa Purāṇa* because it is the closest to the plot of the Khaṇḍaśilā tale and contains the clearest structure.

Wendy Doniger in *Śiva, the Erotic Ascetic*,[22] argues that these variants in which Śiva assumes his erotic aspect reflect the more basic theme of the story cycle,while the variants in which Śiva is depicted as chaste and only falsely accused by the sages require a great deal of "complex rationalization" to support Śiva's disinterest in the women. This episode recounted in the *Brahmāṇḍa Purāṇa* also assumes that the husband's anger is justified.

Śiva and the wives of the Pine Forest sages

> Śiva went to the forest to excite the wives of the sages who were practicing asceticism. When the sages saw what he was doing, they cursed this madman to cause his liṅga to fall off. "When your liṅga has been abandoned, you will then be worshipped." . . .
>
> "When the lord had vanished and the liṅga was cut off, there was no manifestation of the deity among all the beings in the triple world, and there was confusion everywhere. Nothing shone forth; the sun gave no heat, purifying fire had no lustre, and the constellations and planets were all topsy-turvy. The seasons did not come about for the sages of mighty souls who had become involved in worldly ways for the sake of offspring and who went to their wives during the fertile season. They continued to practice dharma, free from egoism, free from possessiveness, but their virile powers were destroyed, and their energy was destroyed. Then their opinion about dharma wavered, and they all went together to the world of Brahmā . . ."[23]
>
> When they told Brahmā about their problems, he told them that the madman they had cursed was Śiva and he advised them to worship this great god in the form of the liṅga. When the sages had propitiated the liṅga, Śiva restored order to the earth, and instructed them to bathe in ashes always, in order to purify themselves from all sins, conquer anger and subdue the senses.[24]

The parallel structure of the two stories is clear. Śiva seduced the sages' wives just as Kāma attracted Pūrṇakalā; Śiva was cursed by the group of sages just as Kāma was condemned by Hārīta. With Śiva's castration, all creation stops and chaos ensues, just as when Kāma was afflicted with leprosy. Kāma's loss of beauty functions in the same way that castration functions in the Śiva story. Kāma's charming appearance is the source of his power in the same way that Śiva's power resides in his liṅga.

The storyteller consciously builds the tale of Kāma and Khaṇḍaśilā on this Pine Forest episode, not only by using the motifs and structure of this story, but by telling us explicitly that Kāma has taken refuge at the shrine to Śiva's fallen phallus. The leprous Kāma was propitiating the great god at the Kāmeśvara Liṅgam to no avail when the gods advised him to worship Pūrṇakalā, who holds the more powerful antidote to his condition. Kāma stands at this Śaivite shrine as a reflection, or even multiform, of the great god, who must also be made whole again to regain full power and stature. For the god of desire to regain this wholeness, he must prostrate himself at the feet of the woman he has wronged. The two stories diverge at this point, but the Khaṇḍaśilā authors have made their point, that the loss of Kāma causes suffering equal to the world's loss of the great god, Śiva. The universe truly needs desire.

Yet on another level, the two stories function as reverse mirror images highlighting their opposing messages. The Khaṇḍaśilā tale instructs people to bathe in the Saubhāgya Kūpikā, performing a pūjā to Pūrṇakalā to purify themselves from the sin of adultery, and worshipping Kāmadeva to gain physical beauty. Śiva, on the other hand, should be propitiated at the Kāmeśvara Liṅgam for help in *subduing one's senses.* The instructions in the Khaṇḍaśilā story assume the continued seeking of bodily pleasure, while the Kāmeśvara Liṅgam stands as a reminder of the chaos and torment produced by Kāma's arrows. Listeners hear both messages, the complex reality of the human need for desire and the longing to be free of its sometimes painful consequences.

DEVOTION TO KĀMADEVA

Devotion to Kāmadeva parallels the worship of the god Kubera[25] by thieves who seek his protection for their unlawful acts, and rituals to Devī who protects the Hijra community, transvestites who live on the margins of society as prostitutes and performers. Rituals to these deities do not encourage all to become prostitutes or thieves, but they do create a place within the religious tradition for people who violate social norms thereby living on the margins of society. Though socially ostracized, thieves and prostitutes are included in the religious community by worshipping at their own shrines and performing rituals to deities who offer them solace and protection.

The famous shrine of Kapālamocana in Varanasi provides such a refuge for those guilty of brahmahatyā, the killing of a brahmin. According to the account in the *Śiva Purāṇa,*

> Rudra, angry at Brahmā's superior manner, created a being called Bhairava to cut off Brahmā's fifth head. Śiva then created a maiden called Brahmahatyā and told her to follow Bhairava, begging for alms with the skull and teaching the vow that removes brahmahatyā, until reaching Varanasi where she would be unable to enter. Arriving in Varanasi, Brahmahatyā died and the skull of Brahmā fell from Bhairava's hand, becoming the shrine of Kapālamocana.[26] At this shrine, Bhairava devours the sins of devotees, and those who perform ablutions at Kapālamocana are freed of brahmahatyā.[27]

Of course, there is a difference between the adultery offered to Kāma and the killing of a brahmin, one of the most serious of all transgressions. But religious rituals in each case offer a means of purification and reentry into the community.

Devotion to Kāmadeva keeps desire within the framework of the religious tradition. An inescapable component of the human condition, desire is acknowledged by the religious authors of the purāṇas and accepted within the framework of devotion and ritual. But the rituals to Kāmadeva function in another way as well. The rituals create an acceptable outlet for the frustration of living within the restrictions imposed by society to create a certain order. Folklore and folk drama perform a similar function, allowing social beings to vicariously participate in taboo behavior by identifying with characters on stage or within the story.[28]

In the course of the ritual, desire itself is offered to Kāmadeva and Khaṇḍaśilā. That which is uncontrolled is given to gods who accept and transform these offerings. The original problem of controlling passionate desires evaporates as the consequences are turned over to the god of desire. The ritual offers divine assistance to mortals caught in the quagmire of desiring that which is forbidden.

Like the worship of deities conducted by murderers, thieves, and prostitutes, devotion to Kāma and Khaṇḍaśilā follows the pattern of worshipping the deity who has fallen in the same way as the penitent. Devotion to the deity who has slipped, suffered, and been purified offers the possibility of one's own purification. In perfect symmetry, the religious tradition accepts human weakness and transgression by providing a way to return to ritual purity and begin anew.

WHAT KĀMA AND KHAṆḌAŚILĀ SAY ABOUT DESIRE

As other narratives have stressed, Kāmadeva/kāma is essential for continued procreation, even for the survival of the universe. But outside the bounds of society's norms, action based on desire can make the beautiful ugly, engender disease, violate taboos, and be unmindful of dharma or duty. Indeed, the story makes a strong case against physical intimacy outside marriage. Yet even within this framework, the tradition recognizes the complexity of human psychology and interactions, and offers a potential loophole, a way out if someone has ignored its clear warning to control desire outside the conjugal bonds. By worshipping Kāmadeva or his paramour, desire can be satisfied without the negative consequences of ugliness and disease, the violation of taboos and dharma.

Yet while the story makes this extraordinary offer, pleasure without consequence, and describes the ritual necessary to attain this freedom, we are still left with haunting images of Pūrṇakalā as a broken rock and Kāmadeva riddled with leprosy.

This tale expresses the ambivalence toward desire that is found throughout Indian story literature. A necessary human force, desire must be acknowledged but not given the reins, followed but guided within boundaries, reveled in but never fully surrendered to. Respecting the complexity of human psychology, the tale offers rituals at the Saubhāgya Kūpikā of Khaṇḍaśilā for those overwhelmed and weakened by desire.

The next chapter examines colorful devotional rituals to Kāmadeva designed to fill the senses with pleasure and to indulge the voluptuous energy of the spring season as it calls forth the fertile monsoon rains.

The Tale of Khaṇḍaśilā and the Well of Good Fortune

1. The Ṛṣis said [to the poet]: When long ago, Himadyuti [Having Snowy Radiance, the Moon] was cursed by the anger of Dakṣa, you told the little story of Somanātha.

2. Also long ago, Kāma's speech resulted in leprosy. Through what fault was that curse laid upon him?

3. At that same place, the lady became Śilākhaṇḍā [Broken Rock] and the Well of Good Fortune sprang up. Tell us [what happened].

4. The poet began: In ancient times there was a famous brahmin named Hārīta who lived in a forest ashram practicing austerities.

5. His wife was a good woman with a noble form, beautiful to behold in all the three worlds [the universe], just like Lakṣmī is always beautiful to Madhudviṣa [Kṛṣṇa].

6. Possessing all good qualities and called by the name *Pūrṇakalā,* she excited desire [kāma] in even Brahmā, the lotus-born one, as soon as he saw her.

7. One day, Kāma, the One-Who-Exists-in-the-Mind [Manobhava], arrived at that place[29] with his wives, Rati and Prīti, all longing to see Śiva, Lord of Desire [Kāmeśvara].

8. But at the same time, a woman had also come there to bathe. Taking off her clothes, this woman entered the water.

9. Seeing this most beautiful woman, Kāmadeva pierced [his] heart with his very own flower arrows.

Skanda Purāṇa 6.134.1–80 (Bombay: Veṇkaṭeśvara Press, 1867, 1910.)

10. Pierced with these arrows, he left Rati and Prīti and went to a secluded place, where he sat under a tree and fell into a reverie.

11. All the hair on his body standing up,[30] Kāma repeatedly let out sighs of very long fiery breaths and his eyes filled with tears.

12. Remaining in sight of her, with one eye he gazed at the woman, transfixed like a yogi sitting in deep samādhi, meditating on Brahmā.

13. The woman also gazed at the passionate Kāma, whose mouth was yawning and body trembling.

14. Pierced by his arrow, she, too, was filled with longing [abhilāṣa]. In the presence of the god of desire, she was entranced by his singular beauty.

15. As a result, she emerged slowly from the water with a pure smile. Approaching the edge of the shore, she stood within range of his vision.

16. Slowly getting up, Kāma walked toward her. Doing añjali with cupped hands, he spoke with devotion:

17. Who are you, O Beautiful-Eyed One who has come here to bathe in the water? You are my destruction, O Beautiful-Limbed One. Listen to my words.

18. I am famous throughout the world as the one-with-Flower-Arrows, O Beautiful Smiling One. By these arrows, I lead even the gods into confusion.

19. Though unhurt by my arrow, Rudra [Śiva] shamelessly supported the One-with-Beautiful-Hips [Pārvatī] in his own body, as half of himself.[31]

20. Brahmā, pierced by my arrow, desired his own daughter, thereby giving birth to those trembling beings, the Vālakhilyas.

21. Śakra [Indra] desired Gautama's own dear wife, Ahilyā.[32] Struck deeply by my arrows, he went from heaven to earth [to see her].

22. O You of Beautiful Eyebrows, if the great gods are broken to pieces by my arrows, how much more easily men who tremble like worms?

23. O Beautiful Smiling One, from the smallest insects to Brahmins, all creatures are subject to the greatest deception because of my arrows.

24. O Beautiful One, even I am led to this state of shyness because of you.

25. O Auspicious One, give me the gift of pleasure. If not, the breaths will leave my body.

26. His arrows embedded in her heart, she listened to his words. At the same time, the woman felt her most important duty, her vow to her husband, being destroyed.

27. This pure one was ignorant of Kāma's dharma.[33] Having been raised alone with ascetics, she knew nothing but ascetic life.

28. Those who speak about this subject are those who have experienced Kāma/kāma [that is, not the ascetics in the hermitage]. She stood for a long time with her face looking down, writing on the earth with her toe.

29. As the sun reached his home over the mountain, the one who tends the sacred fire [the man of the house, Hārīta] entered the dwelling.

30. Expecting his meal, Hārīta looked around for a long time and was worried that his wife had not come back home.

31. He knew that for those who bathe on the bank of this tīrtha, seeing the Candra Well and the Kāmeśvara [liṅgam], Śiva satisfies all desires [kāma] and grants happiness.

32. So Hārīta, along with a student, began looking here and there until they reached the place where the two were standing.

33. As he talked and talked, Kāma was being destroyed by his own arrows. In Kāma's magnetic presence, the woman stood with her face down in shame.

34. Concealed in a clump of trees, the Brahmin heard all that Kāma was mumbling, and saw her feelings of attraction. Out of anger, he spoke:

35. O Evil One, since you pierced with an arrow my wife who was so innocent and devoted to her husband, you will be cursed with leprosy, displeasing to behold.

36. Because of this sin against me, you will be abandoned by your own wives. [Pūrṇakalā] stands with her face downcast in shame at your presence.

37. For her part, she who is like a stone will become without consciousness [vicetana]. Upon seeing you, she was filled with passion and abandoned her dharma.

38. Propitiating the brahmin by prostrating himself, Kāma said: I did not know she was your beautiful wife, O Sage.

39. After speaking these ridiculous words, Kāma continued: She was not at fault. She was simply pierced quite deeply by my arrows.

40. O Muni, she became excited but she said nothing at all. Therefore you should not place any curse on her.

41. The fault lies with me, so restrict the curse to me. Again, O Best-of-Brahmins, do not curse her.

42. [When] Rudra and the gods are not able to endure my arrows, O Best-of-the-Twice-Born, why should she become a stone?

43. The wise say there are three kinds of sin: mental, spoken, and that born of action. In the interaction between the two of us, only one occurred for her, the mental.

44. [If] you restrain [yourself] completely [in your anger] toward this beautiful woman, you should have no fear in the next world.

45. The mind can atone for sins of the mind through performing austerities. Bestowing gifts of apology can atone for sins arising from speech.

46. Through these prescribed acts of expiation, the sin born of action may also be expiated. This is described in detail by all the *dharmaśāstras,*[34] O Great Muni.

47. Hārīta said: Her sin is of one order, O Kāmadeva, [while yours is of another]. Your dharma is traditionally known to be of the mind.

48. She [behaved] as that kind of woman and will always be so.

    O Vile One [Aghama Kāma]. What more is there to say? Do what must be done.

49. All is first conceived by thought, by the mind. Then, it is spoken in word and performed by an act.

50. According to authority, the mind resides in all actions.

    For this very reason, my curse on her remains unchanged.

51. With this statement, that Best-of-All-Munis, Hārīta, went to his home. From that moment, the woman was changed into a stone.

52. Kāmadeva was afflicted with a violent case of leprosy. And, O Brahmins, because his hands and feet withered, he was no longer pleasing to the eyes.

53. Afflicted with this disease, Kāma was totally without energy, O Leaders of Brahmins. Procreation [sṛṣṭi] was blocked in this world.

54. Not only was the world withering, but no new growth was beginning. Even those who were sweat-born[35] were dying away.

55. At this time, all the gods were troubled. Why was the world being destroyed, all that grows in water and on land?

56. Absolutely no child could be seen, anywhere or in any form. There were no pregnant women. The happiness of Smara could not be found anywhere.

57. Knowing that he who had been afflicted with leprosy had taken refuge at this place, the Haṭekeśvaratīrtha of the Kāmeśvara Liṅgam, all the troubled beings went there.

58. As they looked upon the Flower-Armed One in his greatly deformed appearance, standing in front of the Kāmeśvara Liṅgam, contemplating the Great Lord Śiva,

59. They were greatly distressed and said: What is this? O Flower-Armed-One, you have become lethargic, distressed by the leprosy.

60. He put his head down in shame and moved away, saying: All of this is born of Hārīta's curse.

61. The learned ones spoke: Without any doubt, that sin which was committed will be completely wiped out by propitiating her.

62. O Heart-Born, you should propitiate the woman who is now a stone. Through this act, the leprosy will be destroyed and your vitality will return.

63. Let there be great procreating in the world, O God. Whatever must be done, let it be done. There is no sin with the body. Thus released, there is only speech.

64. Here at your well, anyone bathing with faith should touch that rock which has been released from sin. [Thereby others will be released of sin also.]

65. Through raising up the body [to the stone], one who is afflicted with leprosy will be released from the disease and healed.

66. This place is called the Well of Good Fortune [*Saubhāgya Kūpa*]. Without a doubt, the water will make all disease disappear.

67. When the bather sees the Well of Good Fortune, various skin diseases leave almost immediately.

68. Upon saying this, the gods went to the abode of the thirty gods [heaven]. Kāmadeva stood at the well and performed pūjā to her.

69. O Best of the Twice Born, having done penance for a number of months, Kāma again became the one known as Smara.

70. Having completed the ritual at her sacred abode in faith, he went to his beloved land for the purpose of creation [sṛṣṭi]. He was now ready for the effort.

71. Her face bowed down because of the curse, she became the one with the appearance of being broken. Thus she is remembered as Khaṇḍa [Broken] Śilā [Rock].[36]

72. If adultery occurs, there is no blame or censure [*apavāda*] for one who conscientiously does this special pūjā to her on the thirteenth day,

73. Nor for his lover. Thus the son of Śiva, Kārtikeya,[37] spoke, and I have truly recited.

74. Propitiating the image of Kāmadeva and the god Kāmeśvara [Śiva] in this manner on the thirteenth day [of the lunar cycle], all desires should be satisfied.

75. The embodied Smara, joined with Rati and Prīti, takes the highest seat.

76. [When] one who is unfortunately deformed offers pūjā on the appointed thirteenth day with the blossoms born of the kumkum [crocus, saffron].

77. This one will meet with good fortune and gain a beautiful form.

A woman who has been neglected by her husband, laid aside for other wives,

78. Should also offer this pūjā to that god who is rich in good wives [Kāma], on the thirteenth day, with the filaments that rise from the kumkum.

79. Blessed with good fortune, this woman will become wise and fertile, rich, and without pain and sorrow. Freed from all sin, she is praised on the earth.

80. Thus says the Śrī Skanda Mahāpurāṇa, in the sixth [part] of the eighty-one thousand verses, in the Nāgarakhaṇḍa, in the Śrīhāṭakeśvarakṣetra Māhātmya. The one-hundred thirty-fourth adhyaya is named the description of the Māhātmya of the origin of the Saubhāgyakūpikā of Khaṇḍaśilā.

CHAPTER FIVE

Worshipping Kāmadeva

Puranic texts and Sanskrit dramas describe a number of rituals, identified as *pūjās, vratas,* and *utsavas,* that are devoted to the god Kāmadeva. The word *pūjā,* literally meaning "worship," designates a particular set of prayers and offerings to a deity. Pūjās are performed at home or in public gatherings, most often during the morning or evening. The term *vrata,* usually translated as "vow," describes a particular ritual or group of rituals performed over a period of time, and making a specific request of the praised deity. For example, wives often undertake vratas (or vrats in the vernacular languages) for the protection of their husbands and children. Usually performed by women, though not exclusively, such vratas might involve a promise to fast every Tuesday for six months or to eat only specified foods on certain days. An utsava is a festival during which a deity is worshipped in particular ways. For example, in Maharashtra, a weeklong festival honors the god Ganeṣa with rituals performed in homes and in public areas. Like ritual prayers and liturgical festivals in Christianity, pūjās, vratas, and utsavas are common forms of worship in the Indian religious tradition.

However, devoting a pūjā, vrata, or utsava to the god Kāmadeva is not at all common. Over a period of twenty years, I have found no one in contemporary India who knows any place where devotional rituals to Kāmadeva are currently practiced. Indeed, the very idea of devotion to the god of desire strikes most people as odd. So while the following rituals are not performed in India today, and may never have been, the numerous descriptions of these rituals in puranic texts and Sanskrit dramas are significant because they integrate desire as a natural component of human existence into a religious context by placing Kāmadeva at the center of ritual devotion.

Rituals like the damanaka festival, prostitute vrat, and the pūjā for couples seeking happiness demonstrate how the religious tradition has integrated these day-to-day elements of ordinary life. Acknowledging and even celebrating human desire and sensuality, these rituals offer a balance to other tales and rituals that warn of the dangers of desire. Rituals to Kāmadeva reflect an acceptance and enjoyment of desire without creating a dichotomy between this enjoyment and living as a religious person. Both perspectives, enjoying the sensuality of existence and creating boundaries for this sensuality, are represented in the stories and their related rituals. Indeed, the rituals offer an additional way to understand and integrate the force of desire within one's life.

KĀMADEVA'S FESTIVALS AND PŪJĀS: THE DAMANAKOTSAVA

Bhasa in his drama *Cārudatta* mentions a festival called Kāmadeva's Festival (Kāmadevamahotsava), which became an occasion for many love-marriages. Other texts describe Kāmadeva's day, the thirteenth or fourteenth day in the month of Caitra (March–April), when a festival is performed at the Ahalyā Tīrtha.[1] On this day rituals are performed by worshippers hoping to be reborn as handsome men who will be loved by women, indeed like Kāmadeva.[2]

The *Agni Purāṇa* describes a number of pūjās devoted to Kāmadeva. These pūjās are performed to attain particular desires,[3] ranging from the birth of a child to increased prosperity to regaining the attention of a disaffected lover or spouse. This text also specifies pūjā days and rituals dedicated to Kāmadeva, such as Ananga Trayodaśi, and Damanaka Tṛtīya,[4] which specify the use of the damanaka plant to symbolize the presence of the god, Kāmadeva.

Drawing from varied sources including the purāṇas, Hemādri's *Caturvargacintāmaṇi*[5] describes numerous vratas and pūjās dedicated to the god of desire.[6] Other compilations of vratas and pūjās in Sanskrit and regional languages[7] describe many of the same Kāmadeva devotions. For example, a number of texts mention Madana Dvādaśi,[8] the worship of Kāma-Madana on the twelfth day of the lunar cycle; Kāma Trayodaṣi, the worship of Kāma on the thirteenth day in the form of the damanaka plant; Caitrāvali, the celebration of Kāmadeva during the month of Caitra, spring; Madana Bhañji and the Madanotsava, the festival to Kāma-Madana; Kāmadeva vrata and the Kāmadeva pūjā.[9] Many of these rituals describe the use of pictures or figures of Kāma and Rati along with music to invoke and praise the deities.

According to the texts, these devotions are performed for many reasons including health, progeny, a husband, happy married life, merit, and all desires. Several are more specific in their orientation, such as the vrata[10] for prostitutes seeking better life circumstances in their next births. A similar aspiration for a more auspicious future life motivates those performing a ritual mentioned earlier, the Kāmadevadina pūjā offered at the Ahalyā Tīrtha. This ritual is performed by men seeking rebirth in a body which will be as irresistible as the figure of Kāmadeva.[11]

Common elements of the worship of Kāmadeva in these rituals include the use of a plate with a picture or idol of Kāma and Rati placed on a pot of water; an appointed day, usually during the spring month of Caitra (March–April), an identification of Kāma with Viṣṇu[12]; and the use of the damanaka plant[13] as a symbol of the god of desire.[14]

The practice of substituting an image of Viṣṇu or the damanaka is referenced in the following passage from the *Padma Purāṇa*[15] describing a ritual to Kāmadeva called the Damanakotsava.

This celebration is to be performed on the twelfth day of the bright half of the month of Caitra, by faithful Vaiśṇavas guided by their guru [*gurvājñayā*]. [This pūjā] will bring joy to all people. (1–2) Devotees should worship the damanaka flower, identified with Kāmadeva, with perfume, flowers, incense, and arati [flame of fire]. (4–11)

In this pūjā, performed at night, the worshipper should bow to Kāmadeva in the eight directions, and recite the gāyatrī hymn to the damanaka identified as Kāmadeva-Anaṅga. (11–14) Kāmadeva should then be saluted with many of the epithets of Viṣṇu [devadeva, śrīviśveśa, jagannātha, sarva-bīja, janārdana]. (17–19) After offering the damanaka to Viṣṇu and other gods, there should be a great festival, pouring water over the god's feet, and honoring the guru with gifts and food. (22)

Kāmadeva as the object of this worship is addressed by Viṣṇu's epithets (jagannātha, śrīviśveśa, keśava) as well as his own (rati-pati, viśva maṇḍana, madana) in what is clearly a Vaiṣṇava ritual dedicated to the god of desire. Throughout the ritual, the worshipper blends Kāma and Viṣṇu, using the damanaka flower interchangeably for the two gods and associating Kāmadeva and Viṣṇu in the same prayers: "O Kāmadeva, Namaste to you who delude the whole world. For Viṣṇu, I worship you. Have compassion on me."[16]

In this pūjā as in others, Kāmadeva is worshipped indirectly through the medium of the damanaka flower[17]or the god Viṣṇu. Substituting the flower or Viṣṇu for Kāmadeva might appear to be a way to refocus devotion to Kāma away from the sexuality with which he is associated. But the use of the damanaka actually highlights the sexual aspect of the deity, as this flower is understood to have aphrodisiacal properties. In fact, Kāma remains a symbol of sexual desire in the rituals. But linking Kāma with the supreme Viṣṇu brings devotion to the god of desire within more acceptable boundaries. In the Damanakotsava, Kāma becomes a multiform of Viṣṇu, receiving praise and prayers of supplication while granting his devotees' petitions, behaving much like the great god. The damanaka, a more subtle symbol of sexuality, remains at the center of the ritual mandala reinforcing the centrality of human needs spawned by desire.

Speaking to informants from Maharashtra, Tamil Nadu, Kerala, Karnataka, Gujarat, and Uttar Pradesh, I could find no evidence of rituals to Kāmadeva performed today.[18] Because the extant sources for most of these Kāmadeva rituals are collective anthologies rather than writings linked with specific communities or geographical locations, we can only speculate when and where they were once performed.

KĀMADEVA AS FERTILITY GOD, AND VRATAS FOR PROSTITUTES

The vrata[19] for prostitutes seeking a higher rebirth is described in the *Padma Purāṇa* and the *Matsya Purāṇa.*[20] This narrative tells the tale of a group of prostitutes who go to the sage Dālbhya asking him to explain why they must suffer such hard lives. The prostitutes also petition Dālbhya to help them find a way out of their circumstances.

In days gone by, the sage explains, the prostitutes were nymphs, daughters of Agni, quite impressed with their own beauty and their desire for Kṛṣṇa. One day, the sage Nārada walked by and they petitioned him to make Kṛṣṇa their husband. Unfortunately, however, in their eagerness, they forgot to perform the correct salution to Nārada first. So while he granted their request to become wives of Kṛṣṇa, he also cursed them to be subsequently cursed by Kṛṣṇa.

In their next birth, these nymphs did become the sixteen thousand wives of Kṛṣṇa. However, one day while sporting in the lake, they were pierced by Kāma's arrows and immediately felt tremendous lust for Kṛṣṇa's son, Sāmba, who was passing by.

Because Kṛṣṇa knows all things with his supreme vision, he knew what had happened and cursed the women to be captured by bandits who forced them to become prostitutes. Seeing the women overcome with grief, Kṛṣṇa mitigated the curse by saying that they would remain prostitutes until they met the sage Dālbhya, who would teach them a vrat to release them.

First, Dālbhya explained, they should satisfy all men who come to them except those who are proud. [Only in the *Matsya* 70.29.] Secondly, he described the vrat they should practice to obtain release from their lives as prostitutes. Worshipping all parts of the body of Viṣṇu, identified here with Kāmadeva, the women should worship a brahmin who has mastered the Vedas and is without any physical deformity, by giving him food and sexual enjoyment. Certain gifts should also be given to the brahmin and his wife.

After worshipping the brahmin in this manner every Sunday for thirteen months, the women should place images of Kāmadeva and Rati with eyes made of gold on a copper plate. This copper plate with the two images should then be placed on a vessel filled with jaggery.[21] These objects, along with a sugar cane, a pot made of bell-metal, and a cow, should be given to the brahmin, saying, "As I see no difference between Kāmadeva and Viṣṇu,[22] so Lord Viṣṇu, please satisfy all my desires." After the brahmin accepts the gifts and has been circumambulated, he should recite this mantra[23] from the *Atharva Veda*.[24]

> Ka idam kasmā adāt kāmah kāmāyādāt
> Kāmo dātā kāmah pratigrahīitā kāmah samudram āviveśa
> Kāmena tvā prati gṛhnāmi kāmai tat te[25]
>
> [Who gave to whom? Desire gave to desire.
> Desire is the giver and receiver; Desire entered the ocean;
> With desire, I accept you; this is for you, for desire].

This ritual is called the vrata of the gift to Kāma-Anaṅga [Anaṅga-dāna or Anaṅgadauvrata] and all who practice it will obtain a place in the presence of Viṣṇu.[26]

In this ritual, Kāmadeva is identified with Viṣṇu, but also with the brahmin receiving the gifts, food, and sexual pleasures. In other rituals to Kāma, other men or gods take the place of Kāmadeva for women performing the rituals. For example, the Madana Festival (Madanamahotsava),[27] which also begins in the spring month of Caitra, instructs the woman doing the pūjā to worship her husband as the god of desire, satisfying him sexually as part of the devotion. The *Bhaviṣya Purāṇa* promises that "wherever this ritual (in which the husband is seen as Kāmadeva) is performed, the rains (will) come on time and prosperity (will) prevail,"[28] indicating that the purpose of the Madanamahotsava ritual is to ensure fertility, for this woman offering the pūjā as well as for the earth.

While the prostitute vrata would not involve the same concerns for fertility as the Madanamahotsava, the gifts given by the prostitute (pot, milch cow, and vessel filled with jaggery) do represent fertility, as well as prosperity, for the brahmin receiving them.[29] Ordinarily, the mundane occupation of the prostitute gives her a very low status in the community and makes her presence inauspicious for others. But this vrata offers her a way out of these circumstances immediately. By performing the vrata, the prostitute becomes a more auspicious presence because she is the consort of a deity. Then, because she has achieved this fortunate state, her presence can bring fertility and good fortune to the brahmin and his family. The underlying association of sexuality with fertility can enter the ritual.

Fertility is celebrated in the worship of Kāmadeva during the festivals and vratas performed in the spring months of Caitra (March–April) and sometimes Vaiśākha (April–May), a favorite time for marriages. The story of the god who dies and is resuscitated from burnt ashes can also be observed in the dying of the earth in the dry season and its blossoming again in the rainy season. This association of Kāmadeva with fertility is underscored in the story of Khaṇḍaśilā when Kāmadeva has been stricken with leprosy and all creation [sṛṣṭi] withers and dies. No babies are born among any class of beings, from the sweat-born to the egg-born. Until Kāma regains his health, no fertility on the earth is possible.

But the aim of the prostitute vrat is not fertility but a higher birth. The women worship a deity associated here with extramarital sexual liaisons in order to gain release from the negative karmic consequences associated with their lives as prostitutes. The vrat offers a way for these outcaste women to gain a legitimized place within the religious tradition, a higher birth in their next life, and the protection of Viṣṇu/Kāmadeva in the present.

A variant of this tale found in the *Sāmba Purāṇa*[30] explains the previous lives of these prostitutes in greater detail. In this version of the story, it is Sāmba who fails to greet Nārada respectfully because he is so wrapped up in his beautiful body and amorous activities. In order to teach Sāmba a lesson, Nārada arranges for his father, Vāsudeva (Kṛṣṇa), to think that Sāmba is seducing Vāsudeva's wives. Convinced by Nārada's juxtaposing of events, Vāsudeva curses his wives to be carried off by "thieves from the land of the five rivers" after his death, and curses his son, Sāmba, "to become an ugly leper."[31]

In the course of this story, Sāmba finally attains release from his curse by worshipping the sun, Sūrya, who is able to cure many skin diseases and physical defects.

This variant shifts the role of protagonist from the women to Sāmba. Sāmba is obsessed with his beauty, offends Nārada, appears to seduce some women, and is cursed by Vāsudeva/Kṛṣṇa. Although the *Padma* and *Matsya* storytellers explain that they are providing a context for the prostitutes' vrat, and the *Sāmba* raconteur states his purpose as teaching about the worship and curative powers of Sūrya, each variant communicates the same perspective on the hazards of sexual desire. The vanity of desire prevents both the women and Sāmba from behaving properly, and the ritual provides release from the negative consequences of such behavior. Indeed, devotion to the deity provides the cure for a variety of diseases rooted in the body.

A multiform of Kāmadeva and Indra, Sāmba receives the same curse for lustful behavior outside marriage: the loss of his beautiful body. This *Sāmba Purāṇa* narrative explains that when a man is controlled by desire, he loses his sense of good judgment, and ultimately his attractiveness. Following the pattern laid out in other tales about the consequences of lust, like Śiva in the Pine Forest and Kāmadeva seducing Khaṇḍśilā, Sāmba charms another man's wives, is caught by their husband and cursed to lose his beauty/health/virility. Finally by performing acts of worship, in this case honoring Sūrya, the sun, Sāmba's body is restored. Others suffering from skin diseases are then invited to worship Sūrya in the same way in order to be cured like Sāmba.

The pattern of these tales repeatedly warns that the powerful pull of desire brings unpleasant and immediate consequences in its wake. In some parts of India, there is a belief that promiscuity causes leprosy, a disease that not only disfigures but produces an extraordinary sexual desire which leads to further promiscuity. Though no medical evidence confirms this connection between leprosy and lust, the link between extramarital sexual liaisons and leprosy in the tales may be rooted in this belief.

On a metaphoric level, the loss of physical beauty is the appropriate poetic consequence for an illicit liaison. On a physical level, without a beautiful and well-functioning body, future liaisons are curtailed.

RITUALS FOR BEAUTY AND HUSBANDS: TĪRTHAS FOR COUPLES

In the stories of Khaṇḍaśilā, Ahalyā, and the prostitutes, the rituals grow naturally out of the events of the tales. Equally common are the stories which are themselves accounts of devotees performing rituals to gain relief from a painful situation. Such are the stories of Apalā in the *Ṛg Veda* and Karṇotpalā in the *Skanda Purāṇa*.[32] Although the story of Apalā does not directly involve Kāmadeva, Indra in his role as seducer of women heals Apalā by making love to her. A god with all of the erotic charms of Kāmadeva, Indra heals her skin disease not through his kingly power to rule, but by seducing her. Using the common motif of a love affair between a mortal and a god, the story of Apalā graphically illustrates that divine intervention does heal. But in terms of understanding desire, this story reverses the pattern of other tales because the divine action that cures Apalā is love-making, the same act for which Indra, Śiva, and Kāmadeva have been cursed in other tales.

Though the seven verses found in the *Ṛg Veda* are quite elliptical, later commentaries fill in the gaps. Wendy Doniger tells the story in this way:[33]

> Apalā was a young woman hated by her husband (v. 4) because she had a skin disease (v. 7). She found Soma (v. 1), pressed it in her mouth and offered it to Indra (v. 2). Indra made love to her, which she at first resisted (v. 3) and then consented to (v. 4). She asked him to cure her and also to restore fertility to her father and to his fields (vv. 5–6). This triple boon is accomplished by an obscure triple ritual. Later tradition states that being drawn through three chariot holes caused her to slough her skin three times; the first skin became a hedgehog, the second an alligator, the third a chameleon. The Vedic verse merely states that her skin became sun-like (i.e. fair), and the ritual has obvious sexual symbolism.

The story presents a straightforward relationship between the boon that is Kāmadeva's to bestow (or in this case Indra's), a physical beauty that attracts, and the desire to be cured of a disease that creates a repulsive appearance. But the story of Apalā also provides an interesting contrast with the story of Khaṇḍaśilā.

The two stories are reverse images of the same tale. Apalā starts out ugly and becomes beautiful, while Khaṇḍaśilā/Purṇakalā is a beautiful woman who becomes a stone. In the case of Apalā, sexual interaction with a libidinous god results in enhanced beauty, while for Khaṇḍaśilā, the divine sexual encounter transforms her into a stone, though with the important twist that this stone Khaṇḍaśilā has the power to heal. Although the stories work with opposite images, they comment similarly on the appropriate behavior of a married woman.

The Apalā story teaches that a woman who petitions Indra to win the affections of her own husband will become even more attractive. With her mind completely focused on her husband, Apalā's sexual encounter with Indra enhances her position as wife. By contrast, Khaṇḍaśilā becomes mesmerized by the presence of Kāmadeva and forgets her husband for a few moments. For this lapse, Khaṇḍaśilā is cursed. Reinforcing the same image of a proper wife, the didactic narratives depict Apalā and Khaṇḍaśilā being appropriately rewarded and cursed according to their actions. The story of Ahalyā also teaches wives how to behave. When Ahalyā forgets her husband in the presence of a charming god, she too is cursed to lose her beauty and become a stone.

These tales of Apalā, Khaṇḍaśilā, and even Ahalyā present a consistent instruction for wives. If a wife remains absolutely committed to her husband, like Apalā, she will never be tempted by another man and good fortune will come to her. On the other hand, if a wife even inadvertently forgets her husband for just a moment, like Khaṇḍaśilā and Ahalyā, she will certainly fall under the spell of desire and suffer dire consequences.

Another ancient story that underscores the importance of a wife's loyalty is the tale of the old and decrepit Cyavāna and his beautiful young wife Sukanyā.[34] As the tale begins, the twin horse-headed deities, the Aśvins, decide to seduce the beautiful Sukanyā, who appears to be wasting her youth and beauty married to an old man. But the young woman, loyal to her husband, rebuffs them. As the story unfolds, the Aśvins reward Sukanyā for her purity by restoring her husband's youth.

A perfect wife like Apalā, Sukanyā uses her seductive charms, not for her own enjoyment, but to gain greater pleasure for her husband. These early Vedic stories are the precursors to later stories describing women's vrats performed for the well-being of their husbands. Women's vrats, often performed weekly or monthly throughout the year, are understood to generate a power that protects these women's husbands, even, in some cases, restoring them to life.

The story of Karṇotpalā,[35] the second wife of Kāmadeva, also reflects the Apalā pattern, describing how a good woman does tapas to attain youthful beauty and thereby a husband. Like Apalā, Karṇotpalā performs austerities for her own healing, but more importantly, for the sake of her father, who is despondent at not finding a husband for his daughter. When the goddess rewards her for the sincerity and discipline of her austerities, Karṇotpalā asks for a husband "richly endowed with beauty and youth" so that her father will no longer have to worry about her. After performing the ritual prescribed by the goddess, Karṇotpalā receives the most attractive of husbands, the god Kāmadeva. As the story ends, Kāmadeva, filled with affection for his new wife, changes her name from Karṇotpalā to Prīti meaning "affection." Following her dharma as a good daughter and good wife, Karṇotpalā gains both youth and beauty, as well as the charming god of desire as a husband, the appropriate rewards for the righteous woman-who-wears-lotuses-as-earrings, the meaning of her name, *Karṇotpalā.*

Of course Gaurī herself, the bestower of Karṇotpalā's beauty, is the ultimate role model for wives doing penance to gain more beautiful bodies. Though Gaurī acts out of anger rather than the wish to please her husband, she performs tapas to shed her dark skin and gain a golden body in the well-known story recounted in the *Skanda Purāṇa.*[36] Loyal to her husband, Gaurī returns to Śiva after these austerities, presenting her more beautiful form to him.

Just as Karṇotpalā/Prīti gains Kāmadeva by doing penance to attract the attention of the goddess and then bathing in the water of the tīrtha, others are advised to do penance and bathe in particular wells or ponds to attain their desires. In the *Skanda Purāṇa,*[37] two wells are designated for a ritual performed by a man and woman together. Appropriately, these wells are called Rati Kunda and Kandarpa Kunda (Kāma Kunda). After performing ablutions together at each of these wells, a couple will receive from Kāma and Rati beauty equal to that of the god of desire and his consort.

Though rituals to Hindu deities often involve ablutions in wells or bodies of water, this ritual is unusual in that the wells themselves are perceived as a couple, and the man and woman who perform the ritual are instructed to bathe in the wells together. While the purāṇa states only that the couple will obtain beauty, the structure of the ritual suggests that if the two behave like Kāma and Rati at the kundas dedicated to them, they will become as happy as the god of desire and his consort.

WHY RITUALS TO KĀMADEVA

The number of utsavas, pūjās, and vrats dedicated to Kāmadeva described in the purāṇas demonstrates one way that the tradition acknowledges the significance of desire as an integral part of human existence. The rituals very naturally weave the complexity of human desire into religious practice.

Incorporating desire with no inhibitions, several of the rituals describe how to identify an intimate partner as a proxy for Kāma, often a brahmin lover or the popular god Viṣṇu. Flowers like the damanaka, aśoka, kumkum, and jasmine, associated with Kāma for millennia, along with the spring months when these flowers bloom with sensual fragrances and colors, continue to represent the god of desire and his interests. These flowers are understood to possess aphrodisiacal qualities, and the spring months of Caitra (March–April) and Vaiśakha (April–May) are still the most popular months for weddings. Indeed, in many parts of the country,[38] Kāmadeva is still invoked in the marriage ritual.

However, today the direct worship of Kāmadeva does not appear to be an acceptable practice. Although women commonly pin fragrant strings of jasmine in their hair and bathe in flower-scented water, they wear the fragrance much as men and women around the world wear scented oils and waters, simply appreciating fragrances without consciously associating them with desire. While fragrance sellers who work in Indian bazaars behind rows of colored bottles, like their counterparts on Madison Avenue, have never stopped exploiting the sensuality of fragrances and thus witnessing the connection between flowers and Kāmadeva, they do not sell their scented oils for devotional rituals to the god of desire.

P. V. Kane in the *History of Dharmaśāstra* takes a somewhat cynical view of the vratas performed both in earlier days and in the present. He castigates religious practices performed only to gain one's desires as not being truly religious:

> The bulk of the vratas practised in medieval and modern times are kāmya, i.e., performed for the purpose of securing some object in this world or sometimes the next world or both. Most of the vratas are really secular though under the garb of religion and, though certain disciplines (such as fast[ing], worship and celibacy, truthfulness) have to be observed, [the vratas] breathe a frankly materialistic attitude; [and] they are meant to appeal to the ordinary human cravings that rule the whole world.[39]

Though Kane sounds rather disdainful in his statement, perhaps the most compelling reason for the great number of vrats, pūjās, and utsavas devoted to Kāmadeva is precisely that which he deprecates. Kāma's rituals respond to people's immediate problems and concerns by addressing those "ordinary human cravings that rule the whole world."

The Damanaka Festival (Damanakotsava)

The great god, Śiva, said to Pārvatī:

1) In the month of Caitra,[40] the damanakotsava is celebrated on the twelfth day,[41] according to the specific precepts.

2) This celebration should be performed with gaiety by Vaiṣṇavas. It is auspicious, and increases the joy of all people.

   The divine flowers of the damanaka[42] tree are born out of the joy of the gods.

3) O Daughter of the Mountain [Pārvatī], petitioning Vaiṣṇavas should perform all pūjās on the twelfth of the bright half of Caitra.

4) O Faultless One [Pārvatī], one who is determined to perform this pūjā should do it with the highest devotion. He should go first to his own garden.

5) At the command of the guru, the pūjā should be performed. "O Kāmadeva, homage to you who, along with Rati, hypnotize the whole world."

6) "For the sake of Viṣṇu, I beseech you. Have compassion on me." Now the damanaka flower[43] is to be led into the home in a procession with songs and loud music.

7) O Best of all goddesses, on the eleventh day, after purifying the damanaka with perfumes, the devoted Vaiṣṇavas should perform a night pūjā there.

8) In front of the damanaka, the devotee should make a mandala, establishing there the Lord of the Gods and Rati.

Padma Purāṇa, Uttarakhaṇḍa, Ānandāśrama edition, 1894. 86.1-35.

9) Covering the damanaka with a white cloth and placing it there, the best of all twice-born Vaiṣṇavas should then perform the pūjā.

10) Placing Kandarpa [Kāmadeva] in Indra's direction [east] and saying the Hrīm mantra, the wise one should worship him, [saying]

> Klīm, Homage to Kāmadeva.
> Hrīm, Homage to Rati.

11) O Empress of the Gods, the pūjā should be offered by the devotees at night with an oil lamp, perfume, flowers, and incense.

12) In the east [Indra's direction] salutation to Madana;

in the southeast [Agni's direction] salutation to Manmatha;

in the south [Yama's direction] salutation to Kandarpa;

in the southwest [the rakṣas' direction] salutation to Anaṅga;

in the west [Varuṇa's direction] salutation to him whose body is ashes;

in the northwest [Vāyu's direction] salutation to Smara;

in the north [Kubera's direction] salutation to Īśvara

in the northeast [Śiva's) direction] salutation to the one who wields flower arrows.

13) There, the pūjā should be performed in the four directions and in all directions. When Keśava [Viṣṇu] has been worshipped, all the gods are honored.

14) Worshipping the damanaka with the purest perfume, incense, betel, and other offerings of food, say: We know him as the puruṣa; We are fixed on him as Kāmadeva; this Anaṅga should encourage us.[44]

15) While consecrating the damanaka with the Kāma-gāyatrī hymn one hundred and eight times, one should pray.

16) One should give homage to the flower-arrowed, the one who confers delight on the world, the churner of the mind [manmatha], the one who creates the sensuous pleasure and love [prīti] seen in the world.

17) One should pay homage in this way:

O God of Gods,[45] O Lord of Srī, O Husband of Rati, O Confuser of All,

18) We salute you, O Lord of the World, O Seed of All, with these various mantras, as they are meticulously described in the ritual texts [*āgamas*].

19) The exciter of men who, along with Rati, is worshipped with great effort is awakened by performing this ritual.

20) O God of Gods, O Lord of the World, O One Who Grants All Wishes,

Fulfill the desires of my heart, O Viṣṇu, you who are dear to the lady of Kāma.

21) Abode of Śrī, Lord of the World [Viṣṇu], he who desires tranquility for all devoted to him should be worshipped with these mantras and with sincere effort.

22) Afterwards, grasping the damanaka by the flower and [saying] the mantra, the worshipper should offer it to the gods, beginning with Lord Viṣṇu. Then a great pūjā should be performed with perfumes, as a great festival with singing, musical instruments, and dancing.

On this day, after placing a water pot in front of the god and pouring water over the god's feet, people should play in the water. The worshipper should honor his guru with clothes, ornaments, and money; he should also eat with his Vaiṣṇava relatives.

23) Then one should worship Viṣṇu with a cluster of damanaka. When the Lord of the World is worshipped thus, indeed I [Śiva] am always honored.

24) O Goddess, even by watching the damanakotsava one is freed from the worst sin, (even) brahminicide, stealing gold, drinking wine, and eating meat.

25) O Goddess, O All-Bestowing Daughter of the Mountain, the damanaka is always honored in this way by these Vaiṣṇavas. When the pūjā is performed with a cluster [of damanaka], it is equivalent to making all pilgrimages.

26) By performing the pūjā with a cluster [of damanaka], all offerings are abundantly made: the earth offering, the cow offering, and the great offering.

27) Indeed, a study of the Vedas and the śāstras has been done. Even the Vedic fire sacrifice has been performed by one who worships Hari with the cluster (of damanaka).

28) The family of this worshipper should be known as great, whether brahmin or kṣatriya, śūdra or vaiśya. A family traditionally regarded as wealthy will become even wealthier.

29) When the damanaka festival is handed down and performed in a family, this Viṣṇu worshipping family will become even more prosperous.

30) When the two spring months arrive, O Goddess, worshipping with the damanaka will bring the prosperity of 1000 cows.

31) One who devotedly propitiates the Garuḍa-Bannered One [Viṣṇu] in the spring with jasmine flowers will be blessed with liberation.

32) The madhuka[46] and damanaka are always immediately pleasing to Hari [Viṣṇu]. So this pūjā should be performed by Vaiṣṇavas, those best of men.

33) By doing this pūjā to Viṣṇu, one has made a gift of the earth, a gift of a daughter, and a gift of 1000 cows.

34) One who worships the Lord of the Gods [Viṣṇu] in the two spring months by picking damanaka one by one,

35) Gains so much merit that it cannot be measured, O Daughter of the Mountain. Becoming four-armed[47] in this world and the hereafter, he enjoys dharmas, arthas, and kāmas,[48] and the place of Viṣṇu.

CHAPTER SIX

Recognizing Kāma: Perspectives of Early Texts—Anger, Puruṣārtha, Invincible Power, Tantric Energy

In the *Kālikā Purāṇa,*[1] a tenth-to-eleventh-century work from Bengal or Assam, a story is told of a being who springs forth from the mind of Brahmā just as Brahmā is desiring a woman he has just created.

> A beautiful man appeared, shot forth from the mind. Charming, the color of butter or topaz, with a broad chest and a fine nose. (44)
>
> He had broad thighs, hips, and calves, blue-black hair twisted into a crown. His pair of joined eyebrows were arching and his face shone like a full moon. (45)
>
> The hair (growing) near the heart made (his chest) appear as broad as a door. He had beautiful limbs, and plump, round arms. (46)
>
> His hands, eyes, face, legs and feet were reddish. He was slender-waisted with fine teeth. He was captivating like a rutting elephant. (47)
>
> His eyes were like the petals of a full-blown lotus, and he was pleasing to smell like the filaments [of a flower]. He had a conch-like neck [with three folds], was tall, and carried the makara banner. His vehicle was the makara. (48)
>
> Armed with five flowers as arrows and a bow, his eyes moved back and forth in charming side-glances. (49)

A fragrant wind was blowing and he was accompanied by the sentiment of love [śṛṅgāra rasa]. Produced from the mind, in front of Dakṣa, he was quite astonishing. (50)

The man then said to Brahmā: What will I do? What work [karma] will I be appointed to? (53a)

Brahmā replied: With your charming beauty, and bow and flower arrows, you will do [the work of] creation eternally, bewildering men and women. (57)

No devas, no gandharvas, no kinnaras, no great serpents, no asuras, no daityas, no vānavidyās, no rākṣasas, (58)

No yakṣas, no piśācas, no bhūtas, no vināyakas, no guhyakas, no vāsiddhās, no mortals, no birds, (59)

No cattle, no deer, worms, insects, or any water-born, none of all these will be exempt from the mark of your arrow. (60)[2]

This man was called Kāma, linking him to the broadest conception of desire, kāma, and to sexual desire in particular.

Of course, this story of Kāmadeva was far from unfamiliar by the seventh century. Kāmadeva was well established in Indian oral and written traditions by this time, as the mind-born god of desire who possessed the power to arouse desire in all beings and who had been burnt to ashes by Śiva. However, in the ancient Indian texts, the word *kāma* connoted a more narrowly abstract concept of desire. In the verses of the *Ṛg Veda, Atharva Veda,* Upaniṣads, and the *Mahābhārata* examined in the following sections, the character called Kāma appears in different forms, only gradually becoming the deity known as Kāmadeva.

KĀMA IN THE *ṚG VEDA* AND *ATHARVA VEDA*

Kāma in the creation drama and firstborn son of mind

In *Ṛg Veda* X.129, an abstract essence, kāma, participated in the initial creation drama:

> Darkness was hidden by darkness in the beginning; with no distinguishing sign, all this was water. The life force that was covered with emptiness, that one arose through the power of heat. Desire [kāma] came upon that one in the beginning; that was the first seed of mind. Poets seeking in their heart with wisdom found the bond of existence in non-existence.[3]

Franklin Edgerton describes this abstract force called kāma, highlighted in this hymn from the *Ṛg Veda,* as "a sort of cosmic Will" or "force behind the evolution of the universe," an essential part of the creation drama.[4]

In the *Atharva Veda,* a deity called Kāma is requested to satisfy the needs of the petitioner. Praised and supplicated in the hymns, the deity retains characteristics of the primal force, in such epithets as "first seed of mind," *mano-ja,* the mind-born one. The following verses from *Atharva Veda* IX.2 express one poet's conception of the deity. In his translation of these Vedic hymns, W. D. Whitney titles these verses, "To Kāma":

> The rival-slaying bull Kāma do I desire to aid with ghee, with oblation, with sacrificial butter; you, praised with great heroism, make my rivals fall downward. (1)
>
> What of my mind or my sight is not agreeable, what of me gnaws, does not enjoy that evil-dreaming I fasten on my rival; praising Kāma, may I shoot up. (2)
>
> Evil-dreaming, O Kāma, and difficulty, . . . want of progeny, homelessness, and ruin, O formidable masterful, fasten [these] on him who seeks to devise distresses for us. (3)
>
> Thrust, O Kāma; thrust forth, O Kāma; let them who are my rivals go to ruin; thrust them to the lowest darknesses; O Agni, burn out the abodes. (4)
>
> O Kāma, slay those who are my rivals; make them fall down to the blind darknesses[5]; make them all senseless, sapless; let them not live any day at all. (10)
>
> Kāma was first born; neither the gods, the Fathers, nor mortals reached him; to them you are superior, always great; to you as the superior one, O Kāma, do I pay homage. (19)[6]

A deity capable of inflicting a wide range of calamities, Kāma is supplicated here to summon help against rivals or enemies. To assure this intercession, the supplicant wisely extols Kāma's powers and superiority over the gods, the fathers and mortals, making specific reference to the superior position ascribed to Kāma in *Ṛg Veda* X.129, first-born [*eka-ja*] in the creation of the universe.

In *Atharva Veda* hymn XIX.52, the purpose is not stated so clearly. Whitney entitles this hymn "Of and to desire [kāma]," and explains that the hymn may have been intended to accompany the acceptance of sacrificial gifts.

> Desire [kāma] here came into being in the beginning, which was the first seed of mind; O desire, being of one origin with great desire, do you impart abundance of wealth to the sacrificer. (1).
>
> Desiring [kāmayamānā] this, O desire [kāma], we make this oblation to you, that all may succeed with us; then eat of this oblation: hail! (5)[7]

The kāma addressed in these verses is not a god of love, but a deity who fulfills all desires. In this respect, Kāma functions in the same way as other gods petitioned in the *Atharva Veda.*

The only quality that sets Kāma apart from other Vedic deities is his link with the kāma of *Ṛg Veda* X.129. The *Atharva Veda* poet echoes the earlier *Ṛg Veda* description, calling him the "first-born," he who "came into being in the beginning . . . the first seed of mind," who is "of one origin with great desire." The poet presents Kāma as a god whose power is rooted in the fundamental essence of the universe; a god who, therefore, can tap this essence to grant desires. The stature of this Kāma is enhanced by acknowledging his origin in the cosmic generative principle of the universe.

Kāmadeva's Passion-Arousing Arrows in *Atharva Veda* III.25

Atharva Veda III.25, titled by Bloomfield, "Charm to arouse the passionate love of a woman,"[8] and by Whitney, "To command a woman's love," provides another description of Kāma which approximates even more closely the character of the god found in the epics and purāṇas. In this hymn, the supplicant entreats Kāma to arouse desire in a woman who has caught his eye, so that she may be receptive to his advances:

> May the up-thruster[9] thrust you up; do not abide in your own lair;
> with the arrow of kāma that is terrible I pierce you in the heart. (1)
>
> The arrow feathered with longing, tipped with love [kāma], necked with resolve, let love pierce you in the heart. (2)[10]

Though nineteenth-century Vedic scholars translated *kāma* in these verses as *love,* the word more accurately connotes desire. This petitioner clearly wants the woman to desire him, and to desire him with such intensity that she will resolve to meet his desires, something quite different from simply wishing for her affection.

This hymn calls upon Kāma whose arrow pierces hearts. In verse 1a, the supplicant pierces his lover with Kāma's arrow, while in verse 2, Kāma does the piercing. This focus on the "terrible" (*bhimā*) arrow of Kāma indicates that these shafts were one of the first prominent characteristics ascribed to him. From this early period, Kāma is described as shooting hearts with an arrow, a metaphorical yet tangible vehicle for his power.

Influenced by the social biases of the 1920s, Keith states that the *Atharva Veda* is a work that "reflects the practices of the lower side of religious life, and is closer to the common people than . . . much of the *Ṛg Veda.*"[11] Contemporary scholars do not see the *Atharva Veda* as a text associated with the "lower side of life," but rather a work that appealed to all levels of society. The charms and magical rituals for defeating enemies, giving birth to children, and recovering from disease would have appealed to a broad spectrum of society, much as such charms and rituals do in many societies today. Given the popularity of these practices described in the *Atharva Veda,* it is also likely that Kāmadeva as wielder of the "terrible" desire-arousing arrows was a familiar figure in some rudimentary form, even in this early period.

Although it is impossible to know exactly when each of the hymns of the *Atharva Veda* was written, it may indeed be that this hymn describing the charm to arouse the desires of a longed-for woman was composed later than the hymns in books nine and nineteen, because this hymn presents a more clearly defined image of the god of desire. But regardless of the chronological sequence of these three hymns, the *Atharva Veda* as a whole is a later work than the *Ṛg Veda,*[12] and displays a distinct change in the concept of kāma, moving from cosmic generative principle to identification with various forms of human desire. Among these three hymns, only III.25, the love charm, begins to develop the image of Kāmadeva as he comes to be known later, as a deity whose arrow is terrible as it carries desire in its tip [kāmaśalyamiṣu], and burns [vyosa] the heart that it pierces.

In the *Atharva Veda,* kāma is associated with the broad range of human desire: wanting enemies to be defeated; wanting lovers to reciprocate feelings of infatuation, lust, affection; wanting more money and more power; in short, wanting to be successful in love and work.

KĀMA IN THE BRĀHMAṆAS

In the Brāhmaṇas, the word *kāma* most commonly refers to the desires a sacrificer hopes to have fulfilled by the proper perfomance of ritual. This reference to kāma is presented clearly in a passage from the *Śatapatha Brāhmaṇa:*

> Whatever desire [*yatkāmā*] the Ṛṣis entertained when they performed that sacrifice, that desire of theirs was accomplished [*samṛdhyate*]; and accordingly whatever desire he [the sacrificer] entertains in having this sacrifice [*yajña*] performed, that desire of his is accomplished [samṛdhyate].[13]

Another passage, also in this first khaṇḍa, describes the results of a ritual to Prajāpati, here identified with the sun:

> Whatever desire [kāma] he [the sacrificer] desires [kāmayate], that wish [kāma] is fulfilled [samṛdhyate].[14]

The word *kāma* in this verse, and throughout the Brāhmaṇa, expresses generic desire, but is often translated into English with the related connotations of longing, wishing, hoping.

In the fourth khanda of the *Śatapatha Brāhmaṇa* the writer quotes a passage from the *Atharva Veda* which the adhvaryu recites while offering gifts to the deity. In this section, the adhvaryu is described as offering gifts to gain strength, joy, and immortality, while saying:

Who has given this and to whom? Desire [kāma] has given to desire [kāma].

Desire is the giver, desire the receiver. O Desire, that is for you.[15]

This verse, intended to be recited by the adhvaryu, is almost identical to a verse from the *Atharva Veda* (III.29.7)[16] still used in some Hindu wedding rituals. Although it is tempting to interpret this verse as a short hymn to a personified Kāma, there is no other such reference to Kāma in the *Śatapatha,* and thus not enough evidence to support such an interpretation.

Like the *Śatapatha* creators, the authors of the *Jaiminīya Brāhmaṇa* also use the word *kāma* to mean generic desire. In the Jaiminīya, there is a discussion of the offering of the *agnihotra* ritual, in which the sun is offered in fire, and the fire is offered in the sun. Each of five brahmins in turn explains that when these two offerings are made, of sun and fire, one is led to "all things one may desire (*yatra sarve kāmāḥ*)."[17]

Also found in the Brāhmaṇas is an adverbial form, *kāmam,* meaning "at will" or "at one's pleasure" or "as much as you like." In this passage from the *Jaiminīya Upaniṣad Brāhmaṇa,* a text closely related to the *Jaiminīya Brāhmaṇa, ṛk* (speech, exhalation) has a conversation with *sāman* (the mind, breath) about the purifying or cleansing properties of the various components of the Vedas, and what foods Vedic students should and should not eat. The author says that a Vedic student should not eat honey, "but he may eat with pleasure (*kāmam*) what his teacher gives him."[18]

In the Brāhmaṇas, the word *kāma* again is used to connote "generic desire," the hopes and wishes of the sacrificer or patron, as well as the adverbial sense of acting according to one's desires or pleasures. Within this broad context, *kāma* might at times connote sexual pleasure, as in the stories from the *Jaiminīya* translated by Doniger,[19] but not always. Although the word *kāma* is used frequently in the Brāhmaṇas, there is no reference to a personified or deified kāma in these texts.

KĀMA IN THE UPANIṢADS

In the Upaniṣadic writings, the word *kāma* continues to mean "desire" in the generic sense of a longing for any object. But these texts present several different understandings of the way desire functions in the world.

In the *Chāndogya Upaniṣad,* the Udgatṛ or chanting priest is called a "procurer of desires" (āpayita kāmānām).[20] The *Bṛhadāraṇyaka Upaniṣad* explains that "an Udgatṛ priest who has this knowledge (the purificatory formulas and hymns of praise) is able to procure by his singing whatever he desires, either for himself or for the patron of the sacrifice."[21] Again in the *Chāndogya,* it is said that "an Udgatṛ priest who possesses this knowledge (Sāman chants and their meaning) may truly say: "What desire [kāma] shall I obtain for you by my singing?" For one who sings the Sāman chant with this knowledge has, indeed, the power to fulfill desires by singing."[22] In other words, knowledge of a particular ritual or sacrifice and its proper performance brings the satisfaction of desires, according to compilers of the *Chāndogya* and *Bṛhadāraṇyaka.*

This idea that desires are satisfied or prayers answered through the correct performance of the sacrifice or ritual strongly reflects the perceptions and attitudes of early Vedic writings, the *Sāma* and *Yajur Vedas* in particular, which held that sacrifice was the central religious ritual and its performance was necessary to preserve the cosmic order (ṛta). In contrast to these early Vedic writings, the Upaniṣads introduced a new emphasis on knowledge as a vehicle of internal power. Upaniṣadic writers maintained that possessing knowledge of the deeper meanings of the Vedic rituals and hymns could fulfill all desires.

New understandings of desire also emerge in the Upaniṣadic writings. Composers of these texts speak of breaking free from *saṃsāra,* the endlessly turning wheel of birth and rebirth, and attaining union of the personal self, *ātman,* with the ground of all being, *brahman.* In this process, one inevitably must come to terms with desire. But this desire is understood differently in the various Upaniṣads, and sometimes even within the same Upaniṣad.

According to Chāndogya 8.7.1, when one has attained the state of liberation or identification with brahman, all desires are satisfied.

> "The self [ātman] that is free from evils, free from old age and death, free from sorrow, free from hunger and thirst; the self whose desires and intentions are real [*satyakāmaḥ*]—that is the self that you should try to discover, that is the self that you should seek to perceive. When someone discovers that self and perceives it, he obtains all the worlds, and all his desires are fulfilled." So said Prajāpati.[23]

To the writer of this verse, all desires are immediately satisfied upon attaining this knowledge. But to another writer, all desires must first be given up in order to attain this state.

> A man who is attached goes with his action to that very place to which his mind and character cling. Reaching the end of his action, of whatever he has done in this world—from that world he returns back to this world, back to action. That is the course of a man who desires [*kāmayamānaḥ*].
>
> Now a man who does not desire—who is without desires, who is freed from desires, whose desires are fulfilled, whose only desire is his self—his vital functions [*prāna*] do not depart. *Brahman* he is and to *Brahman* he goes.[24]

In a later Upaniṣad, the *Muṇḍaka,* the composer combines both of these attitudes toward desire.

> The wise men, free from desires, who worship the Person [Puruṣa, knower of the ātman] go beyond what is here bright [rebirth].[25]
>
> Whatever world a man, whose being is purified, ponders with his mind, and whatever desires he covets; that very world, those very desires, he wins. A

> man who desires prosperity, therefore, should worship one who knows the self [ātman].[26]

Both attitudes toward desire (kāma) are expressed in the Upaniṣadic writings: that all the desires of one who possesses knowledge of the real, or of truth (satya), are completely satisfied, and paradoxically, that one must be without desire in order to attain this knowledge. On a first reading, these two statements sound like a chicken-and-egg proposition. But in fact, many of the Upaniṣadic teachers taught that both goals are achieved simultaneously. When one has worked for many years and practiced deeply in the ascetic disciplines, that person will both become a knower of the ātman and no longer experience desires as forces that cannot be ignored.

Robert Hume, in his introduction to *The Thirteen Principal Upanishads,* describes the earlier Upaniṣadic thinking as being preoccupied with the power of knowledge, a power which granted a position almost beyond the confines of moral precepts and judgments.

> As water adheres not to the leaf of a lotus-flower, so evil action adheres not to him who knows this [that the Self is Brahman] (*Chāndogya Upaniṣad* 4.14.3)

> As to a mountain that's enflamed
> Deer and birds do not resort—
> So, with the Brahma-knowers, faults
> Do never any shelter find. (*Maitri Upaniṣad* 6.18)

However, as human desire continued to maintain its presence and exert its seductive influence alongside Vedic knowledge, the thinkers began to realize that issues of moral conduct were as important for the seekers of Brahman as they were for ordinary people. Hume says of this development: This unrestricted freedom of the earlier Upanishads could not long continue. It probably went to excess, for in the middle of the period it is sternly denounced. Good conduct was declared to be an equal requisite with knowledge.[27]

The change in attitude toward ethical conduct seen in the comparative study of earlier and later Upaniṣads also results in a corresponding change in attitude toward desire. In the earlier teaching, the satisfying of desires was emphasized as the reward for those who became knowers of the Veda. But as the focus on satisfying one's own desires became problematic for the community, more attention was given to the necessity of ethical conduct, thus restricting the attention given to kāma.

In the historical development of attitudes toward desire, the Upaniṣadic writings present a perspective very different from that presented in the *Atharva Veda.* In the *Atharva Veda,* the primary goal is to gain the object of one's desire, whether the affections of a spouse or the death of that spouse's lover. Moral or ethical standards are not given a high priority. Early Upaniṣadic writing, too, evidences this same lack of concern with ethics, and speaks primarily of the attainment of religious power through knowledge of the Vedas.

However, the later Upaniṣads, reflecting a frustration with Vedic priests who used their power for selfish purposes, teach that kāma must be disciplined and not served, an attitude that survived through the epics and purāṇas into contemporary Indian writing.[28] Living by the dictates of kāma becomes the diametrical opposite of practicing the virtues of dharma (sacred duty) and mokṣa (spiritual liberation).

KĀMA AS A HUMAN GOAL, A PURUṢĀRTHA (*MAHĀBHĀRATA*)

The Indian epic the *Mahābhārata* is a Sanskrit work in eighteen volumes containing numerous stories, philosophical passages, and descriptions of battle scenes, told within a frame that recounts the story of a prolonged feud between royal cousins. Because the epic is a compilation of the writings of many different authors, complicated by different manuscript versions copied and miscopied and sometimes intentionally changed over the centuries, the *Mahābhārata* contains different perspectives on almost any given topic, including how to think about or understand kāma.

In the Śānti Parvan, a discussion of kāma takes place among the five Pandava brothers and Vidura, a man who counsels their cousins. Yudiṣṭhira, the eldest Pandava, frames the discussion by posing a question to his brothers and to Vidura: "The course of the world rests upon dharma [performing moral or religious duty], artha [governing successfully], and kāma [satisfying of desires]. Which of these is the most important, which is the second and which is the last one?"[29] Vidura ranks dharma first, artha second and kāma last, while Arjuna, the Pandava son of the famous warrior-king Indra, places artha as the most important. Arjuna argues that "without artha, neither dharma nor kāma can be achieved." Nakula and Sahadeva begin by agreeing with Arjuna that artha should be first with dharma and kāma following, though they subsequently acknowledge that without dharma, no artha is possible.

The huge and strong Bhīma, mighty fighter and son of the wind god Vāyu, joins the discussion, strongly stating that kāma must naturally be placed before all else. "One without kāma does not strive for artha, one without kāma does not wish for dharma; one without kāma is not striving for anything; therefore kāma is pre-eminent." However, at the end of his presentation, Bhīma changes his position to say that, "Dharma, artha, and kāma should be practiced in the same way."[30]

Finally Yudhiṣṭhira, son of Dharma, speaks, changing the parameters of the discussion by declaring the fourth aim, mokṣa, liberation from the continuous cycle of karma and rebirth, to be the highest because it presupposes nonattachment to dharma, artha and kāma. The other Pandavas and Vidura agree with him.

This passage from the Śānti Parvan is important for our discussion because it reflects the different points of view that existed regarding kāma's proper position within the hierarchy of these three or four puruṣārthas or "aims of life": artha, dharma, kāma, and mokṣa. Though the arguments of Arjuna in favor of artha and Bhīma in favor of kāma are finally defeated by the claims of Yudhiṣṭhira for dharma and ultimately mokṣa, the inclusion of these perspectives demonstrates the author's respect for these positions as substantive enough to require refutation.

However, in this passage as in similar discussions in Manu and even in the *Kāmasūtra,* dharma or mokṣa retains the position of first importance, while kāma is confirmed as that aim which, although a significant part of life, should never be pursued at the expense of dharma or mokṣa. Artha, kāma, and dharma are attainable within the life of a householder, but mokṣa is a goal that transcends the everyday course of existence.

Among the puruṣārthas, kāma is usually ranked last in order of precedence. However, it is significant that kāma is among the three valid aims of life in a tradition that views each person as a responsible member of family, society, and cosmos. Within this framework for living a healthy and full life, one should pursue the art of good government and fulfill moral and religious duties, but one should also satisfy the natural desire for pleasure.

KĀMA AND KRODHA: DESIRE AND ANGER (*MAHĀBHĀRATA*)

In the Adi Parvan, Śānti Parvan, and Anuśāsana Parvan of the *Mahābhārata,* Kāma is closely allied with another god called Krodha (Anger). Describing these two, the narrator often speaks the two names together, Kāmakrodhau, in a compound word indicating that the two are as much a single unit as two characters. Personified abstractions, Kāma and Krodha reflect the psychological or emotional connection of desire and anger, understood as different reflections of the same phenomenon, two sides of the same coin. For teachers warning of obstacles to living a religious life, desire-anger often begins the list.

A common vow for people undertaking a pilgrimage is to abstain from *kam, krodh, lobh,* and *moh*—desire, anger, greed, and delusion—at least for the duration of the pilgrimage. Buddhist iconography places in the center of the wheel of life a cock, snake, and pig running in a circle each biting the tail of the animal in front of it. These three interconnected animals represent respectively, desire, anger (sometimes hatred), and delusion. Attached to one another through mouth and tail, they symbolize the perpetual turning of the wheel of life, or samsāra.

In the Adi Parvan, the powerful Kāmakrodhau are embodied, personified, and described as two beings "never conquered even by immortals . . . defeated only by the tapas [ascetic practice] of Vasiṣṭha," whose feet they massaged.[31]

Earlier in Book I of the *Mahābhārata,* Kāma and Krodha, along with Mahādeva (the Great God, Śiva) and Antaka (Death), are described as having formed, from portions of themselves, the heroic son of Drona, Aśvatthāman. "[Drona's] son the heroic Aśvatthāman, with eyes like the leaves of a lotus [*kāmalapatrākṣa*], gifted with surpassing energy [*mahāvīryaḥ*] and the terror of all foes, the great oppressor of all enemies, was born on earth from portions of Mahādeva, Yama, Kāma, and Krodha merged into one."[32]

Describing Aśvatthāman as a being composed of desire, anger, and death (giving him no fear of death), the narrator foreshadows that Aśvatthāman will embody these powerful forces in the story. Near the end of the epic war when the enraged Aśvatthāman is one of the few surviving members of the Kaurava side, he enters the enemy Pandava camp at night and kills the five small Pandava sons of Draupadi in their sleep. Clearly, Aśvatthāman's action in this episode reflects desire, anger/rage, and death.

In the Śānti Parvan, Kāma and Krodha appear as two ugly and misshapen characters called Virūpa and Vikṛta (Deformed, Disfigured) in a story recounting a dispute between Kāla (Time), Mṛtyu (Death), Yama (Lord of the Underworld), and a religious Brahmin.

There was a certain Brahmin of great fame and pious behavior, who was a reciter of prayers [*jāpaka*]. Possessed of great wisdom, he acquired spiritual insight into the Angas [sacred texts] by practicing austerities. Residing at the foot of Himavat, he was devoted to the Vedas. Silently reciting, he practiced severe austerities for a thousand years. (12.192.2–6)

After a thousand years had passed, the goddess Sāvitrī appeared, offering him any boon he wished. The Brahmin asked only that he be allowed to continue reciting the Vedas, and that his mind be absorbed more completely into samādhi. Although the goddess granted these requests, she also told him that the gods Dharma and Yama would approach him and begin a dispute on a question of morality. (12.192.7–18)

After reciting the Vedas for another thousand celestial years, the Brahmin was greeted by Dharma, who offered to take him to the enjoyment of heaven as a reward for his asceticism. The Brahmin explained that he did not want to go to heaven without his body. Dharma explained that in order to be free of passion [rajas], the body must be thrown off. Still, the Brahmin insisted that he did not want to give up his body and go to heaven. So Dharma simply informed him that Kāla [Time], Yama [God of the Underworld], and Mṛtyu [Death] were all quickly approaching. (12.192.19–27)

This trio arrived and each member stated that he had come to take the Brahmin to heaven. As the Brahmin was offering his guests water to wash their feet, and asking what he might do for them, another visitor arrived, King Ikṣvāku. So again the Brahmin brought water and asked what he might do, this time for the King. (12.192.28–37)

But the King responded: As a king, I cannot ask to be given anything, but you are a Brahmin observing the six duties, so tell me how much [wealth] I should give you. The Brahmin spoke: There are two kinds of dharmas for Brahmins, renouncing and continuing to act in the world, and I am one who has renounced. Therefore, I cannot accept any gift. Rather, I will give you whatever you wish, accomplishing this by means of my tapas. Again the King said: I am a Kṣatriya. I do not know how to say the word *give.* So the Brahmin said: Then we are both happy doing our own dharmas, and there is no need to make an offering to one another. (12.192.38–42)

This bantering about giving and receiving continued until finally the King said: Give me the fruits of the recitations you have done for the past one hundred years. The Brahmin gladly offered these merits but the King declined. He said he had no need of these merits. Yet he also wondered what these fruits of the recitations were exactly. The Brahmin told him that he didn't know, but it was important that he give them to the King in order to keep his word. The King asked why he should want these merits if the Brahmin didn't know what they were. (12.192.43–52)

The Brahmin presented a long discourse on the power of truth [satya] and the importance of keeping one's word, trying to convince the King to receive what was given to him. (12.192.53–72) At this point, Dharma and Svarga [Heaven] attempted to intervene but the disputants were unmoved. Then two other unpleasant-looking characters arrived, Virūpa and Vikṛta.

Virūpa and Vikṛta were also feuding over who was to give and who to receive. In this case, the merits under dispute were those accrued by the righteous act of giving a cow. Upon seeing the King, they asked him to settle the dispute. (12.192.75–86)

In pondering their dispute, the King decided that the one who refused to receive, Vikṛta, was really the one at fault. Thus the Brahmin pointed out to him that he had judged his own position vis-à-vis the Brahmin himself. The King realized that he must now take the gift given by the Brahmin, and stated that both courses, giving and receiving, earned equal merit.[33] (12.192.87–110)

Virūpa then introduced himself to the King as Kāma and Vikṛta as Krodha, and explained that there really had been no quarrel between them. They had assumed these guises to test the King. He continued, explaining that Kāla, Dharma, Mṛtyu, and Kāmakrodhau [Desire-and-Anger] had all observed the king through his actions in this interchange. "Now you may go with the merit attained by your actions." (12.192.114–116)

In the final scene, the Brahmin and the King decide to share the merits of the Brahmin. (12.193.7–8)[34]

This story poses several questions and uses the scenario to answer them. Do Kṣatriyas or Brahmins gain greater merit by their actions? Which is more meritorious, giving or receiving? What is the relationship of Desire and Anger to the issues involved in giving and receiving? How do Desire and Anger interact with Death, Duty, Time, and Heaven?

The allegorical framework of the story sets up the Brahmin as the giver whose acts parallel those of Kāma (Desire); and the King as receiver, with actions paralleling those of Krodha (Anger). Out of his desire to pursue his religious goals, the Brahmin wishes to give the merits he has attained to the King. But the Brahmin's offer makes the King angry because, as a King, his dharma requires him to give to others, especially to Brahmin renunciates. Immediately, a triangular tension exists among Duty, Desire, and Anger. Making things even more complicated, Time and Death get involved, indicating that the consequences of these actions reach beyond the present and immediate future. Within the framework of karma and rebirth, the forces of desire and anger extend beyond the boundaries of an individual lifetime.

At the end of the story, the Brahmin and Kṣatriya agree that giving and receiving are of equal merit, and they will share the merits of the other. In this way, they settle the dispute between the two castes over which caste earns greater merit through performing its dharma. They agree that giving and receiving are mutually meritorious. Yet, the story is more complicated. Both the giving and receiving remain messy from an ethical or moral point of view because each appears to be motivated by a mix of desire and anger. Neither action is performed simply for its own sake, with no thought of gain. Given these tangled human motivations, Desire and Anger emerge as more effective teachers for this Brahmin and Kṣatriya than the traditionally powerful teachers, Duty, Time, and Death.

Kāma and Krodha teach the obvious truism that the willingness to receive on the part of one person allows another to give. Simultaneously, they exemplify in their own characters that desire and anger exist in an equally reciprocal relationship. Just as giving and receiving, though separate actions, are inherently connected, so also anger and desire. Finally, however, Kāma and Krodha are revealed to be working in tandem with Dharma, Kāla and Mṛtyu (Duty, Time, and Death). All have helped the Brahmin and the King understand the ultimate significance of their actions; and all five have judged these actions to be worthy of heaven. Human beings, agreeing to give and receive, will eventually merit heaven.

Though ugly, crooked, and misshapen, the personified human motivations Kāma and Krodha, Desire and Anger, act as teachers and as judges, roles normally ascribed to other deities. Placing them in these unusual roles, the writer emphasizes that anger and desire do indeed act in both these capacities if one carefully observes human nature.

KĀMA: UPHOLDER OF THE EARTH AND COSMIC WILL (*MAHĀBHĀRATA*)

In the "Udyoga Parvan" of the *Mahābhārata,* several chapters are devoted to describing the rulers, residents, activities, and attributes of each of the four directions.

One *śloka* describing the northern quarter says that Kāma, Roṣa [Wrath], Śailas [Mountain], and Umā [Pārvatī] all came into existence in that quarter.[35] As Mt. Kailasā, the residence of Śiva and Pārvatī, is located in this northern quarter, Kāma who arouses passion between these two, is also placed here.

The Anuśāsana Parvan, Book XIII, describes Kāma as a *dharaṇīdhara,* an upholder of the earth, and identifies Kāma with Samkalpa (Will). The elder teacher, Bhīṣma, tells Yudhiṣṭhira whom to propitiate for protection from evil and fear, and for the furtherance of prosperity. As he enumerates the many beings who should be saluted in this prayer, he mentions the seven dharaṇīdharas, whom he describes as seven Ṛṣis [sages] who live in various places, not confined to any specific direction: Dharma, Kāma, Kāla, Vasu, Vāsuki, Ananta, and Kapila.[36]

Kāma stands in this reference as one of a group of seven which in turn is part of a larger group. This list, like many of the lists in the didactic writings, is intended to glorify the particular characters mentioned. However, the inclusion of Kāma, as a dharaṇīdhara, an upholder-of-the-earth not fixed to any particular location, is an appropriate image for the god of desire called Anaṅga, the bodiless one, in later writings. Although this is a minor reference to Kāma not emphasized in later mythology, the older idea of desire as an essential principle in creation and the later representation of desire as a powerful invisible being are both present in this image.

Another reference to Kāma in the Anuśāsana Parvan occurs within a story explaining the birth of Skanda from the fiery seed of both Rudra and Agni, with the help of Gangā. In this episode, Rudra becomes sexually aroused and spills his seed into the fire, really Agni, the god of fire, even though Agni is an unwilling receptacle. The poet comments on Rudra's loss of control: "Eternal indeed is the will [samkalpa] known as desire [kāma]."[37]

Kāma in this passage, as in earlier passages cited, represents an abstract essence or force, rather than a personified character, and this essence is associated with creation or possibly the will to create. Desire as will echoes from the earliest reference to kāma in *Ṛg Veda* hymn X.129, where kāma is said to be born from the void as the first seed of mind and described as one of the elemental forces of creation. Associated with desire, the Sanskrit term *samkalpa* connotes a firm intention, decision, or wish formed in the mind or heart.

A number of the Sanskrit epithets of Kāma, found in the classical literature and purāṇas, continue to reflect this connection between samkalpa and kāma: the most common, *Samkalpaja,* "born from will"; as well as *Samkalpajanman, Samkalpabhava, Samkalpayoni,* and *Samkalpasambhava,* meaning "born from will or desire," "having an origin in will or desire," and "rooted in will or desire," respectively. As these epithets illustrate, the word *samkalpa* contains both concepts, desire and will or volition, indicating the concepts of will and desire to be very closely related.

This integral relatedness of will and desire continues to be reflected in that distant descendant of Sanskrit, English. In Webster's New World Dictionary, *will* is still defined with this association: "the act or process of volition, specifically, a) wish; desire; longing b) inclination; pleasure c) [obsolete] appetite; lust." The longing for an object of desire often produces the will to seek or work for possession of that object. In the epic, samkalpa as "cosmic will" and kāma as "cosmic desire" are understood to function in an integrated fashion.

The *Manavadharmaśāstra,* the first-century-BCE-to-first-century-CE law code, also comments on the relationship between kāma and samkalpa in a brief discussion of kāma:

> Acting out of desire [kāma] is not approved of, but here on earth there is no such thing as no desire; for even studying the Veda and engaging in the rituals enjoined in the Veda are based upon desire.
>
> Desire is the very root of the conception of a definite intention [samkalpa], and sacrifices are the result of that intention; all the vows [vratas] and the religious duties of restriction [yamas] are traditionally said to come from the conception of a definite intention.
>
> Not a single rite is ever performed here on earth by a man without desire; for each and every thing that he does is motivated by the desire for precisely that thing.
>
> The man who is properly occupied in these [desires] goes to the world of the immortals, and here on earth he achieves all the desires for which he has conceived an intention.[38]

Stating that "kāma is at the very root of the conception of samkalpa," this text emphasizes the importance of recognizing the presence of desire in even the most lofty of intended acts, the rituals. Like the authors of the *Mahābhārata* 13.83–84, the writers of these dharmaśāstras explain the origin of will and intention (samkalpa) in desire.

SONG OF KĀMA (KĀMAGĪTĀ): THE POWER OF DESIRE (*MAHĀBHĀRATA*)

When the great epic war is over, Yudhiṣṭhira falls into a terrible depression, becoming paralyzed thinking about the suffering caused by the war. In particular, he remembers the episode in which all of Draupadī's children were killed by Aśvatthāman while they lay sleeping. Feeling personally responsible for all the suffering, Yudhiṣṭhira cannot perform his duties as a king and decides he will live in the forest as a meditating hermit.

Vāsudeva (Kṛṣṇa)[39] explains to Yudhiṣṭhira that he must not get lost in remembering, but must fight the new battle within his mind. Only by winning this struggle will he be able to rule his kingdom. "The time has now arrived, when you must fight the battle which each must fight single-handedly with his mind.... In this war there will be no need for any missiles, nor for friends nor attendants. That battle which is to be fought alone and single-handedly has now arrived for you." Even more directly Vāsudeva tells Yudhiṣṭhira that by carefully watching his internal and external enemies, he will see the true nature of reality (tadbhutam) and be liberated from the deepest fears (mahābhayāt). Vāsudeva recites two verses to Yudhiṣṭhira, telling him that: "In the world, the essence of desire [kāma] is not seen. [But] there is no act whatever that is not from desire. Indeed, even giving, reading the Vedas, tapas [asceticism], and actions ordained by the Vedas [are performed] by means of kāma."[40]

Vāsudeva continues to instruct Yudhiṣṭhira about the nature of desire by telling him to listen carefully to a *gāthā,* or song, called the Kāmagītā (Song of Kāma). This song is recited by those who know the ancient wisdom.

Song of Kāma

> I cannot be destroyed by any creature by any means. He who tries to destroy me by attacking my strength with knowledge; in this very attack of his, I will appear again and again. (14.13.12)
>
> He who tries to destroy me with sacrifices and offerings; I will appear like a man of action in the essence of these actions, among all the mobile creatures of the world. (13)
>
> He who tries to destroy me with the Vedas and the sādhanas [ascetic practices] of the Vedanta; I will appear like the essence of stillness [śāntātmā] among all the immobile creatures. (14)
>
> He whose attack is truth, who tries to destroy me with firmness; I will be the essence of him and he will not be aware of me. (15)
>
> He who firmly adheres to his vow, who tries to destroy me with the heat of asceticism [tapas]; I will appear again and again in that very tapas of his. (16)
>
> He who is a man of learning, who tries to destroy me by being intent on mokṣa; I will dance and laugh at the intentness of his resolution to gain mokṣa. I am eternal. I am the only one among all creatures who is indestructible.[41] (17)

This Kāmagītā, or Song of Kāma, found in a later part of the epic, the Aśvamedhika Parvan, reflects the attitude toward desire found in many of the Upaniṣadic writings, that desire must be struggled against and overcome in order to attain mokṣa. But even more emphatically and graphically than in the Upaniṣadic writings, this text highlights Desire's power to trick his adversaries into believing that they have succeeded when such a victory is impossible. Even when Desire appears to be defeated, to be gone, he is simply hiding within the perception of victory.

A master magician and historian of dice and card games, Ricky Jay, explains that a card shark's favorite opponent is the person who thinks he has everything figured out, who thinks he cannot be tricked. This description of a card shark's mark reflects Kāma's description of the person most easily subject to his power, the person who thinks he has overcome his desires and is no longer vulnerable.

The writer of the Kāmagītā describes desire as existent within every action, whether a person is aware of this presence or not. When an individual attacks him, Kāma is present in that very attack. When a Vedic sacrifice is performed, Kāma participates in that sacrifice. Even when a person meditates in order to fight desire, Kāma exists in that very meditation. When one fights desire with action, Kāma is a part of that action; and when one fights desire by cultivating tranquility, Kāma stands within that calmness.

The Kāma of this passage is not a deity who shoots arrows arousing sexual passion, but a being who interferes with everything an individual does. In the case of Yudhiṣṭhira, kāma interfered with his attempts to leave behind a sorrow-filled past and to perform his duties as king. Sorrow, fear, grief, and despair: all are rooted in kāma. Yudhiṣṭhira's attempt to leave this despair means battling desire, the ever-powerful opponent.

This image of kāma as a powerful force with which all beings struggle is also the deity who wields a sugarcane bow and shoots flower arrows. But here in the Song of Kāma, words placed in the mouth of the god are meant to pierce the mind with poignant truths about the indestructible nature of desire.

KĀMA IN SERVICE TO A TANTRIC GODDESS: CHINNAMASTĀ

Reversing the traditional thinking about Kāma/kāma as an enemy to be fought, to thinking about desire as a necessary element in attaining spiritual power, one Tantric tradition presents an unusual image of the god of desire playing a significant role in the depiction of the Tantric goddess Chinnamastā. In the most common image of this goddess, Chinnamastā is either seated or standing upon the copulating figures of Kāma and Rati.

Focusing on desire as an essential component of spiritual discipline, this iconography suggests that the sexual energy of the copulating god of desire and his consort empowers this goddess. Hindu forms of Chinnamastā always emphasize her connection to sexual energy either through Kāma and Rati or in other ways, and the ritual worship of this goddess almost always includes sexuality as an essential element.

All forms of Chinnamastā show her holding her severed head as blood gushes from her neck in a fountainlike flow into the mouths of her two female yoginīs. Unlike traditional Hindu goddesses seated on an open lotus, Chinnamastā stands or sits on the copulating Kāma and Rati as she enacts her own beheading and directs the blood spurting from her neck into the mouths of her devoted yoginīs. In a variant text, Chinnamastā performs this self-sacrifice as she sits on top of Śiva, engaging in sexual intercourse with him. Both the Buddhist and Hindu tranditions prescribe rituals for this Tantric goddess, but only the Hindu images focus on her sexual energy by depicting her standing or seated upon the copulating God of Desire and his consort. By contrast, the Buddhist Chinnamastā stands on the Hindu goddess Kālī,[42] another Tantric goddess.

The image of Chinnamastā atop Kāmadeva and Rati occurs within the Tantric traditions that prescribe the use of the body in ritual exercises intended to help the practitioner (sādhaka) gain spiritual release (mokṣa) or enlightenment. In left-handed Hindu Tantra, certain rituals that challenge orthodox practice are understood to release the sādhaka even more quickly than other practices precisely because these rituals involve otherwise forbidden acts[43] usually described as five: drinking liquor, eating meat, eating fish, eating a particular grain (perhaps with a drug effect), and engaging in illicit sexual intercourse. Considered to produce powerful effects that may be hard to control, these rituals are prescribed only for those of a heroic nature who have attained a high degree of self-discipline. Tantric texts explicitly warn that these *pañca tattva* practices require an absolute purity of mind difficult to maintain even for highly disciplined sādhakas, and should be avoided by anyone who has not attained this heroic level of mental discipline. As a result, for the majority of Tantric practitioners, the texts instead prescribe rituals in which mantras, yantras, and the worship of specific deities comprise the central practices. One of most colorful of these Tantric deities is the goddess Chinnamastā, though she is worshipped only by left-handed tantric practitioners guided by experienced teachers.

Several Tantric texts and late Śaktā Purāṇas describe a group of ten goddesses called the ten Mahāvidyās, or Great-Knowledge Goddesses, who figure prominently as devotional deities. Chinnamastā is one of the ten Mahāvidyās. Chinnamastā and the other nine Mahāvidyās are fierce goddesses, often depicted as dominant to Śiva, who exhibit characteristics that challenge the norm of accepted behavior for Indian women. Most often naked, the goddesses are sexually dominant, aggressive, and inhabit polluted places such as cremation grounds. One of the body's most visible polluting fluids, blood, figures in much of their iconography. With little or no connection to the characteristics that typify most Hindu goddesses, the Mahāvidyās are identified not as mothers, consorts, or protectors of the cosmic order; but rather as powerful goddesses who exhibit fearsome qualities. Ultimately, the Mahāvidyās represent Tantric practices [sādhanas] and the heightened consciousness and mental or psychic powers understood to result from Tantric discipline.

Prominently associated with the inauspicious—for example, corpses, cremation grounds, skulls and severed heads, as well as female sexuality and the conjunction of death and sexuality—the Mahāvidyā goddesses are seen by Kinsley as "social anti-models."[44] "These goddesses are frightening, dangerous, and loathsome. They often threaten social order. In their strong associations with death, violence, pollution, and despised marginal social roles, they call into question such normative social 'goods' as worldly comfort, security, respect, and honor." Worshippers of these goddesses strive to reach a state of liberation beyond the norms of everyday life in which the dichotomies implied in social norms dissolve. Tantric rituals, especially those of the left-handed path, are intended to help the adept "liberate his or her consciousness from the inherited, imposed, and probably inhibiting categories of proper and improper, good and bad, polluted and pure."[45]

Viewed from this Tantric perspective, the unusual imagery of Chinnamastā, a naked goddess standing on a copulating Kāmadeva and Rati (in reverse position, *viparīta,* with the woman on top of the man) and holding her severed head while blood spouts from her neck, effectively jolts the viewer out of the ordinary, and challenges the norms of the social order. With Rati on top of Kāma, and Chinnamastā on top of the couple, the image appears to signify female domination over the male, and the great goddess's control over sexual desire. For advanced adepts of the left-handed path, this view of the goddess in control may be what is intended. Demonstrating the goddess's control over sexual desire, this Chinnamastā image offers a model for the sādhaka's own physical practice. However, Kinsley suggests a very different way of looking at this image:

> A quite different interpretation of the presence of Kāma and Rati in the Chinnamastā icon emphasizes that the goddess is being charged with the sexual power of the copulating couple. On the analogy of a lotus seat conferring its qualities and power on a deity, Chinnamastā may be thought of as acquiring the sexual energy of the copulating couple upon whom she stands or sits. . . . In this interpretation the copulating couple is not opposed to the goddess but an integral part of a rhythmic flow of energy symbolized by sex and blood.[46]

For a Tantric practitioner, this understanding of the goddess energized by rechanneled sexual energy makes good sense. In the Tantric tradition, the energy represented by the god of desire and his consort exists as a positive force, not to be subdued but to be directed in a form of worship that leads to liberation.

An image of reversals, Chinnamastā removes her head, has her blood flow outside her body, stands or sits not on the lotus, the typical symbol of enlightenment, or on an animal vehicle but on the deities responsible for engendering the desire that prevents the attaining of enlightenment. As a Tantric image clearly positing reversals, if Chinnamastā is supported by the god of desire, the system must assume that desire is ordinarily an obstacle to liberation. But because in a Tantric context the obstacle becomes the path, sexual energy becomes the path to spiritual release.

The Tantric symbols here can be read quite literally, meaning that the practitioner also must remove his or her analytical head, give away the concern with physical life, and use the energy generated in sexual union to reach liberation.

Indeed, the left-handed practice does advocate the practice of maithuna, sexual intercourse with a consort, as a spiritual discipline. Just as Chinnamastā's iconography highlights her sexuality, depicting her either in union with Śiva or using the copulating Kāma and Rati as her seat, the practice of the highly disciplined sādhaka is focused around the use of sexual energy.

As noted earlier, Hindu deities are usually depicted with an animal vehicle or *vāhana.* This animal embodies some characteristic or strength of the deity. For example, Gaṇeśa, remover of obstacles, is accompanied by the rat who gets in and out of impossible places, while Durgā, the fierce mother protector, rides a tiger, a wild animal known to fight to protect its young. In the iconography of Chinnamastā, Kāma and Rati become her mount; they focus attention on the sexuality which is the foundation of her power. An image of untamed nature, Chinnamastā revels in her nakedness, offers her blood with abandon, and is literally empowered by sexual energy as she touches her body to the copulating god of desire and his consort. Her alternate image communicates this idea even more explicitly by depicting the goddess herself in sexual intercourse with Śiva while she performs the self-sacrifice. For Chinnamastā and her worshippers, sexuality is presented as an energy that empowers, an energy that can be tapped to realize spiritual identity.

"Sexual imagery in Mahāvidyā iconography and worship . . . may be understood metaphorically as suggesting the dynamic polar rhythm of reality, the interaction of Śiva and Śakti (male and female principles) that creates and suffuses the cosmos. The *Kulārnava-tantra* says that the world . . . [bears] the likeness of the lingam and the yoni, thus reflecting the form of Śiva and Śakti."[47] Within this tantric view of the cosmos, the god of desire and his consort operate on several levels, embodying the fundamental tension between the male and female principles that fuels the continuous cosmic process of union and separation, creation and destruction; as well as the force of desire that enters individual men and women, compelling them to join with one another. On a physical level, Kāma and Rati enact the tantric ritual of maithuna, sexual union, joining the micro- and macrocosmic processes in their own bodies. As the sādhaka contemplates the image of Chinnamastā mounted on the joined male and female, he contemplates the power of his own sexuality as it reflects, but also connects him to, the larger cosmos.

A nineteenth-century text detailing Hindu tantric practice, the *Śākta Pramoda,* describes the elements of daily Chinnamastā worship. One component of this devotion is the ritual worship of the sacred seat of the goddess, *pīthapūjā.*[48] In this part of the ritual, the sādhaka concentrates on visualizing the power and nature [śakti and prakṛti] of the seat supporting Chinnamastā. The sādhaka then visualizes the various elements associated with the creation of the universe, all of which form part of the goddess's seat. Finally, within all the other elements, he sees the "lotus of the nature of all categories of existence," including the three *gunas* (elements that comprise all of nature). Inside this lotus lie the prostrate Kāma and Rati. When the sādhaka has finished visualizing the seat of the goddess, he requests her to come into his heart, where he has prepared his own seat for her. Ultimately, the sādhaka himself becomes Chinnamastā.

As this Tantric manual details, within Chinnamastā imagery the god of desire and his consort function as the cosmic seat of the goddess, the abstract and material reality supporting her existence in the universe. The text explains that the tension between male and female lies at the center of "all categories of existence." To attain knowledge of the fundamental reality of the cosmos, the sādhaka must explore the nature of desire within himself, the nature of male and female, the Kāma and Rati who form the foundation of his own life. The sādhaka who works with the energy of desire through these tantric rituals will ultimately gain knowledge of the cosmos and release from the dualities of the ephemeral world.

The Tantric traditions view desire as important not only as that which fuels the continued existence of the cosmos, but also as a spiritual path in itself. The culminating pañca tattva ritual is sexual union (maithuna) with a ritually pure consort in order to physically redirect and use one's sexual energy to attain a deeper consciousness. However, because the necessary purity of mind is so difficult to maintain, this ritual is advised for very few. In effect, the tradition warns that sexual energy, while immensely powerful, is not easy to control or direct. Consequently, most practitioners are advised to harness this energy by using only visualized or ritualized devotional forms, not physical enactments. A powerful Mahāvidyā, a Great-Knowledge goddess such as Chinnamastā, makes it look easy, but would-be practitioners be warned.

This Tantric message about the nature of desire resonates with other perspectives on desire expressed in Indian Hindu and Buddhist story texts. Desire, here specifically sexual desire, is a powerful natural force with the potential to generate wisdom and knowledge when viewed as a path to enlightenment rather than gratification. The Chinnamastā imagery teaches that the desire embodied in Kāmadeva is not to be defeated, but rather respected as an essential and multilayered force that supports creative human existence on all levels. For disciplined and well tutored practitioners, the energy of desire can become a vehicle for liberation.

As the untamed Chinnamastā expresses, desire is the seat upon which all existence is formed.

HISTORICAL PROGRESSION OF KĀMA AND HIS GREEK COUSIN, EROS

While it is clear that the character of Kāma in the Indian tradition evolved from an abstract concept in the *Ṛg Veda* to a demigod associated most often with carnal desire, tracing this development historically is very difficult. The dating of ancient and classical Indian texts has always produced a myriad of debates, and the relationship of the written material to the oral traditions pushes the historian to define periods of history very broadly and acknowledge quite fluid boundaries for these periods.

Certain parameters for dating the writing in different parts of the epics have generally come to be accepted by Sanskrit scholars. Epic scholar van Buitenen dates the origins of the *Mahābhārata* story to the eighth or ninth century BCE but the composition of the written text to the period between 400 BCE and 400 CE, with the didactic portions being much later than the narrative sections.[49] References to the god Kāmadeva occur in the later didactic writings of both Sanskrit epics, the *Mahābhārata* (XII, XIII, and XIV) and Vālmīki's *Rāmāyaṇa* (Bālakāṇḍa).[50]

In the Vedic Samhitās, Brāhmaṅas, Upaniṣads, and Sūtra texts, there is no reference to Kāmadeva as the handsome god of desire known in the later epics and purāṇas. In Vedic writings, Kāma connotes primarily the abstract principle of desire, and secondarily a deified form of this abstract principle with the power to grant petitions. Although impossible to date with any exactness, the character and image of Kāma as the charming divine youth armed with sugarcane bow and passion-tipped arrows appear in written literature no earlier than the second century BCE.

Kāmadeva's Greek Cousin, Eros

As a final note to this chapter tracing the history of Kāma/kāma in the Sanskrit texts, we should examine for a moment the question of whether Indian storytellers may have borrowed some elements of the Greek Eros in creating Kāmadeva. Or, alternatively, might traveling Greeks have borrowed some aspects of Kāmadeva for their god of desire?

If the character of Kāmadeva is not found in written texts until the second century BCE, then the Greek Eros is the older of the two images, at least in the written traditions. The oral traditions may reveal the opposite, but that information is not available to us. In Euripides' *Iphigeneia at Aulis* (406 BCE), Eros appears as a youthful god with bow and arrow, and in the works of the Alexandrian poets of the fourth century BCE, Eros is described as being quite mischievous. Within the respective cultures, both gods are named in the earliest creation stories (in the *Ṛg Veda* and Hesiod's *Theogeny*); and both Eros and Kāma represent the abstract principles of desire and/or love in literary works. Both gods evoke desire by shooting arrows, though Kāma's bow and arrows are more metaphorically expressive: his arrows formed by fragrant flower buds and his bow a bent sugarcane strung with honey bees.

However, Eros seems to have acquired a personality in the Greek written literature earlier than Kāma grew into a youthful deity in the parallel Sanskrit works. Of course it is possible that the characters of these two gods evolved in the oral storytelling traditions before they found their way into the written works, but the evidence of extant literature suggests that the deity of desire was developed by the Greek poets before the figure of Kāma was fleshed out by those writing in Sanskrit.

Because communication did exist between the two cultures during this period, it is possible to hypothesize that some sharing of ideas and stories may have taken place. During the fifth century BCE, Darius extended the rule of the Persian empire from the Mediterranean to the Indus, bringing Greek and Indian trade and ideas together. Both the Indians and the Greeks sent soldiers to the Persian army, and learned men from both cultures traveled to learn from the scholars of other cultures.

With the coming of Alexander to India in the fourth century BCE, and continuing relations between Indians and Greeks under Chandragupta into the third century, it seems quite probable that the development of both the Indian Kāma and the Greek Eros might have been affected by this interchange. While it is not possible to say who influenced whom, the mutual exchanges between the two cultures may indeed account for the similar iconographic images of the two gods.

In spite of these similarities, however, each developed according to the patterns and thinking of his own culture. The most important relationship for Eros is that he is the son of Aphrodite, even in the story of his love affair with the mortal Psyche[51]; while Kāma's primary companion is his amorous wife or consort, Rati. The male Kāma remains in a superior position vis-à-vis his female companion, in contrast to Eros, who remains always second to his mother. Similarly, Kāma acts as the full embodiment of the force of desire, while Eros functions mainly as assistant to the goddess of love. The two figures may have developed during a period in which there was communication between Greece and north India, but more significantly, Kāma and Eros were shaped by their own cultures' expectations and perceptions, and remain symbols most meaningful within their own traditions.

CHAPTER SEVEN

Kāmadeva's Assistants: Celestial Beings, Birds, and Crocodiles

In puranic literature and art, Kāmadeva is associated not only with his two wives, Rati and Prīti, but also with other biological and mythical creatures who further define the character of desire. Kāma is depicted with two classes of heavenly beings called apsarases and gandharvas, a parrot as his vehicle or *vāhana,* and a mythical water creature known as a makara. This chapter explores the attributes of Kāma's assistants to understand how they further nuance the image of desire. Apsarases, gandharvas, parrot, and makara play no roles in the stories involving Kāmadeva, but they have been prominently depicted with him in visual representations from an early period. Typically, apsarases and gandharvas are positioned next to Kāmadeva and Rati, as they are in an eighth-century sculpture in the Kailash Cave Temple in Ellora (figure 7.3), while the parrot is placed at his feet and the makara on his banner.

Early in the twentieth century, Gopinatha Rao gathered into four volumes many of the instructions for artisans presented in the *Śilpa Śāstras,* texts describing the formalized iconographic details identifying each deity. According to these texts, Manmatha (Kāma) should be depicted with his wives, Rati and Prīti, and with two companions, Vasanta, personification of the brilliant and sense-delighting spring season, and a "flag-bearer having the face of a horse (and) carrying the *makara* banner." Kāmadeva should also carry a sugarcane bow and five flowery arrows, and be "adorned with appropriate ornaments and a closely knit garland of flowers." However, Rao observes, not all artisans followed these instructions. For example, sculptors of the important twelfth-century Halebid temple compound portrayed Manmatha with only his horse-faced flag-bearer, not with Vasanta.[1]

Although in written texts Vasanta is often described as accompanying Kāmadeva, visual representations rarely include him. In fact, I have never found a visual image portraying these two together. Perhaps when depicting the beautiful God of Desire, iconographers were careful not to distract viewers with another male deity with a handsome body. According to the Śilpa Śāstras, the pleasing-to-behold Vasanta, Mr. Spring Season, should be clothed in the leaves of the aśoka tree and adorned with pomegranate flower earrings and a garland of keśava flowers.[2]

As for Kāma's standard bearer displaying the face of a horse, this image is most probably a reference to the stallion's prominent genitals and reputation for siring offspring with many mares. Although the horse reflects an obvious connection with Kāma, the Halebid temple portrayal of Kāma with a horse-faced standard bearer is unusual. Much more common are depictions of the God of Desire with makara, parrot, apsarases, and gandharvas. Appearing regularly in the iconography of Kāmadeva, these assistants also came to symbolize desire, along with Kāma and his two wives.

APSARASES

Apsarases[3] are heavenly female beings associated with water and air, or more specifically with the water-laden air of clouds. Residents of Indra's heaven, *svarga,* apsarases move easily between heaven and earth and, like clouds, appear

7.1 Apsarases and gandharvas on Buddhist cave doorway, Ellora. *(Photo by Cathy Benton, 2003)*

in countless forms. The word *apsaras* is used in the *Ṛg Veda* to connote that which moves in or between the waters, meaning clouds.[4] Identified with a more defined role in the *Mānavadharmaśāstra*[5] and other texts, apsarases are also known as the dancers of the gods.

A story is mentioned elliptically in the *Ṛg Veda,*[6] and then further developed in the *Śatapatha Brāhmaṇa* and the *Mahābhārata,* of an apsaras, Urvaśī, who marries a human king, Pururavas. Fleshing out this story in his wonderful drama, *Vikramorvaśīyam, The Hero and the Nymph,* the Sanskrit playwright Kalīdāsa tells us about the nature of apsarases as he tells the story of the beautiful and independent nymph Urvaśī. Building on the kernels of the story found in the epic and oral traditions, Kalīdāsa's drama revolves around the apsaras and her ability to appear from and dissolve into water, change forms, maintain her independence in a relationship with a mortal, and move between heaven and earth. These characteristics of Urvaśī, along with her irresistible seductive charm, describe the primary qualities of apsarases.

Enchantingly beautiful creatures whose voluptuous bodies are barely covered by filmy diaphanous robes and billowing tresses, apsarases are said to seduce even the most determined of ascetics. By sensuously moving her limbs and eyes, casting sidelong glances at her current love-interest, an apsaras can distract even a powerful yogi from the ascetic practice which is the very source of his

7.2 Detail of apsarases and gandharva in fig. 7.1.
(Photo by Cathy Benton, 2003)

power. A familiar narrative pattern tells how the king of the gods protects his kingdom with the help of apsarases.

When Indra, king of heaven, determines that an ascetic is gaining so much power through his yogic practice that he rivals him for the heavenly throne, Indra sends several of his apsarases to seduce this man whose power is rooted in asceticism. As the story unfolds, the ascetic slips from years of practiced discipline into the embrace of an apsaras or two, typically experiencing sexual union for the first time. As he falls under the spell of his intensely stimulated desire, the yogi inevitably loses his hard-won ascetic powers. Empathizing with the ascetic's plight, listeners sigh with disappointment even while nodding their heads in recognition. When the story ends, Indra's throne is safe once again, thanks to the charmingly skilled apsarases.

Yet, at the same time, this paradigmatic tale of Indra's victory over ascetic rivals always carries a somewhat ironic edge, as Indra himself is hopeless at resisting the charm of a beautiful woman.[7] Because of his own weakness, he knows well the power seductive women exert over men, and thus how to use his apsarases as effective weapons. The implication of this tale for ordinary mortal men attempting to discipline themselves in the presence of charming women is obvious.

Like Indra, Kāmadeva also commands the charms of apsarases for his purposes; and countless heavenly nymphs await his command. The *Skanda Purāṇa* numbers the apsarases as thirty-five million, although it specifies that only 160,000 are important, while the *Mahābhārata* speaks of seven times six thousand.[8] These figurative numbers assure us that apsarases are truly countless. Embodying passionate fantasies, disappearing into clouds but reappearing to fan the flames of desire, apsarases are exquisitely effective assistants to Kāmadeva, his seductive troops. As they take on the appearance of a man's ideal female, apsarases personify the fantasy component of desire, the self-created mental images of perfect happiness. Just as an apsaras embraces her lover but remains outside his grasp, visions of true happiness permeate our imaginations but remain unattainable.

Various stories describe the origin or first appearance of apsarases. In several purāṇas we learn that apsarases were born at the churning of the ocean of milk,[9] the creation event that produced all the creatures and components of the universe. In other texts, apsarases and gandharvas are understood to be the offspring of Brahmā or one of his sons.[10] This close association with the god Brahmā who begins the process of creation again and again, and with the origin of the universe at the churning of the oceans, presents apsarases as fundamental to the nature of human existence. Indian narrative frameworks consistently place these evokers of desire at the beginning of creation, but also at those points when the seeker of spiritual enlightenment must learn once again the hubris of believing he has overcome desire. The appearance of an apsaras as soon as a yogi or king thinks he has reached his goal of absolute power adds just enough fantasy to bring reality back into focus, for him as well as for the audience.

As a result of their power to seduce and charm men, apsarases were noted in Vedic texts as causing madness.[11] This association of desire and madness is also reflected in Kāmadeva's epithet *Madana,* bringer of madness. Such desire-driven madness is felt by lovers separated by distance or death, like Śiva pierced by Kāma's arrow while he mourns the death of his wife, Satī, carrying her corpse on his shoulders as he wanders the earth.

At the same time, apsarases may bring good luck. In the *Atharva Veda,*[12] apsarases are petitioned to protect wedding processions, during which bride and groom are particularly vulnerable to the evil eye, and to bring luck to dice players.[13] Specifically, the Vedic hymn asks apsarases and gandharvas not to injure the bridal car. Apsarases, like their gandharva consorts, are ambivalent figures in the *Atharva Veda* thought to cause madness especially at dawn and twilight when they haunt wooded areas and forest pools, but also to bestow good fortune. As a result, apsarases are propitiated as much to stay on their good side and escape their mischief as to ask that they bestow good luck and good fortune.

In later periods, when apsarases were viewed more consistently as auspicious symbols of prosperity and good fortune, their images adorned the outside entranceways of temples, often alongside figures of amorous couples. People used to North American Christian churches influenced by Puritan sensibilities are surprised and confused to see images of men and women in amorous poses surrounding the entrances of Indian Buddhist and Hindu Temples. But these images are understood to be auspicious symbols as well as bringers of good fortune in their own right. Like a house protected by an auspicious rangoli design on the doorstep, a temple adorned with images of amorous couples offers all who enter the good fortune of passion and fertility. For the same reason, images of Kāmadeva and Rati are also welcomed in temples as auspicious images.

Depictions of amorous couples acquire meaning partly because they ward off their opposite situation, that of the widow whose presence brings bad fortune to all who meet her.[14] In contrast to the inauspicious widow, images of amorous couples, apsarases, and gandharvas call forth the potential of happiness and prosperity for all who see them.

But like the god of desire himself, his heavenly nymphs also embody fantasies that generate intense longing, complete with frustration and disappointment. Apsarases contribute to the never-ending cycle of desire that ensures Kāma's success as he snares creatures with their own desires.

GANDHARVAS

Gandharvas, male counterparts and consorts of the apsarases, also reside in Indra's heaven, playing music for the gods and pairing with the dancing celestial nymphs. But gandharvas hold a unique place among the deities associated with desire as their activities arouse specifically the erotic passions of women. The male counterparts of apsarases, gandharvas are known to love women; and

7.3 Gandharvas accompanying Kāma and Rati (depicted in adjacent panel), Kailash rock-cut temple, Ellora. *(Photo by Cathy Benton, 2003)*

women fall instantly for the charms of gandharva men. Associated, like apsarases, with air and water, these demigods draw women into their arms with the captivating tones of their celestial singing and the beauty of their "godlike" bodies. In a hymn from the *Atharva Veda*[15] presenting a marriage ceremony, gandharvas are invoked for their blessing. According to some Vedic scholars including Monier-Williams, gandharvas are included in this Vedic marriage text precisely because they awaken sexual passion in women. In the larger context of the hymn, both the groom and society benefit from the wife's greater openness to sexual intimacy, as she gives her husband pleasure and society offspring. This gandharva blessing of mutual desire bonds the new couple and contributes to the stability of the community.

Another reference to gandharvas arousing passion in women is found in the name of a union called *gandharva-vivāha* or gandharva marriage. In a gandharva marriage, a man and woman are so drawn to one another in mutual passion that they run off together without ceremony or consent of their families. (Indeed, as in western cultures, the eloping couple often makes this choice because of parental or societal disapproval.) Motivated by consensual passion, a gandharva marriage is considered legally valid by the *Mānavadharmaśāstra,*[16] though far from socially acceptable. Although the term *gandharva vivāha* belongs to another era, there are still couples who run away to marry, fearing the disapproval of their families or society.[17] But, most couples in contemporary India describe themselves as having arranged marriages, love marriages, or love-cum-arranged marriages, with parents consenting to any of these three.

Gandharvas are also said to have healing powers, particularly the power to restore virility. In Vedic texts, the term *gandharva* is used in two ways, to indicate a particular deity referred to as the Gandharva, sometimes "called Viśvāvasu . . . guardian of the celestial *soma,* i.e. rain, or . . . the rain-cloud itself,"[18] and a class of beings known as celestial musicians associated with water. References in the earliest texts are to the individual deity, the Gandharva, while later texts treat gandharvas as a class of supernatural beings. Gandharvas sometimes appear in texts as healers or as providers of herbs that promote virility. This aspect of their character is probably due to an incident described in the *Atharva Veda,*[19] in which Varuṇa, Vedic god of the waters and lord of gandharvas, is cured of impotence by the Gandharva, who brings him a healing herb.

Not always healers, however, gandharvas, like apsarases, are described as dangerous because they are thought to cause insanity or madness.[20] As noted earlier, this apsaras- or gandharva-induced madness may recall Kāmadeva's epithet Madana, producer of madness, and its clear reference to the overwhelming experience of falling in love.

Because of their mutual connection to horses, gandharvas are also associated with Varuṇa, known primarily as the Vedic god of the waters but also connected to the stallion. This association of gandharvas with Varuṇa in Vedic texts is significant from the perspective of a study of Kāmadeva as this Vedic

7.4 Celestial gandharva, Kailash rock-cut temple, Ellora.
(Photo by Cathy Benton, 2003)

deity also shares some other attributes with the god of desire. In the *Atharva Veda,* Varuṇa is petitioned by men and women to arouse passion in lovers who are not returning their affections.[21] And Varuṇa is associated with horses, in particular with the generative force of the stallion and the fertility aspects of the horse sacrifice, the aśvamedha, recalling Kāma's horse-faced standard bearer, symbol of male sexuality.

Varuṇa's vehicle, the makara, connects him through yet another aspect with Kāmadeva. An early deity designated Lord of the Waters, Varuṇa was often depicted standing on his aquatic makara vehicle, the water creature who came to be associated almost exclusively with two other deities, Kāmadeva and the river goddess, Gaṅgā.[22] In addition to sharing the symbolism of stallion and makara, both Varuṇa and Kāma command the services of gandharvas.

Beautiful, seductive, and charming, these heavenly musicians, along with their apsaras dancing partners, embody the fantasies of women and men for the perfect lover. And like all fantasies, they beckon with promises of personalized happiness, even as they refuse to be possessed. Like Hallmark greeting cards promising endless love and boundless happiness, paradises where fantasy transforms reality, apsarases and gandharvas are always welcome as they offer gilded futures. After all, they have been known to bring good luck and good fortune.

On a narrative level, these ephemeral cloudlike dancers and musicians, impersonate desired lovers as they engage individual desires. Evoking passion and emotion, apsarases and gandharvas abound in Kāma's army like the countless fantasies generated by human desire.

Kāma's *vāhana,* or vehicle, the bright green parrot with intently gazing eyes and talkative nature, represents another element of the passion instilled by Kāma's arrows.

PARROT: KĀMADEVA'S VEHICLE

Kāmadeva's vāhana is the parrot, a bird long enjoyed as a caged pet for its bright colored feathers and ability to mimic human sounds. Although there is no evidence to suggest that parrots know what they are repeating, their ability to sound almost human has cast them as characters in poetry, songs, and folktales in many parts of the world.

Parrots are particularly suited to their role as Kāmadeva's vehicle because many parrot species, especially those called lovebirds (agapornis) exhibit behaviors people associate with an affectionate couple. "Together almost constantly, nibbling each other's feathers," parrot couples are monogamous and, to human eyes, appear quite affectionate to one another. Parrots maintain this closeness with their mate by "bill-caressing, mutual preening, and bowing." Like other courting birds, parrots raise their wings and spread their tails to get their mate's attention. They also feed one another, a behavior that appears tender and caring. Similarly, when their mates disappear, many parrots die, apparently of loneliness.[23]

7.5 Indian Hooded or Alexandrine Parakeet, Sanskrit *śuka*, psittacula eupatria. Drawing from Edward Lear's *Illustrations of the family of Psittacidæ, or parrots,* published in 1832. The Academy of Natural Sciences of Philadelphia, Ewell Sale Stewart Library. Used by permission.

Like humans, parrots are naturally gregarious and talkative, flying in large flocks between trees in different parts of a city and screeching loudly through the entire flight. In one area where I lived in Pune, we could set our watches by the parrots who flew between two sections of the city at 6:55 each evening. In an instant, the sky was transformed into a bright parrot green and our ears were filled with the raucous chattering of hundreds of parrots. And then they were gone. With their bright color, loud voices, and flocking behavior, parrots naturally draw all eyes to their presence. Like Kāmadeva, they flaunt their beauty and song, and even the affection they lavish on their mates.

Prized as pets for centuries, especially by royalty who have had elaborate cages designed and built for these humanlike but controllable companions, parrots fascinate people as they return intent gazes and stay on perches rather than fluttering about. Long-lived (some birds are said to live eighty or even one hundred years) and able to speak wordlike sounds, parrots are often described in folklore as wise and experienced, capable of giving sage counsel to those who befriend them. Thought to be wise and affectionate, parrots perched at eye level appear to engage in conversation with people, or perhaps allow people to imagine they are conversing with an intelligent being attentive to their every word.

In a well-known Indian collection called the *Shuka Saptati,* or *Seventy Tales of the Parrot,* a parrot narrates seventy tales in order to distract a young wife from finding a lover while her husband is away. The sagacious parrot tells stories as a way to make the woman forget to look for a lover. On a more substantive level, the parrot helps the young woman realize the long-term consequences of her actions, consequences she is too inexperienced to see. The young wife and husband gain wisdom vicariously through hearing the parrot describe the adventures of other couples who did betray their lovers. Some of the stories are bawdy, with women two-timing their husbands both successfully and not, and clever men engineering such deceptions as stealing the services of a prostitute without paying her. Altogether, the stories are entertaining rather than moralistic, though by the end the young couple gains a deeper understanding of marriage and an appreciation for the virtue of forgiveness. Throughout, the parrot retains the moral and wise high-ground in matters of the heart, helping humans to see further than their immediate desires and gratifications.

Placing the parrot in pictures of Kāmadeva and Rati combines the sensuality of the god of desire and his wife with the projected wisdom of the parrot in matters of love. A bird thought to be amorous with his own mate, and a communicative and caring husband, the parrot is ascribed the role in folktales of imparting animal wisdom to bumbling humans. As this wisdom often pertains to the complicated and messy matters of lovers quarrelling, misunderstanding one another, and simply falling in love with the wrong people, the parrot makes a perfect vehicle for Kāmadeva, the god who revels in the desire that fuels such romantic intrigues. Like apsarases and gandharvas, the lovebird parrot expresses the amorous behavior evoked by the God of Desire.

MAKARA, EMBLEM OF THE GOD OF DESIRE

The connection between the mythical makara and Kāmadeva is more obscure than the association of the deity of desire with apsarases, gandharvas, and parrots. The epithet *Makara-Dhvaja,* the Makara-Bannered, has identified Kāmadeva for centuries, but the meaning of this epithet, an understanding of the connection between Kāma and the makara, has eluded scholars. In this section, depictions of makaras by artists and storytellers combined with the biological attributes of two makaralike aquatic creatures, a reptile and a mammal, explain how the makara further defines the God of Desire.

What do makaras look like?

References in puranic literature describe the makara as a water creature with a curved shape formed by a raised head and tail. Though this curved shape and association with water are its two primary characteristics, other elements include scaly skin, short legs, a long snout, and a huge tail. However, no one form describes the makara as it was imaginatively reenvisioned from region to region. One makara appears to be formed out of the swirling white foam of a breaking wave, while others are composites of several creatures. For example, in western Maharashtra, a makara might be described as having the body of a crocodile, feet of a lion, and tail of a peacock,[24] or as a sea

7.6 Red sandstone makara carving on Kushan Architrave (cross beam), Mathura, India, first to second century c. CE. *(Photo by John Bigelow Taylor, courtesy of Arnold H. Lieberman.)*

monster with the body and tail of a fish fitted with the head and forelegs of an antelope.[25]

Although the first images of makaras appear to be stylized representations of crocodilelike creatures, in time makaras were described as mythical water beasts that combined features of real and imagined animals to form fearsome but decorative figures. Adorning temples, archways, and fountains, makara images functioned much like European gargoyles. Ornamental archways called "makara toranas" display the jaws of makaras spewing forth flowers and creepers often wrapped around a mango tree laden with fruit. Transforming an archway into a makara torana with intertwined symbols of fertility and good fortune—namely, the creepers, flowers, and mangos—would create an auspicious entrance or enshrine a beneficent deity.

A popular symbol from early periods, makaras were carved on Jain, Buddhist, and Hindu temples. The first-century BCE Bhārhut stūpa depicts the mount of the ninth Jain tīrthankara, Suvidha or Pushpadanta, as a makara with

7.7 Makara water spout, seventeenth c., Jaswant Singh I Chattri, Mandore. *(Photo by Stuart Whatling. Used by permission.)*

7.8 Makara as dragon of abundance on silver carving.

crocodile snout, hoofed feet, and curled tail. Viṣṇu wears makara *kundalas,* earrings in the shape of the makara.[26] The symbol of Capricorn, tenth house of the zodiac, is a makara usually depicted with prominent antelope legs, reminiscent of the goat symbol for Capricorn in European symbology. Stylized makaras were worked into many scenes carved on ancient temple walls, giving a sense of flowing water or movement. Often the tails of makaras flow on and on, swirling in plumes to create abstract designs.

The makara appears also as the vāhana of the gods Varuṇa and Gaṅgā and as the banner emblem for the god of desire. Indeed, the makara on Kāmadeva's banner is one of his primary identifying symbols, along with his signature sugarcane bow and flower arrows. However, the connection between Kāma and the makara is not immediately clear, as it is for the water deities Varuṇa and Gaṅgā, often depicted standing in their watery habitats upon their makara vehicles. The question that has long puzzled scholars is what attribute Kāma must share with the makara.

The answer to this question lies in the character of the marine animal understood to be the model for the makara, most probably the Indian crocodile or river dolphin, both formerly found in great numbers in the Ganges and Indus rivers. Because animal vehicles and emblems reflect prominent characteristics of the deity with whom they are associated, the makara must also represent some aspect of the god of desire. For example, bulls are known as fierce fighters and as virile males with the capacity to mate with numerous cows. In Indian iconography, the bull is Śiva's vehicle, mirroring the god's prowess as a powerful creator and destroyer. Similarly, the lion, ferocious predator and protector of its offspring, offers its back as a vehicle for the goddess Durgā, protective mother and powerful demon-slayer.

As the patterns and correspondences of symbols become regularized over time, they are employed as standard ways to communicate stories, ideas, and teachings to both literate and nonliterate viewers. In a society permeated with these symbols, people know that even the most rudimentary stone image of a god shown with a bull and trident must be Śiva, while the male deity reclining on a serpent will always be Viṣṇu. Though not as prominent a deity as Śiva or Viṣṇu, Kāmadeva, too, is recognized by his animal symbol. Indeed, the epithet makara-dhvaja ties the god of desire expressly to the makara.

Makara as Vāhana of Varuṇa and Gaṅgā

The river goddess Gaṅgā and the Vedic god of the sea, Varuṇa, are also deities associated with the makara. Varuṇa, identified with water and part of a triad including fire (Agni) and sky (Indra), was usually depicted in early sculptures either standing on a makara or seated in a chariot under a makara banner.[27] Standing next to him on a makara would often be the river goddess, Gaṅgā. Because the makara was understood to have come from the sea, artisans placed a makara under the feet of this male deity to identify him as lord of the seas.[28] Similarly, a makara positioned under a female deity identified her as Gangā, embodiment of the great north Indian river.

An image of goddess, river, and fertility, Gaṅgā Mātā (Mother Ganges) is believed to bestow fertility, health, and prosperity to all who pray in her waters, the river which also nurtures makaralike crocodiles and river dolphins. Placing the goddess on the back of one of the river's strongest water creatures identifies her as the manifestation of the river but also demonstrates her unquestionable power. In familiar images of the goddess, the fierce makara appears to offer its back in submission as it supports the mighty Gṅgā Devī.

In depictions of Varuṇa and Gaṅgā, the makara identifies them as water deities and highlights their power over the many demons who live in their waters. But Kāmadeva differs from these deities in having no obvious connection to water or bodies of water. So, too, Kāmadeva's makara must be associated with different attributes. To better understand how people perceived the makara during the period when puranic storytellers were ascribing its characteristics to Kāmadeva Makara-Dhvaja, we should examine the behavior of Indian crocodiles and river dolphins.

The earliest narrative images of makaras appear to be based on the water creatures people knew, reptiles and fish that lived in the great north Indian rivers, particularly, the large fish that fishermen battled or the fantastic sea monsters whose jaws sailors feared. River dolphins and crocodiles were always plentiful

7.9 Mātā Gaṅgā on makara, Varanasi water-color painting, Hotel Ganges View. *(Photo by Cathy Benton, 2003)*

in these river systems, and both were formidable predators. Once abundant in rivers and marshes near human settlements, crocodiles figure in numerous South Asian fables, including the well known *Pañcatantra* and Buddhist jātaka tale of the Monkey and the Crocodile, or more precisely the Monkey and the Makara.

Makara as river dolphin

Two species of river dolphins, the *bhulan* and the *susu,* live in the river systems of Pakistan and north India. The bhulan, or Indus River Dolphin (platanista minor), is found, as its name implies, in the Indus River Basin in Pakistan and grows to a size of about eight feet and 200 pounds.[29] The susu, or Ganges River Dolphin (platanista gangetica), similar in size and appearance to the bhulan, inhabits the Brahmaputra, Meghna, Karnaphuli, and Ganges river systems as they flow through India, Nepal, Bangladesh, and Bhutan.[30] Bhulans and susus are so similar that before being more carefully studied in the 1970s they were thought to be the same species.

Susus and bhulans, which share their rivers with gharials, marsh crocodiles, and turtles (before the intense pollution of the late twentieth century decimated these populations), have a unique way of swimming. Sometimes called side-swimmers, these river dolphins propel themselves through shallow waters lying on their sides, using their heads to sweep up and down in a scanning motion and their flippers to trail along the bottom in search of fish. Though almost blind, susus and bhulans use an efficient system of echolocation for finding prey. Much smaller than Ganges crocodiles, these river dolphins have small dorsal fins and long slender beaks lined with peglike teeth. Because their vertebrae are not fused, river dolphins have great flexibility in moving their necks,[31] often giving them a curved or crescent shape.

Although their long slender beaks and naturally curved bodies do give river dolphins some resemblance to the curved makara, especially when viewed side-swimming, their skin is not marked with makara scales nor are their mouths as large. However, the use of its flesh does connect the dolphin to the realm of Kāmadeva. The meat of the susu is eaten to enhance virility and its oil is highly valued as an aphrodisiac.[32]

Texts dating back to the time of Aśoka prohibit the hunting of river dolphins. But both susus and bhulans have long been killed for the layer of fat just

7.10 Ganges river dolphin, Platanista gangetica, shown straight and in side-swimming position

under the skin, processed for an oil valued historically as a healing medication as well as for lighting homes. Today, susu oil is mixed with fish parts primarily as an attractive bait for catfish, a lucrative catch for fishermen. But University of Patna researchers report that susu oil is still used as an aphrodisiac by the fishing community in Patna, as well as in other parts of Bihar, West Bengal, and Assam. A source of oil regarded as a love potion or remedy for impotence, the susu would have been an appropriate emblem for the God of Desire.

A biologist at the University of Patna writing on the environmental fate of the gangetic dolphin mentions one other trait that connects the susu with the makara. Members of the fishing community in Patna, a city located on the Gaṅgā, speak of the susu as the *vāhan,* or vehicle, of the Gaṅgā, the river and deity who provides their livelihood.[33] For these river communities, the susu is known as the makara of Mother Gaṅgā.

Nevertheless, compelling evidence indicates an even closer connection between the makara and the crocodile.

Makara as "Baby-Killer"

The Sanskrit philologist J. Ph. Vogel wrote that "the fundamental sense of the word (makara) is 'crocodile' (and this) is proved by the evidence of the vernaculars."[34] Vogel argued that because the crocodile is called "magar" (cognate with the Sanskrit *makara*) or some variation of *magar* in Hindi, Gujarati, Marathi, and Sindhi, with close variations in Punjabi, Kashmiri, Bengali, Nepali, and even Telugu, then the Sanskrit word *makara* clearly indicates the Indian crocodile. In other words, because the vernacular word for crocodile, *magar,* is cognate with the Sanskrit *makara,* the Sanskrit original must refer to the crocodile.

Vogel also used the well-known *Pañcatantra* fable "The Monkey and the Crocodile/Makara" to demonstrate that this makara in this tale behaves exactly like a crocodile. This fable tells of a makara-crocodile and a monkey who strike up a friendship when the crocodile comes out of the river to lie on a sandy shore under the monkey's rose-apple tree [jambu]. As they chat about their lives, the monkey throws down fruit for the crocodile to enjoy, and the two become friends, spending every afternoon together. However, the crocodile's wife can't believe that her husband's new friend is a monkey (how often do monkeys befriend crocs?) and suspects him of having an affair. She surmises that this new friend must, at least, be a she-monkey. The crocodile wife demands that her husband bring the monkey's heart to cure her own ailing heart and this request leads eventually to the monkey's outsmarting the crocodile.

Since the makara in this tale is an amphibious creature who emerges from his watery home to lie about on the sandy shore, Vogel concluded that it could not be a fish, shark, or dolphin, other suggested referents for the word *makara,* because these creatures would die outside water. Given the amphibious nature of this *Pañcatantra* makara, the character is clearly a crocodile: he lives in a river, suns himself on a riverbank, and is a natural predator of the monkey (the characteristic that creates an irony fundamental to the plot).

Although the Buddhist jātaka versions of the tale (four Pāli narratives and one Sanskrit text[35]) recount slightly different variants in which the character is not called a makara but rather a "kumbhīla" or "sumsumāra," these words are also connected with crocodiles. The Pāli noun *kumbhīla* is directly cognate with the Sanskrit *kumbhīra,* meaning crocodile, and the Pāli word *sumsumāra,* literally "baby-killer," is an apt name for a huge-jawed crocodile who catches baby animals wandering too near the riverbank. Though some Sanskrit references list the Pāli *sumsumāra* as river dolphin,[36] the feeding habits of the two river creatures indicate that crocodiles are more likely to have been labeled "baby-killers" by populations living along the rivers. River dolphins feed only on fish, crustaceans, turtles, and the occasional waterfowl, while crocodiles happily feast on most small mammals that fall within their reach, including unfortunate monkeys.

Finally, over the last two thousand years, translations of this story into South and Southeast languages from the original Pāli and Sanskrit sources have portrayed the aquatic protagonist, the natural foe of riverbank monkeys, as a crocodile. Carved on temple walls and stupas in many Buddhist and Hindu cultures, are clear depictions of a monkey outsmarting his *crocodile* neighbor along the great river Gangā.

Indeed the Pāli-Sanskrit labels *kumbhīla* and *kumbhīra* point not only to the crocodile but to a particular species found most prominently in the Ganges river system, the long-nosed *gavialis gangeticus,* known in Hindi as the gharial. Like the mythical makara, this amphibious reptile bends its body into a curved shape and blows bubbles through its nose. Well known by people living in settled and educated communities along the Ganges, towns where Sanskrit and Pāli literature flourished for centuries, the narrow-snouted gharial is the most convincing prototype for the makara of this fable, the Ganges-dwelling sumsumāra-kumbhiīra-makara.

Makara as gharial

Narrow-snouted gharials, native to the major river systems of north India and Nepal, once populated these rivers in abundance. Its species name, gavialis gangeticus, locates the gharial specifically in the Ganges river system though it was also found in the Brahmaputra and Mahanadi.

Gharials are readily identified by their long thin snout and jaws which contain more than a hundred razor-sharp teeth. One of the world's largest crocodiles, male gharials grow to a length of between sixteen and twenty feet, though some reports indicate that a large male might reach twenty-three feet. Although gharials are not thought to be aggressive toward humans, their enormous size and fearsome teeth inspire a healthy respect. Most at home in the water, where they can swim great distances with highly webbed back feet and

7.11 A gharial, Gavialis gangeticus, at the Honolulu Zoo.
(Photo by Tim Knight, Seattle. Used by permission.)

strong arms, gharials wait quietly to prey upon schools of fish. When fish swim alongside, gharials move with a "lightning-fast sideways swing"[37] to snap their jaws around the fish and swallow them whole. Although gharials are very strong swimmers and efficient predators in the water, they are not as well-adapted for travel on land because of their short, weak legs and heavy bodies. On the riverbank, this reptile awkwardly pushes its huge body forward, dragging its belly along the ground. Still, gharials do leave the water to warm themselves in the sun and nest in sandbanks.

A physical characteristic unique to sexually mature male gharials connects this creature more directly to Kāmadeva and his banner. For the first eighteen to twenty years, male and female gharials look alike. But when the male reaches sexual maturity, he develops a bulbous growth on the tip of his snout called a "*ghara,*" the Hindi word for a pot. When the ghara grows to a certain size, the male begins attracting the attention of females by vocalizing and blowing bubbles through this part of his snout. Because only the males have gharas, scientists believe they also act as visual stimuli to help female gharials easily recognize the males during mating season.[38]

An early literary text, dating from the fourth to fifth centuries CE, Bhartrihari's *Nītiśataka,* cites a proverb that refers to the tusk of a fierce makara. But this "tusk" may in fact be the ghara of the male gharial:

7.12 Indian gharials, Gavialis gangeticus, as depicted in a series of "Asian Wild Life" picture cards, a promotional item from Brooke Bond Tea, 1962.

> A man may forcibly extract a pearl from the sharp tusk of a makara[39];
> he may even cross the sea covered with a mass of agitated waves;
> he may even carry an angry snake like a flower on his head.
> But he cannot conciliate the heart of stubborn fools.[40]

Struggling to pry a pearl, or more accurately a jewel, from a crocodile weighing several hundred pounds certainly qualifies as a difficult if not impossible job, and a wonderful metaphor for trying to change the thinking of stubborn fools. But the proverb's description of the makara snout as having a tusk, or some growth, that holds a jewel, could well describe the distinctive male ghara. After reading this proverb, I reexamined several makara representations and found that many makaras are depicted with a prominent protuberance on the ends of their snouts.[41]

With gharials so abundant in the Ganges, it is hardly surprising that many of the visual representations of makaras found in the folk art and formal art of Varanasi and other communities along the river look very similar to ordinary Ganges gharials with scaly bodies, short legs, and pointed bulbous snouts. As the gharial curls on the sand to sun itself, its curved body forms a symmetrical shape with long thin snout and tail reaching toward one another. Such sunning gharials might easily have inspired the artists who first painted this fierce water creature as the vehicle of the goddess Gaṅgā. Devotees of the powerful river goddess might well have seated their deity on one of their river's most enormous and awe-inspiring creatures. Images of Gaṅgā Mātā show a subdued but fierce water creature as her vehicle. If Gaṅgā's vāhana is the gharial in these

7.13 Gharial with fully developed ghara, San Diego Zoo/ Mindenpictures. Used by permission.

images, the taming of this huge reptile's lightning-quick jaws and huge, powerful tail graphically demonstrates the power of the great goddess.

Pilgrims traveling to the source of the Gaṅgā in the Himalayas, from Varanasi to other pilgrimage sites upriver, would have continued to encounter gharials and artists' renditions of the gharial-makara, fierce vehicle of the powerful goddess and symbol of the god Kāmadeva.

The gharial is associated with the god of desire in several ways. First, the male gharial's visible sign of sexuality, his ghara, would be observed functioning to attract females. But more significantly, many river communities have valued the gharial's long, thin snout and its ghara for their aphrodisiac or virility-enhancing properties.[42] Conservationists have reported that often gharials are killed not because they are perceived as dangerous, but because their snouts can be sold as aphrodisiacs.[43] A personal e-mail from the editor of a conservation publication in Mumbai rues this practice. Describing the buying and selling of gharial parts, he says, "The eggs of crocs are collected for medicinal value and unconfirmed reports suggest that the snouts of gharials are used as aphrodisiacs. There is virtually no reliable information on the trade for this purpose, though all manner of reptile extractions (monitors, spiny tailed lizards) are sold by street side quacks to make stupid men feel more virile."[44]

7.14 Stylized makara at Datta Temple, Ellora.
(Photo by Cathy Benton, 2003)

Valued and feared, the river-dwelling gharial presents an earthy connection with the god who evokes sexual desire. Possessing long, phallic snouts and bodies containing fats and oils believed to enhance human sexual activity, gharials are graphic symbols of the desire evoked by Kāmadeva. His gharial banner suggests feelings of attraction and attractiveness.

Makaras, like apsarases, gandharvas, and parrots, reflect the cosmic purpose for which the god of desire was created: to charm lovers into fools, to swell the experience of irresistible attraction, to engender the depths of desire that ache in separation and produce madness in abandonment. Yet the makara, personified in susu oil and gharial parts, keeps Kāmadeva rooted in the mundane aspects of desire, the mechanics of physical passion. The makara offers the promise of enhanced sexual pleasure, even as the tales of Kāma warn of its painful consequences. Symbol of physical sexuality, the makara on the banner of Kāmadeva epitomizes desire in its most elemental form.

CHAPTER EIGHT

Buddhist Kāmadevas: Māra and Mañjuśrī

The Indian Buddhist tradition identifies two figures with Kāmadeva: Māra, the God of Death who poses obstacles for Śakyamuni Buddha in his quest for enlightenment, and the *bodhisattva* of wisdom, Mañjuśrī. In this literature, Māra-Kāmadeva is vanquished not only by the Buddha but also by other famous Buddhist teachers such as the well-known senior monk Upagupta. Other Buddhist texts describe the bodhisattva, Mañjuśrī, as the eternally youthful God of Desire who carries Kāma's signature sugarcane bow. As in Hindu texts, stories of desire in Indian Buddhist literature portray both the need for desire and the traps created by this dimension of human nature. But amidst the serious philosophical discussions, the stories still bring us to smile at ourselves. One story describes how even the God of Desire in the figure of Māra honors the Buddha.

In order to place Māra and Mañjuśrī within the historical development of Buddhist thinking about desire, it is helpful to first explore the discussions of kāma in early Buddhist philosophical and religious literature.

ATTITUDES TOWARD KĀMA IN EARLY BUDDHIST LITERATURE

In the early Buddhist texts, *kama* is described as one of the four *āsravas,* or "intoxicants." As an āsrava, kāma "refers to the gratification of the fives senses in general, and to sensuality or carnal lust in particular. As a general term, kāma is spoken of as fivefold. There are five *kāma-gunas,* corresponding to the five *indriyas* [sense organs]."[1]

In the *Dīgha-nikāya* and *Majjhima-nikāya* of the *Sutta-piṭaka,*[2] the five kāma-gunas are described as: the eye (*cakṣus*), the ear (*śrotra*), the olfactory organ (*ghrāṇa*), the tongue (*jihvā*), and the body or skin (*kāya*). As in the Hindu Sānkhya and Nyāya-Vaiśeṣika philosophical schools, the *Divyāvadāna*[3] adds a sixth sense-organ, mind (*manas*), because the mind is thought to be the actual source of *kāma.*

In the first-century-CE *Buddhacārita* of Aśvaghoṣa, the Buddha unequivocally connects seeking the kāma-gunas or sense pleasures with death:

> Antelopes are lured to their death by songs; moths fall into the flame (fire) for the sake of the beauty of form; the fish, avid of flesh, swallows the iron-hook. Thus Pleasures [kāmas] bear evil fruit. . . . Pleasures have no absolute quality of their own; for this reason also, I cannot think that they are enjoyments. The same conditions [or things], as point the way to happiness, bring misery again. Heavy garments and aloe-wood give pleasure in the cold, but cause pain in the heat.[4]

In another of Aśvaghoṣa's works, the *Saundarananda,* (*Nanda the Fair*),[5] which tells the story of Nanda's conversion to the monastic ideal, the poet neglects no opportunity to preach against the kāma-gunas. The tale, also told in the Pāli *Udāna* III.2, the *Samgāmāvacara Jātaka,*[6] and the *Dhammapadaṭṭhakathā*[7] (a fifth-century CE work), describes the brother of the Buddha, a prince called Nanda whose love for his wife, Sundarī, blocks his spiritual progress. Early in the poem, the poet paints a picture of the passion of the two.[8]

The two dallied blindly together, as if they were a target for the God of Love [*Kandarpa*] and Rati, or a nest to hold Delight and Joy or vessels for Pleasure and Satisfaction. The pair attracted each other mutually, with their eyes engaged solely in gazing at each other, with their minds intent solely on each other's conversation and with their body-paint rubbed off by their mutual embraces. They sported and shone together as if challenging each other with the glory of their beauty, like a Kimpuruṣa and a Kinnarī standing by a mountain torrent in loving devotion. (Canto IV.8–10)

One day, the Buddha and his followers went to the house of Nanda to ask for alms. When Nanda offered hospitality to the Great Teacher, the Buddha handed Nanda his alms-bowl and continued to walk. Holding the Buddha's alms-bowl, Nanda followed him, expecting to rejoin Sundarī once he had returned the bowl. However, when they reached the camp of the monks, the Buddha asked Nanda to join them in their ascetic practice. Nanda was extremely despondent over the prospect of being separated from his beautiful wife, but felt such respect for the Buddha that he could not refuse. Nanda accepted the robes with tremendous reluctance, his face covered with tears. To help him see more clearly, the Compassionate One explained to him that, "There is no bond equal to affection [*sneha*[9]], no destructive stream equal to desire [tṛṣṇa, thirst], no fire equal to the fire of passion [*rāga*]; if these three did not exist, happiness would be yours." (V.28)

But Nanda could not *hear* these words. (IV and V) Lamenting his suffering, Nanda thought repeatedly, "I have neither the knowledge that leads to peace nor, being kindly by nature, can I be hard-hearted. On the one hand I am passionate [*kāmātmaka*] by nature, but on the other the Buddha is my Guru. I am placed, as it were, between the two wheels of a cart. (VII.16)

When Nanda determined to go home, one of the disciples tried to dissuade him by explaining that youth, beauty and strength are transitory. Putting his desire for Sundarī above the Law was succumbing to a delusion.

> The man who should, in his eagerness for the objects of the senses, deem himself strong, when all that he has is this worthless corporeal aggregate, is like a man who should set out to cross the heaving ocean in an unfired clay pot.
>
> But I consider this body to be even more fragile than an unfired clay pot; for a pot if kept carefully will last a long time, whereas this aggregate must break up, however well tended. (IX.10–11)
>
> For no one can ever have enough of the enjoyments of the passions [kāmabhoga], as a blazing fire is never satiated with oblations; the more prolonged the indulgence in the pleasures of the passions [*kāmasukheśu*], the more does longing [*icchā*] for the objects of the senses grow. (IX.43)

However, none of the monks were able to dissuade Nanda from his decision to leave, so the Buddha went to him. The Blessed One, seeing Nanda wandering in the darkness which is called 'wife' [*bhāryābhidhāne tamasi*], grasped his hand and flew up into the sky to rescue him, like a cormorant which has caught a fish in the water and, wishing to bring it up, comes to the surface. (X.3) The Buddha took him to svarga [heaven] and showed him the celestial nymphs [apsarases] who excited a passion in Nanda that was much stronger than that evoked in him by Sundarī.

> He longed to quench that thirst with the draught of the Apsarases [sic], for he was afflicted by the despair which held him of possessing them. Confused with desire [*jehrīymāṇa*], [in] that chariot of the mind whose steeds are the restless senses, he could not control himself.
>
> For just as a man makes dirty clothes dirtier by putting soda on them not to increase but to remove the dirt, so the Sage caused greater passion [*rajas*] to him [in order to abolish it].
>
> And as a physician who wishes to remove diseases of the body will set to work to cause it still greater pain, so the Sage in order to stamp out his passion [rāga] led him into still greater passion [rāga]. (X.41–43)
>
> Great beauty eclipses minute beauty, a great noise drowns a little noise, severe pain destroys a faint pain. Every great cause leads to the destruction of a [similar] small one. (X.45)
>
> Then the Sage, Himself free from passion [*virāga*], deemed that Nanda's passion [rāga] had been excited by them [the apsarases] and that he had

> turned away from love [rāga] of his wife, spoke to him thus, combating passion [rāga] with passion [rāga]: (X.47)
>
> Listen to me, embrace steadfastness of mind, shake off agitation, restrain your hearing and feelings. If you desire these women, practice strenuous austerities [tapas] in this life in order to pay the fee for them.
>
> For they are not to be gained by force or service or gifts or handsomeness of person; they are indeed only to be obtained by following the Law dharma. If you find pleasure in them, practice the Law intently. (X.59–60)
>
> It is certain that these women in heaven belong to the man who has acquired merit by practice of the Law.
>
> Therefore if you desire to obtain the Apsarases, abide diligently and zealously in the observances, and I stand surety [promise] that, should you hold firmly to your vow, union with them will certainly be yours. (X.62b–63)

Having become infatuated with the nymphs, Nanda applied himself vigorously to the ascetic practices of the monks. Thus it was under the influence of the sense objects that, from having restless senses with his beloved as the sole province [of his senses], he now became controlled in his senses. (XI.3)

However, in spite of achieving this new control through ascetic practice, Nanda was taunted and rebuked by the other monks because he was still motivated by carnal desire. Finally, Ānanda, one of the monks closest to the Buddha, spoke to Nanda affectionately.

> A fire can never by satiated with fuel, or the salt sea with water, or the man who is full of desires [*satṛṣṇasya*] with love [kāma]. Love [kāma] therefore does not lead to appeasement. (XI.32)
>
> If you desire true delight [*riramsā,* lustfulness], then apply your mind to the delight [*rati*] of the inner self; for there is no delight like that, being as it is both tranquil and free from reproach. (XI.34)

Hearing the words of Ānanda, Nanda realized that he must give up his desire for the apsarases. With this understanding, he went to the Buddha to release him from his pledge. [Nanda had extracted a promise from the Buddha that if he practiced asceticism, he would indeed win the attentions of the nymphs.] On being confirmed by the Sage [the Buddha] in this new direction, Nanda was filled "with the highest joy." (XIII.1)

The Teacher converted some by soft words, some by harsh speech and some by both methods. (XIII.3) At the time of giving counsel he made use of now joining, now separating, now pleasant methods, now harsh ones, now fables and now meditation—for the sake of healing, not at his own whim. (XIII.7)

Aśvaghoṣa in this work draws upon the Pāli Jātaka called the *Samgāmāvacara* which tells the identical story though in a shorter form. The existence of this technique for overcoming desire, the instruction to "fight passion with passion," in such an early jātaka tale, suggests that it was certainly understood by, and perhaps practiced by some of the earliest followers of the tradition.

Throughout the Pāli canon, the power of desire and the problems it creates are described in parables and jātaka stories, as well as in the more didactic literature. Desire in all its expressions—kāma, rāga [passion], rajas [emotion, affection, passion], tṛṣṇā [thirst, craving]—was unequivocally understood as an obstacle to spiritual discipline. Given the dominance of this perspective in the religious thinking of ascetic practitioners in north India, this story of Nanda is remarkable in that it presents a revolutionary way to understand desire in the context of achieving religious goals. Acknowledging the deep hold of desire on human beings, the Buddha shows Nanda how to use desire as a tool rather than confronting the force of innate desires with the usual ascetic practices taught to young seekers.

The Buddha completely reframes the traditional ascetic's understanding of deep cravings, to see not obstacles but powerful motivators to perform spiritual practice. This perspective on desire was so radical that the majority of his followers dismissed it, as did the monks in the story of Nanda. But over time, different monastic groups, particularly the Vajrāyana Tibetan tradition, adopted this radical perspective and developed techniques that used the power of desire as an integral part of a spiritual practice. Over time, the psychology presented in this story of Nanda helped others like him who felt drawn to seek enlightenment but found themselves tangled up in the demands of their passions.

For the writers of the *Samgāmāvacara Jātaka* and the *Saundarananda,* there is no doubt about the Buddha's teaching on this matter, although it appears that Aśvaghoṣa may have expected some misunderstanding. In XIII.7 he tells us unequivocally:

> At the time of giving counsel he [the Teacher] made use of now joining, now separating, now pleasant methods, now harsh ones, now fables and now meditation, [all] for the sake of healing, not at his own whim.

Importantly, in neither Aśvaghoṣa's poem nor the jātaka does the Buddha ever chastise Nanda for his passionate love of Sundarī. Rather, in wisdom and compassion, he simply allows Nanda's desire (intensified and refocused on the celestial nymphs) to motivate him. With mind focused on future sexual enjoyments, Nanda rose each day in the early hours of the morning to practice meditational disciplines till the late hours of the evening. In the intensity of this practice, Nanda came to see the superficial nature of his passion and found that he no longer craved sexual pleasure. As both goal and process, desire led Nanda beyond itself.

Although the story of Nanda is told primarily to demonstrate that the life of a monk is superior to that of a householder, the story also teaches that even a mind completely driven by passionate desire may work as the starting point for religious practice. As mentioned above, though this teaching did not gain a broad following in the early centuries of Buddhist practice, it forms part of the foundation of the practices of later tantric communities. (For example, as we will discuss later in this chapter, certain practices performed in devotion to the bodhisattva Mañjuśrī-Vajrānaṅga are understood to transform one's desire for a lover into prajñā, the wisdom of Buddhist insight.)

In contrast to the later Aśvaghoṣa text, the earlier jātaka variant, though narrating the same story, highlights a different aspect of Nanda's actions. Jātaka stories often describe events from the Buddha's teaching years in a loose historical style, and follow this narrative with another story that provides a commentary on the episode recounted in the first story. Typically, this second tale offers a commentary by detailing a similar incident that occurred in an earlier animal incarnation. Following a very early jātaka narration of Nanda achieving enlightenment, the *Samgāmāvacara Jātaka,* describes a previous incarnation of Nanda as a warrior elephant in the service of a king.

This tale of Nanda's incarnation as an elephant emphasizes not how his lustful cravings motivated him to ascetic practice, though this element is mentioned, but rather how the elephant's strong internal will led him to religious practice. In the tale, Nanda is identified as a military elephant trained by the Buddha. He is very well trained for battle but at a point when his efforts are most needed to win, he withdraws in fear. As the tension mounts, the elephant finally hears the encouraging words of his trainer and returns to triumph in the battle.[10] Intended to elucidate the story of Nanda, this tale focuses upon the importance of one's training at the moment when the struggle is the fiercest, mirroring here Nanda's committed efforts to practice asceticism, even if motivated by winning the favors of the apsarases. However, by focusing on the elephant's training rather than his motivation, the story sidesteps the creative method introduced by the Buddha to bring Nanda into the monastic discipline. Unlike Aśvaghoṣa in his later narration of the experience of Nanda, this jātaka writer wanted simply to emphasize Nanda's effort, not the strong carnal desires that led him to enlightenment. Later commentary jātakas do address the more complex issues involved in the Buddha's guiding of Nanda.

In the *Dhammapadaṭṭhakathā,* a compendium of jātakas, probably written before Aśvaghoṣa but after the *Samgāmāvacara Jātaka,* a different jātaka accompanies the story of Nanda and does address the technique of using desire as spiritual practice, though still not as forcefully as Aśvaghoṣa. Here a merchant named Kappaṭa (formerly the Buddha) had a donkey (formerly Nanda) who carried pottery for him.

This donkey becomes infatuated with a female donkey, causing him to become dissatisfied with his job. Kappaṭa tries in various ways to move the donkey but is unsuccessful. Finally, he promises the donkey a beautiful mate in return for his hard work. Working toward this reward, the donkey happily undertakes more work than before. After a few days, the donkey reminds Kappaṭa of the unfulfilled promise. The merchant agrees to get the she-donkey for him but explains he will provide only the same amount of food for two as for one. When the donkey realizes that he will starve under this arrangement, he loses his desire for a mate.

This jātaka variant presents a donkey who is first lured into working by the promise of sexual pleasure, but subsequently sees that achieving this goal would ruin him. The last line of the text reads: "In former times, too, Nanda was won to obedience by the lure of the female sex."[11] The life of the donkey perfectly parallels the life of Nanda, as he is drawn away from his first love with the promise of fantasy females. But this commentary tale emphasizes that although the Nanda/Donkey is lured into the process of achieving insight by his desire for sexual pleasure, finally only his decision to obey the Buddha's precepts guides him to wisdom. Although the strategy of using sensual desire to motivate religious practice is articulated here, it slips into the background with the tale's last verse, which emphasizes instead a monk's practice of the precepts, behavior more acceptable to the mainstream Buddhist teachers of that time.

Yet, it is interesting to note that this early story introduces an idea which becomes central in later Mahayana Buddhism, the use of "skillful means" (*upāya*) to lead people toward enlightenment. In later Mahayana teachings, numerous bodhisattvas bring their students into Buddhist practice with the promise that practice will lead to the attainment of their desires. Mahayana teachers often locate the authority for the technique of skillful means in this story of the Buddha and his half-brother Nanda.

But for most Buddhists in the early centuries, steeped in their Brahmanical heritage, desire remained essentially a force of human nature that had to be overcome before any form of liberation could be achieved. Kāma (or Kāmadeva), referring to sense-pleasures *per se* and the use of the senses in seeking pleasure, was understood to be the source of most obstacles to spiritual progress. Accordingly, Māra, whose name is cognate with death and who came to be associated with Kāmadeva, is understood to send his three daughters, Desire, Delight, and Discontent, to distract seekers from their spiritual goals. In the following tales Kāmadeva appears as the Buddhist god of death, Māra.

KĀMA AND MĀRA: DESIRE AND DEATH

Māra is most famous for his role as the primary adversary of the Buddha in the final days of his struggle for enlightenment under the bodhi tree—a story that has been told and retold in a number of texts.

Because the extant versions of the life of the Buddha were composed at least 500 years after his passing by authors intent on celebrating the Buddha as an epic hero rather than preserving historical fact, these texts record only highly symbolic accounts of his life. As a result, the events and characters of the Buddha's life come to be known primarily through mythological stories and images. Early Buddhist poets offered both legendary and mythic accounts of the Buddha's life, often in allegorical forms. Within this context of myth and allegory, this section explores the character of Māra.

Etymologically, the word *māra* is related to the Pāli *maccu* and the Sanskrit *mṛtyu* meaning death, but *Māra* specifically denotes one who kills or causes death. According to legend,[12] Māra became alarmed at the prospect of the bodhisattva's victory, a victory which meant the bodhisattva would escape from Māra's realm. So using persuasion and argumentation, the demon pushed the bodhisattva[13] to give up his quest for enlightenment.

For example, in the *Samyutta-nikāya,* Māra urges the bodhisattva to use his power to establish a great empire of peace, and to turn the mountain Himālaya into gold. But the bodhisattva responds that such acts would merely be attempts to satisfy the sense-desires (kāmas) which are ultimately insatiable. Māra urges him in these words:

> Let the Exalted One, lord, exercise governance, let the Blessed One rule without smiting nor letting others slay, without conquering nor causing others to conquer, without sorrowing or making others sorrow, and therewithal ruling righteously.
>
> Lord, the four stages to potency have by the Exalted One been developed, repeatedly practiced, made a vehicle, established, persevered in, persisted in, [and] well applied. Thus if the Exalted One were to wish the Himālaya, King of the Mountains, to be gold, he might determine it to be so, and the mountain would become a mass of gold.

But the Buddha replies:

> And were the mountain all of shimmering gold,
> Not e'en twice reckoned would it be enough
> For one man's wants. This let us learn
> To know, and shape our lives accordingly,
> He that hath suffering seen, and whence its source—
> How should that man to sense-desires [*kāmesu*] incline?[14]

In the *Mahāvastu,* Māra, again promoting worldly and seemingly moral values in the form of conventional good works, encourages the bodhisattva to return to his palace and enjoy the sensual pleasures available to a powerful sovereign. In addition, Māra reminds him of the great sacrifices (*mahā-yajñāni*) he might perform for the benefit of his people: "What wilt thou gain by this striving? Go and live at home. Thou wilt become a universal king. Perform great sacrifices . . . [and] when thou diest thou wilt rejoice in heaven and wilt beget great merit."[15] Śākyamuni responds that he no longer needs to gain merit, that he is striving to move beyond the realm of samsāra where merit has meaning.

When the bodhisattva rejects all the possibilities placed before him, Māra sends his daughters, called in the Pāli literature Rati (Lust, Delight), Arati (Aversion, Discontent), and Tṛṣṇā (Thirst, Craving), to arouse the passions of the bodhisattva.[16] The *Samyutta-nikāya* describes the daughters as displaying their bodies and using feminine charms to entice and distract the bodhisattva from his goal of enlightenment. Though unsuccessful, the three daughters appear again four weeks after his Enlightenment to persuade the bodhisattva Gautama, now the Buddha, to enter nirvāṇa before preaching his doctrine.[17] Tradition holds that the Buddha is initially uncertain whether to teach others about the insight he has gained. This early text attributes the cause of this uncertainty to Māra's daughters.

When Māra's persuasive arguments are refuted and his daughters fail to lure the bodhisattva out of his disciplined practice, Māra sends troops of demons to terrify him into submitting. These demons and monsters are described in detail[18]:

> Some are many-headed, many-armed, many-legged; others have no heads, arms or legs at all. Some vomit serpents; others devour them. Some consume the bones and flesh of men; others belch fire and smoke. . . . Some have faces and ears like those of goats, boars, camels and fishes; the bodies of others resemble those of lions, tigers, monkeys, cats, snakes, tortoises and other beasts.[19]

In the account described in the *Mahāvastu,* the struggle ends when the Buddha touches the earth to bear witness to his final defeat of Māra. Then Māra himself acknowledges the Buddha's escape from his realm:

> The bodhisattva strokes his head thrice, touches his couch and strikes the earth with his right hand. The earth shakes and gives out a deep and terrible sound; and Māra's hosts sink down and disappear. Māra writes these words with a reed on the ground: "Gautama will escape from my dominion."[20]

These accounts of the battle between the bodhisattva and Māra are essentially allegorical narratives that describe in vivid terms the victory of the Buddha over Māra, associated with both death and desire. In spite of the linguistic association of the word *māra* with death, in these episodes Māra is identified not so much with Death as with Kāma. Specifically, Māra is called *Kāmādhipati* [Lord of Desire] in the *Lālitavistara,* and directly referred to as "Manmatha" and "Kāmadeva" by Aśvaghoṣa and Kṣemendra.[21] Though Māra represents death in other Buddhist writings, these early allegorical descriptions of the battle between Māra and Śākyamuni Buddha emphasize Gautama's victory over *kāma,* rather than death.

However, the underlying idea that desire and death are combined in the figure of Māra pervades the literature.[22] James W. Boyd in his study of Māra and Satan discusses several early texts that explicitly connect worldly desire and death in the figure of Māra. "(The idea that) Kāma, the god of sensual love and worldly enjoyment in the Vedic tradition, (is) used in the Buddhist tradition as a synonym for Māra, clearly rests on Buddhist views in which death and worldly desire are coordinates."[23] Underscoring this association is a passage from the *Mahāvastu* in which Māra answers the Buddha's question Who are you? with the following verse in which he brags that in his realm he intoxicates god, men, and demons with pleasure:

> I am the lord who intoxicates [*īśvara madakara*] devas and men. The fair suras and asuras who dwell in my domain, though caught in the cage of recurrent birth, are overcome by intoxication and drunk with pleasure [kāma]; [and] they escape the snare of death [*mṛtyupāśā*].

But the Buddha contradicts him:

> Behold how you are deluded. There is no sovereignty for him who is afflicted by sensual desires. . . . [Such persons should be called] slaves of Yama [*yamadāsabhūtā*].[24]

According to this text, one who is a slave of kāma is also a slave of death, for Yama rules the underworld.

Although the demon Māra bears this underlying association with death, he behaves more like Kāmadeva in the early Buddhist story literature as he places obstacles that are clear manifestations of desire (longing, anger, fear, lust) in the paths of contemplatives. However, although the actions of Māra and Kāmadeva are described in similar terms, each uses slightly different tactics. Kāma shoots arrows, external objects intended to penetrate an ascetic's inner resolve and excite desire for objects outside himself, while Māra attempts to awaken fears and/or inclinations latent in the mind and heart of his adversary. Māra is called Kāmadeva in these texts because he steers men and women away from wisdom by guiding them to follow their own kāma-gunas (desire natures). Unlike Kāma, Māra carries no weapons. Even the army of demons summoned by Māra when his arguments and daughters have failed is summoned to evoke an internal sense of terror, not to pose an external threat.

Analyzing the language used in the Pāli literature to describe the actions of Māra-Kāma, James Boyd notes that European translators often give the impression that Māra actively "entices" the Buddha and others, but the Pāli terms indicate rather that Māra *stirs up drives already present* within each being: "As far as can be ascertained there is no Pāli or Sanskrit term used in conjunction with Māra's activities which is equivalent in meaning to the Greek verb "to tempt." The overall emphasis is that Māra's role is essentially one of encouraging man's own inclinations toward sense desires rather than actively enticing him as an external agent away from the path."[25] Boyd primarily distinguishes Māra from Satan, rather than from Kāma who, like Māra, brings to the surface already existing attractions and emotions with his arrows. Indeed, Māra is more often depicted as a mental opponent arguing the pros and cons of staying in the realm of desire. Because Māra duels mentally with the Buddha as opposed to wielding weapons, his opponent has only to touch the earth to demonstrate his victory.

Although Māra is clearly a multiform of Kāmadeva, his nature is described differently perhaps because Buddhist teachers understood the relationship between discipline and desire differently than other ascetic teachers. Śākyamuni chose not to follow the extreme asceticism of his teachers, but to pursue a more moderate discipline that allowed him to reject Māra without killing him, without burning him to ashes.

The Buddhist process of seeking enlightenment acknowledges both desire (and death) as necessary elements in spiritual practice.[26] Early texts prescribe a meditation that focuses on death in the form of a rotting corpse or skeleton to deepen the practitioner's focus on the impermanence of all things but specifically the impermanence of human life. Other texts offer the strategy the Buddha used with Nanda, allowing desire to motivate serious Buddhist practice. Acknowledging the importance of the kāma-gunas is a teaching that distinguished the Buddha's community from other Indian ascetic traditions of that period. Fostered and reinterpreted over time, this perception of death and desire as integral to the process of attaining enlightenment continued to inform Mahayana and Vajrayana teachings. The early Mahayana doctrine of "skillful means" recognized the importance of desire in motivating daily practice; and later Vajrayana bodhisattva called Mañjuśrī-Vajrānaṅga embodied the pursuit of desire as a spiritual practice.

A tale of reversals in the early Buddhis literature, describing an encounter between Māra and the clever monk, Upagupta, highlights desire as integral to Buddhist practice through an unexpected plot twist. The monk who is unafraid of desire outsmarts the arrogant Kāma/Māra who, in turn, becomes a follower of the Buddhist Dharma.

UPAGUPTA AND MĀRA: MĀRA AS THE BUDDHA

In numerous Sanskrit Buddhist texts, a story is told of a famous monk, Upagupta, and his meeting with the demonic Māra.[27] Although Māra is portrayed in this tale as the traditional tempter of monks and laypersons, not only is his life spared (in contrast to Kāmadeva in his encounter with Śiva), but he is converted by the monk and begins to practice the Dharma.[28]

> One day, Upagupta was asked to preach at a Dharma meeting in Mathura. When he was about to "expose the Truth, . . . Māra caused a shower of strings of pearls to rain down on the assembly; and the minds of those who were about to be converted became agitated, and not one of them came to see the Truth."

On the second day, at the same point in the discourse, "Māra caused a shower of gold to rain down on the assembly. . . . And on the third day . . . Māra began a theatrical performance; heavenly instruments were played and divine apsarases started to dance, and the once dispassionate crowd of men, seeing the divine forms and hearing the heavenly sounds, was drawn away by Māra." . . .[29]

At this point, Upagupta realized that it was Māra who was distracting those who had come to hear the Dharma, and Upagupta knew that he was to convert Māra to the Dharma. By means of supernatural powers [*ṛddhyā*], Upagupta bound the carcasses of a dead snake, a dead dog, and a dead human being, transforming them into a garland of flowers which he bestowed on Māra [who had assumed a more pleasant appearance for the occasion]. Thinking he had won over Upagupta, Māra entered into the garland personally, meaning without his disguises [*svayamanupraviśya*], and so he could not remove it. Seeking release from the constant stink and pollution of the garland stuck to his neck, Māra spoke to a number of gods including Indra, Yama, Varuṇa, Kubera, and Brahmā. But none were able to help. Finally, Brahmā advised him, "Go quickly and take refuge in Upagupta. It was after encountering him that you fell from the heights of your magical power [*ṛiddhi*], fame, and happiness. As they say, 'One who has fallen on the ground must support himself on the ground in order to stand up again.'"[30]

When Māra, the Lord of the Realm of Desire [*Kāmadhātu Adhipati*] realized that Upagupta was his only recourse, he went to the monk, asking why he had ridiculed him in this way. He pointed out that the Buddha had never harmed him. Recounting the numerous times he had tormented the Buddha, Māra reiterated that the Buddha had never been unkind to him. Upagupta replied:

> Evil One, how can you, without even considering the matter, refer to a disciple [śrāvaka] in terms of the great virtues of the Tathāgata? How can you equate Mount Meru with a mustard seed, the sun with a firefly, the ocean with a handful of water? The Buddha's compassion for living beings is exceptional, my friend; a disciple does not have great compassion [*mahākaruṇā*].
>
> . . . the farseeing Sage never said anything unkind to you, but addressed you only with pleasant words. By this reasoning, that man of highest wisdom engendered devotion in your heart. Truly, even a little devotion toward him gives the fruit of nirvāṇa to the wise.[31]

Māra then reflected on the virtues of the Blessed One and was filled with faith.

This first half of the story follows a pattern familiar in Indian story literature. In a struggle between a god and a demon, when the demon reaches the point of being trapped, he takes refuge in the protective nature of that same god, thereby saving himself.[32] Māra is often classed as a demon and the figure of Upagupta, with appropriate and significant deference to the Buddha, here acts as the deity.

Yet Māra's act of taking refuge with Upagupta is not simply the following of a typical story pattern. The episode establishes an attitude toward Māra/Desire that is different from that reflected in earlier texts.

From the earliest period Māra is identified as both god and demon, though he always represents obstacles to enlightenment. In her study of evil in Hindu mythology, Wendy Doniger explains that Māra's dharma is to behave demonically. "Although no mention is made in the Buddhist context of his [Māra's] svadharma, it is in his nature to behave demonically, to represent Lust and Death and to attempt to counter at every turn the spread of the Buddha's Doctrine. Māra is thus, at least in early Buddhist texts, a demon by definition, and there is no hint that his nature might be changed by an act of conversion. The Buddha does not convert him, but merely chases him away."[33] Māra Pāpimā, the Evil One, known also as Kāmadhātvadhipati, Lord of the Desire Realm, leads the deities of the desire-world as they attempt to seduce the Buddha and his disciples. But whether demon or deity, Māra's transformation by Upagupta indicates that Buddhist notions of evil and soteriology were changing.

Unlike the Māra who is vanquished and banished by the Buddha, Upagupta's Māra becomes truly capable of devotion to the Tathāgatha. This change reflects the influence of Mahayana ideas concerning the potential buddhahood of all beings and the influence of *bhakti* (devotion) in both Hindu and Buddhist communities.[34] The bhakti movement and the growth of Mahayana ideals within Buddhist communities establish a more integrated role for desire in religious practice. In the context of these influences, the Lord of Desire gains the potential to become a good demon.

Another familiar pattern is reflected in Brahmā's advice to Māra to propitiate the one he has harmed. In the story of Khaṇḍaśilā, Kāmadeva is given this same counsel when he is stuck within the grotesque and polluting garland of leprosy. The two lords of desire are shown to be powerless in these tales when entrapped by their own desires. The powers of Māra-Kāma are restored only when they begin to respect their former adversaries, the Buddha through Upagupta and Khaṇḍaśilā.

For their own healing, both Kāma and Māra demonstrate that desire must acknowledge the polluting and destructive nature of its own actions by making amends to the injured party. This act of respect or devotion is essential for the healing of Māra and Kāma, not for Upagupta or Khaṇḍaśilā, who are not affected in any way. It is Māra-Kāma who gains strength by this act of devotion. The story of Upagupta and Māra clearly establishes the importance of Buddha bhakti. Devotion to the Buddha strengthens faith in the Dharma, Buddhist teaching and practice.

Within the context of Indian story literature, it is no coincidence that the garland constructed to bind Māra, who himself is polluted/polluting[35] and impotent, consists of the carcasses of a snake, a dog, and a human, also polluted/polluting and impotent objects. Although all dead bodies are understood to be polluting objects, these three demonstrate the realms in which Māra wields power: snakes or *nāgas* as traditional inhabitants and guardians of the underworld, dogs as filthy representatives of the animal realm, and human beings who, like reptiles and animals, are controlled by desires that lead to death and subsequent rebirth. The irony here is that in most situations, the appearance of these three traditional victims of Māra's power would signify his prowess. But in the language of this story, these symbols become the fetters that nullify that power and produce his suffering. His pride-filled attachments to the power he wields in these realms become literally attached to him, causing him to experience suffering as the direct consequence of his actions. Māra's garland, which, like a hologram, appears beautiful and alluring from one angle but putrid and horrifying from another, effectively demonstrates the first and second of the Four Noble Truths, that all life is suffering, and that suffering is the result of one's desire.

As the story progresses and the image of Māra practicing devotion to the Buddha turns the traditional role of Māra on its head, we are encouraged to shift our own views of desire. Rather than attempting to attack and eliminate it through ascetic practice, we are encouraged to see desire as an unwitting devotee of the Dharma. Because this is such an unusual teaching for an early text, it does stand out as an exception. However, the continued popularity of the story indicates that this idea of desire transmuted to devotion was accepted from an early period. The second half of this story continues to stretch our understanding of desire by transforming the image of Māra into the actual form (*rūpa*) of the Buddha .

When Māra, after recollecting the virtues of the Buddha, asked Upagupta to release him from the garland of carcasses, Upagupta agreed but with two conditions: that Māra never again harass the monks, and that Māra show Upagupta the physical body [*rūpakāya*] of Gautama Buddha. Māra agreed but with his own condition: Upagupta was not to prostrate himself before this form because Māra himself would be consumed by fire [*dagdho*]. Upagupta agreed to this condition, removed the carcasses, and waited for Māra's performance.

When Māra appeared as the Buddha, Upagupta became so intent on contemplating this form that he began to feel that he was seeing the Blessed One. After bowing in añjali, Upagupta became so enraptured that he forgot his agreement and fell at Māra's feet.

Very worried, Māra begged Upagupta to get up and remember his promise. Upagupta did get up and said with a stammering voice,

> You, Evil One! Of course, I know that the Best of Speakers has gone altogether to extinction, like a fire swamped by water. Even so, when I see his figure, which is pleasing to the eye, I bow down before that Sage. But I do not revere you!

When Māra asked how it was that he was not being revered when Upagupta had bowed to him, Upagupta explained:

> Just as men bow down to clay images of the gods, knowing that what they worship is the god and not the clay, so I, seeing you here, wearing the form of the Lord of the World, bowed down to you, conscious of the Sugata, but not conscious of Māra.

Then Māra returned to his original form and honored Upagupta.[36]

As Māra takes the form of Śākyamuni Buddha, the boundary between desire and the Dharma becomes absolutely blurred. The body of the Buddha is given form by Māra; but in the process of taking on this form Māra begins his own devotion to the Buddha. Though Māra as Death/Desire remains clearly Māra to himself, and separate from the Buddha who perfectly reflects the Dharma, the two figures are not diametrically opposed in the way that they were in the traditional story of Gautama's temptation. Māra moves into the process of seeking enlightenment, following the practice of the Buddha; and the accomplished monk follows his desire to experience the form of the Buddha in order to deepen his own understanding of the Dharma. No longer posited as traditional enemies, the Dharma and desire are purposefully intertwined in these two characters. The story challenges the simple dichotomy of desire versus the Dharma and insists on recognizing the complex role of desire in religious practice.

Shaking up and delighting a traditional audience (as do other Indian stories of demons becoming devotees of deities), the narrative is filled with reversals: a garland which is a traditional gesture of respect is constructed to pollute the recipient; Māra, the mythological and psychological enemy of the Buddha, becomes aware of the Blessed One's virtues and begins to practice devotion to him; the tempter "becomes" the enlightened one; Upagupta as representative of the Dharma bows down to the Lord of Desire; and in the final section of the story (not recounted here), the Evil One himself calls the crowd together to hear the Dharma. Because the narrative goes to such lengths to describe and then to explain away Upagupta's prostration at the feet of Māra, this section of the story becomes particularly poignant.

We hear Upagupta emphasize that he did not revere Māra through his action, even though it appeared that way. We listen as he explains that he was showing devotion only to the being whom Māra's presence called to his mind, the Buddha—and we know that given the stature of Upagupta within the tradition, his explanation must be accepted as genuine. Still, Upagupta's act of fully prostrating himself before Māra crosses dangerous boundaries both for Upagupta and for Māra. The episode reverses the accepted order for both characters.

When Māra first receives what appears to be a flower garland from Upagupta, "he was delighted and thought that he had won over even Upagupta (this senior monk). He resumed therefore his own bodily form (letting go of his disguises) so that he could be garlanded in person."[37] But as Māra resumes his real form, the garland too is manifested in its real form. In other words, Māra would ordinarily have been delighted to receive Upagupta's prostrations, but without the protection of his deceptions, he cannot bear this act which turns the deceptions *right side out.* For Upagupta, too, his order is challenged in the second part of the story when he realizes to whom he has bowed.

In this episode, neither Upagupta nor Māra behaves according to his traditionally ascribed role, and both feel vulnerable. Māra tells Upagupta directly, "If, (with) your mind tender from your recollection of the Blessed One, you should happen to bow down, I will be consumed by fire."[38] To protect both Māra and himself, Upagupta hurriedly explains that he has not bowed to Māra but to the *rūpakāya* (form-body) of the Buddha. Yet his stammering voice indicates that he is indeed shaken by what has happened. This episode remains a central focus of each retelling, though both characters survive the danger. Indeed the story suggests that when monks are able to bow to desire, or in other words to respect the power of desire, their understanding of the Dharma will be deepened. But this process carries the risk that the monk might succumb to its power. However, if the monk can acknowledge desire while remaining focused on the Buddha, his practice will be strengthened, as it was for Upagupta.

Contrary to more traditional attitudes, Upagupta teaches that the forces of desire can be converted and even enlisted in the process of working toward enlightenment; that a respect for desire can enhance one's practice of the Dharma. The Tantric figure of the bodhisattva Mañjuśrī-Vajrānaṅga, discussed later in this chapter, even more explicitly integrates the nature of desire into Buddhist practice, an attitude that meshes well with other Tantric perspectives. But the story of Upagupta originates in these much earlier texts, indicating that this non mainstream attitude most probably existed from the days of the earliest teachings but without receiving the same emphasis as the more traditional view of Māra and desire.

John Strong, in *The Legend and Cult of Upagupta,* discusses this story and its variants at length, pointing out that the story specifically reflects the fundamental teachings of the Buddhist doctrine of impermanence and what he calls "Buddha bhakti" or Buddhist bhakti within a Sarvāstivādin framework:

"... bhakti, engendered in Māra by Upagupta, is responsible for his conversion experience, and ... bhakti is capable of speeding up the process of final liberation (for all beings). The aim of bhakti, far from being that of rebirth in heaven, is unambiguously soteriological. As Upagupta put it, it is something which can bring about nirvāṇa for the wise, that is, for those who realize the impermanence, the nonpresence of the object of worship."[39]

The relationship between suffering and impermanence is reflected in the earliest of Buddhist teachings as two of the three characteristics of existence. Within the framework of samsāra, the endless round of death and rebirth, all objects of desire are impermanent. In other words, no object is unchanging, or forever fixed in one form. That which is desired changes as soon as it is achieved, or indeed, never was the fixed entity it was perceived to be. Because that which is desired is inherently impermanent, the entire cycle of desiring can only bring suffering.

Upagupta uses Māra to gain his desire. But the manipulation of appearances by the Lord of Desire demonstrates that the satisfaction of desire (here Upagupta's desire to see the Buddha) is grounded in ultimately misperceived and misunderstood experience. Desire leads to perceiving momentary apparitions as reality and this false understanding leads to further desire, which inevitably produces suffering: the Second Noble Truth of Buddhist teaching.

Strong discusses another tale "from an important and often-neglected Pāli collection of tales dating from perhaps the fourth century," the *Sīhaḷavatthuppakaraṇa,* which makes an even more direct statement about the monk's desire for the presence of the rūpakāya of Śākyamuni Buddha and the illusory nature of this impermanent phenomenon. In a variant of the Upagupta and Māra episode, a monk named Phussadeva is tormented by Māra, denounces him, and then demands that he magically manifest the form of the Buddha.

In the text, there is "a long, ecstatic description of the Buddha's body (by Phussadeva), starting at his feet and working up to the top of his head ... Clearly, Phussadeva, like Upagupta, is getting carried away by his devotion and vision. Just at that point, however, where one would expect him to prostrate himself on the ground in front of Māra, he abruptly switches gears and declares the truth of impermanence: 'Such is the wholly enlightened Jina, the best of all beings,' he announces, 'but he has succumbed to impermanence, gone to destruction. One cannot see him.'"[40] Phussadeva resumes his description of the Buddha but adds for each part of the body, "(it is) gone to destruction and cannot be seen." Phussadeva uses his desire to experience the form of the Buddha as a means of continuously experiencing the reality of impermanence.

The stories of both Phussadeva and Upagupta reflect the Buddhist perception of the interconnectedness of desire, appearance, and reality. Integrating desire into the process of seeking enlightenment, these stories acknowledge and respect its power, help channel its energy into devotion, and transform desire into another means of gaining insight.

VIMALAKĪRTI AND MĀRA: ENLIGHTENED MĀRAS

Māra appears in another tale doing battle with a practitioner of the Dharma, but in this story, narrated in the *Vimalakīrtinirdeśasūtra,* it is a householder rather than a monk who goes out of his way to take on Māra. This spiritually accomplished householder, Vimalakīrti, converts Māra's army of seductive celestial nymphs, his apsarases. Thurman recounts this story of Vimalakīrti in his translation of the sutra.[41]

> One day the bodhisattva Jagtimdhara was approached by Māra disguised as Indra [King of the Gods] along with twelve thousand heavenly maidens [apsarases]. When the disguised Māra offered his maidens to the bodhisattva as servants, Jagtimdhara politely declined still thinking this being to be Indra. Seeing and understanding the deception taking place, Vimalakīrti intervened, explaining Māra's identity to the bodhisattva and then asking Māra for the maidens himself.
>
> > Then Māra was terrified and distressed, thinking that the Licchavi Vimalakīrti had come to expose him. He tried to make himself invisible, but try as he might with all his magical powers, he could not vanish from sight. Then a voice resounded in the sky, saying, "Evil One, give these heavenly maidens to the good man Vimalakīrti, and only then will you be able to return to your own abode."
> >
> > [So the maidens were given to Vimalakīrti who] exhorted them with discourse suitable for their development toward enlightenment, and soon they conceived the spirit of enlightenment. [When Māra came to take the women home, Vimalakīrti told them to] fulfill the religious aspirations of all living beings [and explained to them how to] live in the abode of the Māras.
> >
> > Sisters, a single lamp may light hundreds of thousands of lamps without itself being diminished. . . . Likewise, the more you teach and demonstrate virtuous qualities to others, the more you grow with respect to these virtuous qualities. . . . When you are living in the realm of Māra, inspire innumerable gods and goddesses with the spirit of enlightenment. In such a way, you will repay the kindness of the Tathāgata, and you will become the benefactors of all living beings.
>
> After bowing to Vimalakīrti, the women left with Māra.

Quite different from Upagupta, Vimalakīrti is a householder rather than a monk, and in his tale the conversion of the forces of desire takes place not through a direct confrontation with Māra, but through teaching his heavenly maidens. Vimalakīrti shows no fear of Māra and challenges him more indirectly by neutralizing his forces. In this way, Vimalakīrti reduces Māra's power by taking his maiden assistants and even retraining them to teach the Dharma in their own realm of desire.

The character of Māra in this narrative reflects the more traditional image of "the evil one" and also more closely resembles Kāmadeva. Māra, like Kāma, sends maidens to seduce those who have taken vows of celibacy. And Māra mimics Kāma by attempting to become invisible when his identity is discovered. However, in this story Māra's magical powers fail him and he is unable to hide from this experienced teacher of the Dharma. Vimalakīrti sees the forces of desire at work, just as Ahalyā's husband, the ascetic sage Gautama, saw the guilty Indra hiding as a cat, and Khaṇḍaśilā's sage husband understood Kāma's intentions toward his wife.

However, unlike the stories of Ahalyā and Khaṇḍaśilā, which portray desire as a force that inevitably leads away from spiritual pursuits, the tale of Vimalakīrti teaches that the forces of desire do not always oppose the Dharma. Desire's troops can be taught the path to enlightenment, and even cultivate Buddhist virtue while remaining in the desire-realm. If creatures of sensuality and passion such as Māra's apsarases can develop virtuous natures, then perhaps pleasure-loving human beings who also reside in a desire-realm can practice the Dharma. Perhaps human beings can refocus natures steeped in desire.

This emphasis on viewing desire as a force more complex than simply an embodiment of evil continues throughout the *Vimalakīrtinirdeśasūtra.* In chapter six of this sūtra, *Vimalakīrti* conducts a discussion with the monastic patriarch Mahākāśyapa in which he explains that positing desire-versus-virtue as evil-versus-good is a perspective that misses the deeper complexities. Desire as represented by the Māras he argues, is an essential part of the process of attaining enlightenment.

> Reverend Mahākāśyapa, the Māras who play the devil in the innumerable universes of the ten directions are all bodhisattvas dwelling in the inconceivable liberation, who are playing the devil in order to develop living beings through their skill in liberative technique.... [Māras] wish to test and thus demonstrate the firmness of the high resolve of the bodhisattvas.... Ordinary persons have no power to be thus demanding of bodhisattvas ... just as a donkey could not muster an attack on a wild elephant, even so, Reverend Mahākāśyapa, one who is not himself a bodhisattva cannot harass a bodhisattva. Only one who is himself a bodhisattva can harass another bodhisattva, and only a bodhisattva can tolerate the harassment of another bodhisattva.[42]

According to the teachings of Vimalakīrti, if Māras, the foot soldiers of the army of desire, can act as strong and skilled forces guiding living beings toward liberation, then both Māras and bodhisattvas are part of an integrated system which cannot be easily separated into good and evil factions. The text shocks the listener further by explaining that Māras are indeed bodhisattvas, beings who are enlightened, not evil. Finally, Vimalakīrti teaches, just as bodhisattvas are tested, strengthened, and thereby assisted by these forces, human beings too must welcome and learn from these creatures of desire.

Both the story of Upagupta and the story of Vimalakīrti demonstrate a pronounced shift from the traditional Indian ascetic view that personified desire as the Evil One [Māra Pāpimā]. These stories give voice to those Buddhist teachings that incorporate desire into the very center of Dharma practice. In the next section, Tantric devotion to Mañjuśrī-Vajrānaṅga offers another admonition to embrace desire as part of the Dharma.

MAÑJUŚRĪ AND KĀMADEVA: DESIRE AS A PATH TO WISDOM

The Mahayana Buddhist tradition recognizes many people known as bodhisattvas who attain an advanced state of enlightenment but, rather than leaving samsāra, postpone this final act until all sentient beings achieve enlightenment. Out of deep wisdom and compassion, bodhisattvas choose to be reborn again and again into a life of suffering to assist others.

Mañjuśrī is a popular bodhisattva associated specifically with wisdom. In his most common form, Mañjuśrī stands in a warriorlike pose holding a sword in an upraised hand. He is understood to use this sword to cut through ignorance for those who are devoted to him, bringing them swiftly to enlightenment. However, in a number of his forms, Mañjuśrī carries a flower bow and arrow and is understood to display the śṛṅgāra rasa, the sentiment of passionate love, in his face. These images of Mañjuśrī, who is clearly a multiform of Kāma, are found in texts written for Tantric practicitioners, sādhanas, and for iconographers.

In a study published in 1972, R. S. Gupte studied bronze and stone miniatures of Mañjuśrī as well as descriptions of the bodhisattva in sādhana texts, using primarily the *Sādhana Māla* and the *Niṣpannayogāvalī*. In this study, Gupte listed the characteristics of thirteen forms of Mañjuśrī to examine them comparatively, and found that eight, or possibly nine, of these thirteen figures[43] displayed the śṛṅgāra rasa and/or held a bow made of flowers and an arrow (sometimes more than one), the tip of which was a lotus bud. Because the śṛṅgāra rasa and flower bow and arrow are the most prominent characteristics of Kāmadeva iconographically, they illustrate an intentional link with the Indian God of Desire.

The image of Mañjuśrī most directly associated with Kāmadeva is called "Vajrānaṅga,"[44] a name that calls to mind one of the most popular epithets of the God of Desire, Anaṅga. Vajrānaṅga is described in the *Sādhana Māla* as one who:

> bears the image of Akṣobhya on his jaṭāmukuṭa [hair twisted into a crown shape, like that worn by yogis], stands in the Pratyālīḍha attitude [the posture for shooting an arrow with the right knee advanced and the left leg retracted], appears a youth of sixteen years and displays the intense Śṛṅgāra Rasa [Attitude of Love]. . . . The two principal hands hold the fully expanded bow of flowers charged with the arrow of a lotus bud. The four remaining hands carry the sword [khaḍga] and the looking glass in the two right hands, while the two left carry the lotus and the Aśoka bough with red flowers. In another sādhana the Aśoka bough is replaced by Kankelli flowers.[45]

In addition to the Kāma-like characteristics of the bodhisattva described above, this description from the *Sādhana Māla* designates also that Akṣobhya Buddha is seated on the Bodhisattva's crown or jaṭāmukuṭa. Akṣobhya, whose name means "without anger" or "without agitation," is said to have made a vow while he was a bodhisattva to perform all deeds without anger. As the *Dhyāni Buddha* ruling the family (kūla) of celestial buddhas and bodhisattvas to which Mañjuśrī belongs, Akṣobhya appears naturally in association with Mañjuśrī, and this association recalls the pairing of Krodha (Anger) and Kāma found in the epic and puranic literature. As discussed earlier, the linking of Kāma and Krodha, and of Mañjuśrī and Akṣobhya, metaphorically expresses a recognition that anger is fueled by the frustration of unfulfilled desire. This association of anger with a bodhisattva may at first seem counterintuitive, but the following story makes clear why the tradition places the bodhisattva Mañjuśrī in the family of buddhas associated with anger.

Mañjuśrī as Yamāntaka

This story of the origin of Yamāntaka, the fierce manifestation of Mañjuśrī, graphically reflects the relationship between anger and desire, and demonstrates that the intensity of anger is directly proportional to the intensity of desire.

> A holy man once lived in a cave and remained in deep meditation for forty-nine years, having been promised that at the end of fifty years he would enter nirvāṇa. On the night of the forty-ninth year, eleventh month, and twenty-ninth day, two robbers entered his cave with a bull they had stolen and proceeded to cut off its head. When they noticed the ascetic, they decided they had to do away with him since he had witnessed their theft. The holy man begged them to spare his life, explaining that he had but moments left before he would enter nirvāṇa and that if he died prematurely would lose all benefit of his long penance. But the robbers did not believe him and cut off his head. At that moment, the body of the holy man assumed the ferocious

form of Yama, King of the Dead, and put the head of the bull on its now headless shoulders.

This rage-filled ascetic, now acting as Yama, killed the two robbers and drank their blood from cups made of their skulls. Moving with an insatiable fury, he threatened to depopulate the whole of Tibet. When the Tibetan people appealed to Mañjuśrī to protect them from this terrible enemy, the bodhisattva assumed the ferocious form of Yamāntaka, meaning "Killer of Yama," and defeated him.[46]

This form of Mañjuśrī as Yamāntaka, Killer of Death, recalls the ferocious image of Śiva, another Yamāntaka. In the Hindu story, Śiva-Yamāntaka kicks Yama, almost killing him, in order to save his devotee Mārkaṇḍeya from an early death.[47] Mañjuśrī-Yamāntaka parallels this role of Śiva-Yamāntaka, as he destroys Yama to protect the people of Tibet.

In this Buddhist variant, the ascetic-become-Yama embodies the rage produced by unsatisfied desire, or kāma become krodha. The story presents the Ruler of the Dead as wrath-filled Desire inflicting death on those around him. When Mañjuśrī-Yamāntaka defeats this raging demon, he also defeats the desire that produced this rage. Like his Hindu counterpart Śiva (and like Śākyamuni Buddha who defeats the demon Māra), the fierce Mañjuśrī-Yamāntaka vanquishes Desire and Death in one stroke.

From a more psychological perspective, the tale illustrates not only how anger is rooted in desire, but how desire can literally become anger. The intensity of desire necessary to approach enlightenment can shift in a moment to become the rage felt at being thwarted. The fact that the object of desire in this story is the selfless state of nirvāṇa rather than a more mundane object of longing makes no difference. Indeed the idea that the desire for nirvāṇa can become a murderous rage makes the point more effectively: desire can manifest as devotion or rage. Finally, the story of Yamāntaka demonstrates a concept taught in many Indian religious traditions, that the most difficult and final desire to release is the desire to be free of desire.

This tale presents an out of control ascetic, desire-rage-death, who can only be defeated by the bodhisattva of wisdom. The metaphor is clear: wisdom's deep insight dissolves desire. The dual image of the bodhisattva of wisdom as fierce Killer of Death reflects a wisdom that transcends not only desire-anger, but ultimately, death.

Mañjuśrī as Vajrānaṅga

While the close relationship between desire and anger is commonly observed in human interactions, Mañjuśrī as the Tantric Vajrānaṅga presents a more subtle insight, the potential of desire to become wisdom. In one Tantric practice focused on devotion to Mañjuśrī as Vajrānaṅga, Mañjuśrī performs the role of Kāmadeva, with the goal of transforming kāma into wisdom.

In this ritual, called *Vaśikaraṇa* or "the bewitching of men and women,"[48] the worshipper visualizes himself first as Mañjuśrī-Vajrānaṅga, and then as the bodhisattva, piercing the bosom of the woman whose affection he seeks with a lotus-bud arrow:

> The woman falls flat on the ground in a swoon, whereupon the worshipper should visualise her legs as being tied by the chain which is the bow. Then he should imagine that the noose of the lotus stalk is flung round her neck, and she is drawn to his side. Thereupon, he should think that he is striking her with the Aśoka bough, is frightening her with the sword, and subsequently he has only to confront her with the mirror by which she is completely subjugated.[49]

Mañjuśrī exhibits the obvious traits of Kāmadeva here, but as a Buddhist Kāmadeva, the bodhisattva breaks through the confines of desire.

The vaśikaraṇa sādhana operates as both an ordinary magic charm to win the affections of a lover and as a Tantric practice to achieve identification with the deepest wisdom, prajñā, often depicted as a goddess. Indeed, the ritual text intentionally intertwines human images with abstract concepts guiding the practitioner to use the human images and feelings as stepping stones to deeper realizations. In the image of Mañjuśrī-Vajrānaṅga, wisdom and desire are joined; in the Vaśikaraṇa sādhana, human desire and the transformation of that desire into wisdom are *integrally* related. Desire and wisdom are not represented as two levels of an esoteric theory, but as one complex experience. The practitioner who identifies himself as Vajrānaṅga mirrors the mundane realities of kāma or desire, while his simultaneous identity as Mañjuśrī embodies the wisdom that lies beyond these realities.

Rather than separating the magical charm from the tantric goal of union with Prajñā, the tradition presents the two as taking place simultaneously, and thus completely integrated in the ritual. In more concrete terms, if a practitioner is so absorbed with gaining the affections of a lover that he cannot focus on ordinary Buddhist practice (like Nanda), then using the object of his desire to motivate meditational practice offers a way to make the obstacle itself the path toward Buddhahood. As the practitioner maintains the rigorous discipline and training necessary to become Mañjuśrī, the desire for his human lover will fall away as his identification with the bodhisattva of wisdom increases.

Other Tantric rituals similar to the Vaśikaraṇa sādhana are described in a text devoted to the goddess Tārā in her form as Kurukullā.[50] One might question how the Buddhist emphasis on purity and the elimination of desire can also promote a practice designed to win the affections of a lover. However, the substantial discipline and time necessary to attain the skills required for this sādhana make it unlikely that any but the most serious would complete this practice. Stephen Beyer in his work on the Tantric Tārā also addresses this issue.

> The most powerful rituals of subjugation and destruction remain those wherein the power of the deity is directed through the practitioner's own person and aimed at the object of the ritual, either directly or through the medium of a magical device. This process requires the practitioner to have acquired the requisite powers of visualization and to have gained the capacity of containing within himself, as a fit vessel, the deity's power through the performance of the preliminary ritual service of that deity. This prerequisite in effect limits the availability of destructive power to those who are able to devote at least a minimum amount of time and effort to its acquisition, for the most part professional contemplatives; and the check placed on its misuse is held to be that the prior contemplations themselves, in their inculcation of moral attitudes, limit the greed and hostility of the practitioner.[51]

The outcome of the long practice necessary to perfect the Vaśikaraṇa sādhana supports the interpretation of this ritual as one which moves the practitioner beyond his initial goal, toward the deeper aim of enlightenment. In the ritual worship of Tārā-Kurukullā, the text explains that the practice is meant to foster concentration on the desire for a lover while the discipline and devotion to the deity simultaneously develop wisdom (prajñā) in the practitioner.

In contrast to the Hindu image of Kāma who smites Śiva with his arrow, jarring him out of meditation and pushing him into a maddening cycle of desire-produced trauma, Mañjuśrī-Vajrānaṅga uses the desire of the devotee as a kind of carrot drawing him into new wisdom. Indeed, the rituals ascribed to Vajrānaṅga allow one to use almost any state of mind as a path to Buddhist wisdom.

A basic tenet of contemporary psychology—a legacy of Freud and the twentieth-century psychologists who followed him, Adler, Jung, Fromm, Horney, Rank, May, and others—holds that when an emotional internal conflict is denied, it gathers such force and momentum that it may eventually erupt in an explosive and uncontrollable form, much like the Yama subdued by Yamāntaka. Devotion to Mañjuśrī-Vajrānaṅga provides a way to harness the force of such conflicting desires and direct it toward enlightenment.

Similarly, the bodhisattva Mañjuśrī-Vajrānaṅga transforms his role as Kāmadeva. Mañjuśrī carries a book identified as the *Aṣṭasahasrika-Prajñāpāramitā* (*Perfection Wisdom Treatise in Eight Thousand Verses)*, and his consort is the female personification of Prajñā. Mañjuśrī in his form as Vajrānaṅga demonstrates that desire is a bonafide path to this wisdom.

In his translation of the Tibetan text by sGam-po-pa, the *Jewel Ornament of Liberation*, Herbert Guenther writes of Buddhist wisdom, *prajñā:*

> Since [Buddhist philosophy] is a way of life concerning the whole man rather than a mere intellectual pastime, *prajñā* is a most difficult term to define. It is usually translated by "wisdom". This is tolerably correct in so far as prajñā is the culmination of a disciplinary process which starts with ethics and manners (*śīla*) and proceeds through concentrative absorption (*samādhi*) to wisdom

> (*prajñā*). By etymology it is *dharmāṇām pravicaya*, "analysis of events and/or entities." ... *Prajñā* therefore is really "discrimination," which in Webster's "Dictionary of Synonyms" means "the power to select the excellent, the appropriate and the true." But as a result of the previous training *prajñā* is more than ordinary discrimination. Unfortunately there is no functional term to express this "more" in Western psychology.[52]

In another work, Guenther attempts to define *prajñā* still more accurately, by reviewing the connotations of the word in Buddhist Sanskrit. "Prajñā refers to the cognitive potentiality that is present in everyone to be developed, intensified, and brought to its highest pitch. To bring this potentiality to its highest pitch means to release it, to free it from all the extraneous material that has accumulated." Guenther speaks of this cognitive potential as being normally imbedded in a "network of relative considerations," such as the web of compulsions resulting from the attachments of interlocking and conflicting desires. Acting in a pure state of prajñā means acting from a position of total freedom from the dictates of desire. Guenther stresses this point when he says that "the opposite of freedom is not [pre]determination but compulsion." He identifies these compulsions as "preconceptions and fixations" that disturb the process of relating to the world and to other people from a position of total openness, a quality that characterizes the state of prajñā.[53]

The visual and conceptual images embodied in Mañjuśrī as the bodhisattva of prajñā, and in Vajrānaṅga as the Buddhist Kāmadeva, express the process of moving from compulsiveness to freedom.

In the *Śikṣāsamuccaya* Śāntideva describes the power of prajñā to liberate the mind from the control of negative emotions:

> All phenomena originate in the mind, and when the mind is fully known all phenomena are fully known. For by the mind the world is led ... and through the mind karma is piled up, whether good or evil. ... The bodhisattva, thoroughly examining the nature of things, dwells in everpresent mindfulness of the activity of the mind, and so he does not fall into the mind's power, but the mind comes under his control. And with the mind under his control all phenomena are under his control.[54]

Accordingly, Mañjuśrī-Vajrānaṅga exemplifies ultimate freedom from the control of the desiring mind in the emptiness and openness of wisdom, prajñā.

CHAPTER NINE

Conclusions: Kāmadeva and the Meaning of Desire

The tales of Kāmadeva as a whole demonstrate how the Indian tradition has understood and presented the concept of desire. In contrast to philosophical texts which analyze the mental and physical functioning of desire, and law books that prescribe behavior, story literature, though part of this same broad Sanskritic tradition, often camouflages the seriousness of its teachings in the caricatured antics of fools, heroines, and heroes. Offering admonitions and advice along with instruction for performing ritual and devotion, the tales of Kāmadeva are also meant to arouse curiosity and tickle fantasies.

Anyone who has sat through a dry, flat lecture with no polite way to exit knows the attention-getting value of the words "Let me tell you a story." But under the guise of providing a respite from dullness and routine, the tales of Kāmadeva teach. As didactic narratives, tales such as the burning of Kāma define the character and symbolism of the god in order to explore the function of desire within the individual and society. The qualities of the God of Desire, especially those highlighted by his epithets, create a picture not only of the deity but of how desire operates as a dynamic dimension of human existence. This concluding section moves from the antics of the Kāma in particular stories to addressing more directly what the tales of Kāma demonstrate about the nature of desire itself.

WHAT DOES KĀMADEVA TEACH ABOUT DESIRE?

The storytellers' thoughtfully crafted descriptions of Kāmadeva focus on the following aspects of desire:

- Originates in the mind (Manoja, the Mind-born)
- Enters through the senses

- Called to action by memory (Smara)
- Manipulates human vulnerabilities
- Deceptively beautiful and charming
- Invisible yet wounding (Anaṅga, the Limbless, Invisible One)
- Kindles passion that burns and maddens (Madana, the Maddener)
- Difficult to conquer completely, or even control
- Incinerated (or controlled) by ascetic self-denial/discipline
- Dies and revives

Even across cultures, human experience offers numerous examples that would testify to the accuracy of this description of desire. English idiom speaks of desire as a force that can be productive or destructive, possess or consume, can motivate to excel, reach new limits or impossible depths. Sanskrit speaks of desire as a force that originates in the mind and becomes activated by memory. The texts ask, "Is it possible to feel the pull of desire without a pleasurable memory of satisfying that desire?" Desire exists inside and outside the mind as an invisible foe requiring mental and religious focus to conquer, or at least control. Even as dead ash, the fire of desire contains the potential to burst forth and consume. When underestimated, desire always emerges the victor.

Desire Originates in the Mind

This first element of Kāma/kāma, the association of kāma with the mind, is graphically portrayed in the tale of the birth of Kāmadeva in the *Śiva Purāṇa.*[1] In this tale, Kāmadeva emerges from the mind of Brahmā when Brahmā experiences lust for the beautiful daughter born of his own mind, Twilight (*Sandhyā*) or Evening Twilight (*Sāyam Sandhyā*). Describing what happened, Brahmā explains:

> Seeing her and being excited [*samutthāya,*[2] being aroused, rising], that which had come to my mind was pondered in my heart. [When] such a thing was thought by me, indeed O Best of Sages, an extremely beautiful and surprising man was conceived by my mind.

This man is, of course, Kāmadeva. The author makes it clear that Kāma is not merely associated with the mind (manas) but specifically owes his existence to the mind, in this case to the mind of Brahmā. Brahmā did not set out to create a being of desire. Kāma simply stepped out of Brahmā's mind reflecting the creator's lustful thoughts. Kāma/kāma is spontaneously created by the mind, as his epithets *manoja* (born of the mind) and *manobhava* (existing in the mind) reflect.

In addition to being born of the mind, Kāma is also Manmatha, the one who disturbs or mixes up the mind, and Madana, the one who intoxicates the mind. Shooting the arrow Unmada, which causes the mind to be mad or insane, Kāma causes mental chaos. As Kāmadeva steps out of the mind of Brahmā, all around him are affected. The storyteller describes the collective effect this new presence has on Brahmā's mindborn sons: "The mind of my sons immediately became deformed, confused [*vikṛta*]."[3] Originating in the mind, desire disturbs one's mental equilibrium.

The tradition insists that the mind creates desire. So the mind must also be able to discipline its creation.

Sensuous Desire Enters through the Senses

Mirroring human experience, the stories present graphic images of desire linked with pleasure. Wherever Kāma goes, he brings with him Madhu/Vasanta, the sensuality of the spring season that offers renewed energy: the cuckoo [*kokila*] singing to its mate, breezes caressing the face, rainbows of blooming flowers, black bees buzzing in blended harmonies, and an avalanche of flowery fragrances.

In the *Śiva Purāṇa,* the storyteller describes Kāma as he emerges from the mind of Brahmā, in terms that allow us to experience this new being with our senses:

> He appeared to be made of gold, with a broad chest and a well-formed nose. His thighs, hips, and calves were wide, and he had a blue lock of hair on the crown of his head. (II.2.2.24)
>
> He had a pair of touching eyebrows that were restless, moving [*lola*], and a face that shone like the full moon. (II.2.2.25a)
>
> Slender-waisted, with beautiful teeth, he smelled like a rutting elephant. His eyes were like the unfolding petals of a lotus, and he had the fragrance of the filament [stamen] [of the flower]. (II.2.2.27)
>
> He was attractive because he moved his eyes back and and forth throwing [coquettish] side-glances. His breath [*māruta*] was a fragrant wind, O dear one, and he was accompanied by the sentiment of love [śṛṅgāra rasa]. (II.2.2.29)

Using the vulnerabilities of the senses as his targets, Kāmadeva uses his skill as an excellent archer, a warrior. Brahmā describes Kāmadeva getting ready to shoot the Creator God and his mind-born sons:

> Standing in the ālidha position [the posture for shooting with the right knee advanced and the left leg retracted], ready to attack, with his bow bent with careful effort, Kāma, the most excellent of archers created the form of a circle [with his body and the bow]. (III.2.3.17)

The stories portray desire as the physical presence whose beauty attracts all eyes, and as the skilled archer whose arrows find their targets like magnets drawn to metal. Of course desire does attract and find easy targets, because desire is *manoja,* born of the mind, that is, of our own minds. Desire is created by our minds, nurtured by our senses, and acted out by our physical bodies, the aggregate of mind/emotion/body. But by conceptualizing desire as a beautiful warrior, we project responsibility away from ourselves. The tradition emphasizes, that *we create* the passion we curse in the form of a God of Desire targeting us with his arrows. We experience the desire long imbedded in our own minds as an external force.

The story of Kāma's creation is clear: as soon as the woman stepped from the mind of Brahmā, he was overwhelmed with longing. The underside of our vulnerabilities, desire is our need to be loved, our fear of loneliness, our need to touch other living beings and to be touched, our need to care for others, our need to give and be received, our need to feel secure and safe from harm, our need to feel powerful, our fear of losing control, our fear of death. Inextricably linked with human vulnerability, desire is continually created by the mind, projected outward, and then battled as if an external adversary, the good-looking archer wielding powerful flower-tipped arrows.

Memory Evokes Desire

One of Kāmadeva's most prominent epithets is Smara, "Memory." The Indian philosophical tradition explains that what we perceive through the senses leaves an impression in the mind; when that impression is awakened, we experience memory.[4] Desire is associated with memory because people yearn only for what they already know, though this knowing may occur on a level that reaches beyond individual experience. For example, the tenth-century Kashmiri philosopher Abhinavagupta explains a Sanskrit dramatist's use of memory by defining memory as not simply a remembering of past events but rather "an intuitive insight into the past that transcends personal experience, (moving) into the imaginative universe that beauty evokes."[5]

Commenting on the playwright Kālidāsa's use of memory as almost another character in his dramas, Barbara Miller explains that Kālidāsa drew on a tradition that understood memory as a powerful factor in evoking passionate desire. Memory was often used as a literary convention in classical Sanskrit literature.

> "An act of remembering is a conventional technique for relating the antithetical modes of love-in-separation (vipralamabha-śṛṅgāra) and love-in-union (sambhoga-śṛṅgāra). In the *Caurapañcāśika* (attributed to Bilhana), for example, each of the verses is a miniature painting of the princess with whom the poet enjoyed an illicit love. For his recklessness in this love he is condemned to death. The love-thief's final thoughts are details of his mistress's beauty:

Even now,
I remember her eyes
restlessly closed after love,
her slender body limp
fine cloths and heavy hair loose—
a wild goose in a thicket of lotuses of passion.
I shall recall her in my next life
and even at the end of time.

By remembering the exquisite details of her physical beauty and her behavior in love, he brings her into his presence and the lovers are reunited in his mind. Even as a literary convention of intense love, memory has the power to break through the logic of everyday experience—it makes visible what is invisible, obliterates distances, reverses chronologies, and fuses what is ordinarily separate."[6]

As memory propels desire to transcend space and time, writers, playwrights, poets, and lyricists evoke passion in audiences. Tweaked by the smell of hot apple pie, the sound of a clarinet, the sight of a bluebird, memory invigorates desire, old and new, with intensity and passion.

Desire Enflames, Wounds, and Maddens

In the variants of the burning story, Kāmadeva battles Śiva and Devī, and in the story of his emergence from the mind of Brahmā, Kāmadeva attacks Brahmā and his famous mind-born sons, including Dakṣa and Marīci. His weapons are arrows with names that describe their power: Vijṛmbhaṇa (Extending, Becoming Erect),[7] Māraṇa (Killing), Stambhaṇa (Stiffening, Paralyzing), Śoṣaṇa (Drying Up, Withering), and Unmādana (Maddening, Infatuating),[8] names that one Sanskritist describes as "indicating the condition of a person in love-pangs."[9] In another text, the five arrows are listed as Harṣaṇa (Delighting), Rocana (Pleasing, Stimulating the Appetite), Mohana (Deluding), Śoṣaṇa, and Māraṇa.[10]

Kāma's arrows are described as flower shafts, beautiful and fragrant like jasmine, aśoka, and lotus, yet nonetheless deeply wounding, as their names reveal. The image of Kāma/kāma implies paradox: dangerous and not, as easily pushed away as a flower yet as impossible to ignore as the pain of an arrow in the heart.

When Śiva tries to ignore the beautiful god and his arrows, he learns that Kāma is too dangerous to be brushed aside, and so burns him to ashes. Kāma burns others with his arrow Santāpana (Inflaming, Burning), but his arrows are no match for the internal fire of the ascetic Śiva. The fire of desire mingled with the fire of asceticism and anger becomes indistinguishable in one conflagration. A safe receptacle has to be found for both these destructive fires. In the *Matsya Purāṇa,* the fire, described as the "fire of Smara," is distributed among the mango tree, the moon, the spring, black bees, flowers, and cuckoos,[11] while in the *Śiva Purāṇa,* the fire, described as the "anger of Śiva," is molded by Brahmā into a mare that he gives to the ocean because it threatens to burn the entire universe.[12]

Idiomatic Indo-European English, descended from the Sanskrit, speaks of being "burned" in an unhappy romance, of a "burning" desire, of being "burnt up" with anger, and of being "burned" in a business deal in which desired ends were not achieved. English expressions also associate desire, and anger as desire thwarted, with fire or potential destruction.

The stories confirm our sense that desire can drive us literally mad with ecstasy, jealousy, rage, or despair. And English idioms reinforce this association of desire and madness. We speak of people who are "mad with rage," "insanely jealous," "madly in love," "crazy about" a new lover, adolescents who are boy-crazy or girl-crazy. When he loses his wife, Śiva becomes insane with grief, unable to respond coherently or live in one place. Wandering like a madman from place to place carrying her corpse on his shoulder, Śiva behaves in a way that most societies would view as mentally unbalanced or insane. Yet in the context of the story, the episode makes perfect sense: Śiva acts out the intense grief of losing a loved one, the disconnect with reality, the rage—feelings understood as normal but which mimic mental illness or madness if acted upon in ways considered inappropriate by society.

Producing not only the madness of lovers separated from one another, Kāma's arrows evoke the insanities of falling in love described by playwrights and songwriters. Kāma's arrows produce the insanity that allows individuals to idealize and connect with one another, as well as the insanity of grief that allows lovers to separate at death.

Difficult to Control, Desire is Incinerated by Ascetic Practice

The burning story raises the question of mastery over Kāma/kāma. Who or what controls Kāma and over whom or what is Kāma lord? In the variants examined here, Kāma does the bidding of Indra, Brahmā, and Devī, but he also wields power over Indra, Brahmā, Śiva, and even the Goddess in her manifestation as Pārvatī/Gaurī. Kāma is portrayed in different positions, sometimes controlling a situation, sometimes taking orders, never entirely predictable.

In the story of the emergence of Kāmadeva from the mind of Brahmā in the *Śiva Purāṇa,* Brahmā states that Kāma has control over all men and women, all moving and nonmoving beings, and all gods, including the creator god Brahmā himself, Vāsudeva [Viṣṇu], and Sthānu [Śiva].[13] Yet other stories describe Kāmadeva at the beck and call of Brahmā, Indra, or the goddess Lalitā. The tension between controlling and being controlled by desire is demonstrated again and again, with the outcome never certain.

Though the ascetic Śiva and goddess Lalitā demonstrate control over Kāma, and therefore over kāma, neither of these deities ignores desire. When Kāmadeva is repositioned among the troops of Śiva and Lalitā in their tales, the narrative structure emphasizes that the force of desire can be refocused but not totally defused.

Desire Dies and Revives

After his transformation to ash in the fire of Śiva's third eye, Kāma is ultimately identified with his resuscitated form, the Limbless One, Anaṅga, formless and invisible. For some storytellers, this attribute of invisibility becomes so important that it is placed earlier in the narrative, before Kāma has even tested his new weapons and powers. In the *Śiva Purāṇa,* when Kāma has just come into existence and Brahmā is speaking to him about his position in the world, he tells him that he (Kāma) will "enter the hearts of all beings with a concealed form or body (*pracchannarupaḥ*)"—in other words, invisibly.[14] In this later work, Kāma's invisibility has become so important that he is described as formless, even before Śiva has transformed him.

But perhaps more important than Kāmadeva's identity as Anaṅga is his identity as a god who dies and revives, a god connected with birth and procreation in the fertile rainy season, and death in the hot season when rivers and trees dry up, appearing dead. Kāmadeva as a dying and rising fertility deity is evident in his recovery from leprosy and impotence as well as in the burning story where he shoots his flower arrows, dies, and flourishes again. Desire is so intrinsic to human nature that even when it seems to be gone, there is always something that can spark its return, often with unexpected force.

Experience tells us that desire most often arrives in our lives unseen and unheard, invisible like Kāma, wonderfully charming yet wounding us even before we get our fill of its elation. Experience also tells us that passion can produce the death of old ways of seeing, ultimately forcing the generation of new perspectives. Out of the ashes of madness and heartache, desire arises offering new beginnings.

ATTITUDES TOWARD DESIRE IN SANSKRIT STORY LITERATURE

"Human life is based on pairs of opposites or *dvandva* (which could be mutually reinforcing or destructive), and he who denies this fundamental principle is bound to come to grief. It is true that the sannyasi [renunciate] finds spiritual joy only when he succeeds in transcending dualities; even so, one must begin with the recognition that both the terms of a duality are equally important. The problem is not to separate them but to establish a proper relationship between them at a higher, transcendent level. The soul, after all, resides in the body and not independently of it. . . . The human body is a key symbol which bridges nature and culture but does not by itself constitute the totality of being. Any effort to locate the body exclusively in either of these two domains is a bad choice, for it is bound to fail. . . . Those who seek *puṇya* [merit] are dogged by *pāpa* [evil, sin], and those who seem morally derelict turn out to be worthy of being the recipients of divine grace."[15]

These passages from T. N. Madan's essay on "Asceticism and Eroticism" address the same question explored by the stories of Kāmadeva: What does the Indian religious tradition teach about appropriate attitudes toward kāma? In his essay, Madan presents the stories of three contemporary novels,[16] each from a different part of the country, the Hindi-speaking north, Kerala in the south, and the western state of Maharashtra, to demonstrate that Hindu thinking values both the householder and the ascetic, in spite of placing the two in opposition. One cannot live as an ascetic and a householder simultaneously; the life of the householder rests on the guidance of the senses while the ascetic struggles to free himself from these same senses. The resolution of this opposition, says Madan, is the transcendence of the realm of dualities.

"Transcendence is a complex concept and, it seems to me, much misunderstood. . . . [It refers to] raising the level of being in order to free it from the conflict of dualities. This is the ancient goal [rather than object] of *samskrti,* the bringing into being of the mature, refined person. Nothing is discarded or excluded in this process of refinement: everything is included, improved and carried forward into one integrated experience. In this experience eroticism exists no more nor less than does asceticism. The goal is to connect them, to establish a proper relationship between them. The relationship alone is real in the same sense in which the truth of the trader's balance lies in the even beam and not in either of the two pans or their contents."[17]

The stories and rituals presented of Kāmadeva support Madan's assertion that the tradition does not deny the experiences associated with the body but rather encourages their refinement by including them in religious practice.

For example, in the tale of Yayāti and his wives recounted in the introduction, Yayāti's attempt to satisfy his lustful drives for thousands of years leads not only to his realization that desire is insatiable, but to his readiness to become a renunciate. Kāmadeva in the story of Khaṇḍaśilā is led to worship Śiva as the Kāmeśvara Liṅga in order to be cured of the leprosy that was the consequence of his improper desire for another's wife. A ritual pūjā is performed by those involved in adulterous liaisons to ward off any resulting bad karma yet allow them to continue as lovers. Prostitutes, earning a living through the exploitation of others' kāma, perform a ritual to Kāmadeva to gain their own liberation. Karṇotpalā devotes herself to the Goddess to earn a husband for herself and well-being for her father. In the Buddhist tradition, Nanda's sexual desire motivates his commitment to Buddhist discipline and practice.

Each of these stories presents a different progression from desire to some form of ritual practice. In the most common pattern, a protagonist who experiences intense longing propitiates a deity for help in attaining the object of desire, as in the prostitutes' vrata the adulterers' ritual, and the story of Karṇotpalā. In another pattern, the protagonist reveling in pleasure is unable to maintain his euphoric state and the resulting frustration leads to religious practice. This pattern is seen when Yayāti becomes dissatisfied with the perpetual demands of desire and its short-lived pleasures, and when Kāma seeks release from the leprosy which has made him undesirable to new lovers.

In several tales, a related pattern emerges in which the primary character, upon attaining the object of his desire, realizes that his initial desire has dissolved in the process of striving to achieve it, or that the object once attained offers no meaningful satisfaction. In the stories of Yayāti and Nanda, both find that pursuing physical desires is no longer satisfying in any lasting or significant way. After gaining renewed sexual intimacy with his wife, Yayāti takes up the religious asceticism of the forest to move beyond the insatiable drives of his body. Nanda sets his sights on religious enlightenment.

Viewing mundane human desire as an essential element in the process of seeking spiritual goals may appear to conflict with more well-known Hindu and Buddhist teachings. But ancient stories, carefully preserved from generation to generation, indicate that some Hindu and Buddhist teachers did indeed communicate this message, even while contradicting the more mainstream positions in their communities.

For example, familiar passages of the *Upaniṣads* and the *Bhagavad Gītā* teach that desire leads inevitably to anger, delusion, and entrapment in the cycle of death and rebirth.

> A man gets attached to what the senses tell him if he does not turn his mind away.
> Attachment gives rise to desire, desire [kāma] to anger [krodha].
> Anger leads to a state of delusion [sammoha]; delusion distorts one's memory.
> Distortion of memory distorts consciousness, and then a man perishes.[18]

But the *Gītā* also teaches that even better than rejecting the influence of desire, one should rechannel it into love for the divine. The *Gītā,* too, recognizes the potential of human desire to be transformed in the divine.

In the burning story, even after he is reduced to ashes, Kāma continues to flourish alongside the ascetic. The incinerated god of desire is present in the ash the ascetic smears on his body, paradoxically indicating detachment from desire, as well as in the trees and flowers surrounding the yogi in the forest. Śiva projects a wonderfully paradoxical image: ashes of desire protecting the ascetic intent on conquering him; desire ensuring discipline.

The traditional opposition between desire and asceticism is transformed so that each, indeed, becomes the other. Kāma is the ascetic's ash while Śiva is the insatiable lusting lover. This transformation of Kāma and Śiva supports Madan's point that the process is not one of harmonizing opposites but of melding or transcending them: choosing not between restraint and indulgence but rather seeing that desire and religious discipline function as equally essential aspects of the whole. In Madan's view, the ultimate goal is to understand that each is "included, improved and carried forward into one integrated experience."[19] The structure of the burning story reflects this integration.

Desire presents a complex problem for any religious discipline that teaches control of the natural tendency to pursue sensual pleasure. However, the stories present the possibility of accepting this conflict as an essential and ultimately constructive foundation of existence. Kāma and Śiva coexist, their respective strengths enhanced through continuous interaction. The ascetic realizes that his desire nature keeps him alert and committed to religious practice; the householder appreciates the strength that such discipline affords. The ascetic and the householder transcend their inherent conflict by establishing a proper relationship between them. This is the wisdom and teaching of the stories of Kāmadeva, that human beings possess this same ability to integrate, to balance desire and discipline within themselves. Desire permeates religious practice and religious discipline ultimately fulfills desires. The stories assure us such balance is possible, and demonstrate the shifts in perspective that take place in this transformation.

Kāmadeva's stories can be read as models of personal transformation. From a religious perspective, desire is transformed, but only by the force of disciplined effort. Yet, ultimately, both are essential for spiritual progress. Just as the desire for a strong body remains a fantasy without the hard work of continuous exercise and healthy eating, desire and discipline provide the necessary focus and balance within each individual. The stories prod us to realize that we can transform, even as we are transformed by, our deepest desires. Ultimately, the maddening lotus-tipped arrows of Kāmadeva infuse our lives with pleasure, loss, struggle, and infinite possibilities to create ourselves anew.

Notes

INTRODUCTION

1. The Vedas are the earliest sacred texts, dating in the oral tradition possibly to the second millennium BCE.

2. This point of view was explained to me by Professor K. Venugopalan, director of the Sanskrit Dictionary project, at Deccan College in Pune. He helped me think through the symbolism and ideas found in the Kāmadeva stories, during a number of conversations while sitting on his porch during the summer of 1988.

3. The three puruṣārthas or "aims of life" are artha (government or politics), kāma (pleasure), and dharma (prescribed duties). Later texts added a fourth: mokṣa, liberation from the wheel of death and rebirth.

4. B. G. Gokhale, *Indian Thought Through the Ages,* Bombay: Asia Publishing House, 1961, p. 83.

5. D. Chatterjee, "Towards a Better Understanding of Indian Ethics," in S. S. Rama Rao Pappu and R. Puligandla, *Indian Philosophy Past and Future,* Delhi: Motilal Banarsidass, 1982, pp. 165–166.

6. Potter, *Presuppositions of India's Philosophies,* Englewood Cliffs, New Jersey: Prentice-Hall, Inc., 1963, p. 7.

7. Ibid. p. 8

8. The genre of literature called "purāṇas" refers to collections of stories from ancient times. Various frameworks were developed to categorize and organize the puranas according to subject matter and the primary deity praised. Two general lists were devised, the *Mahāpurāṇa*s and the *Upapurāṇa*s.

9. *Bhāgavata Purāṇa* IX.18.1–51 and IX.19.1–19, Bombay: Veṇkaṭeśvara Press, 1830, 1908; *Viṣṇu Purāṇa* IV.10.1–18, Bombay: Oriental Press, 1811; *Liṅga Purāṇa* I.67.1–28, Gurumandala Series 16, Calcutta: Manasukharaya Mora, 1960; *Matsya Purāṇa* chapters 30–35, Gurumandala Series 13, Calcutta: Manasukharaya Mora, 1954; *Padma Purāṇa* Bhūmikhaṇḍa (II).76–83, Gurumandala Series 18, Calcutta: Manasukharaya Mora, 1957; *Vāyu Purāṇa* chapter 93, Bombay: Veṇkaṭeśvara Press, 1895;

Mahābhārata Adi Parvan (I).76–81, edited by V. S. Sukthankar, Poona: Bhandarkar Oriental Research Institute, 1933.

10. *Bhāgavata Purāṇa,* Ganesh Vasudeo Tagare, part III, AITM series, p. 1217, note 1.

11. Wendy Doniger O'Flaherty, *Asceticism and Sexuality in the Mythology of Śiva,* Harvard University Thesis, 1968, p. 800.

12. Ludo Rocher, *The Purāṇas,* vol. II of A History of Indian Literature, edited by Jan Gonda, Wiesbaden: Otto Harrassowitz, 1968, p. 103.

13. Ibid., pp. 96–97.

14. [Just as] "the Rāmopākhyāna in the *Mahābhārata* (3.ch.261–275) is not necessarily based on any manuscript of the Rāmāyaṇa but can very well be derived from an oral version, in the same way the written versions of puranic stories represent only an infinitesimal part of the versions that have existed over the centuries, in different parts of India. Comparing puranic stories is useful because it gives us at least some idea of the vast richness with which certain themes have been treated; drawing other, unwarranted conclusions may be hazardous and misleading." Rocher, *The Purāṇas,* pp. 97–98.

15. Rocher, *The Purāṇas,* p. 102. Rocher is referring to an article by R. N. Mehta, "Puranic Archaeology," *Journal of the University of Baroda* 20–21, 1971–72, p. 6.

16. The Salar Jung Museum in Hyderabad, India, holds a collection of many exquisite art objects from around the world, as well as these carvings of Kāma and Rati. The art was collected by the Salar Jung family, five of whose members were prime ministers to the Nizam of Hyderabad.

17. Stella Kramrisch, *Manifestations of Shiva,* Philadelphia Museum of Art, 1981, p. 55.

18. Dr. C. M. Joshi generously received me and three of my students at his home in Ellora, January 2003, to discuss the images and symbols of the Buddhist and Hindu Caves of Ajanta and Ellora.

19. Vidya Dehejia, *Indian Art,* London: Phaidon Press Ltd., 1997, pp. 107–108.

20. Ibid., pp. 65–66.

21. T. A. Gopinatha Rao, *Elements of Hindu Iconography,* second edition, vol. II, part I, Delhi: Motilal Banarsidass, 1985 [original 1916], pp. 148–149.

22. Fourth- to sixth-century CE sculpture; Badami, Bijapur, Karnataka. Digital South Asia Library, American Institute for Indian Studies, Center for Art and Archaeology, photo archive. Information from the Archaeological Survey of India. http://dsal.uchicago.edu/images/aiis/aiis_search.html?depth=Get+Details&id=21172

23. Desai, *Erotic Sculpture of India, A Socio-Cultural Study,* Delhi: Tata McGraw-Hill Publishing Co., 1975, pp. 178 and 180.

24. P. V. Kane, *History of Dharmaśāstra,* vol. III, Poona: Bhandarkar Oriental Research Institute, 1968, pp. 53–54

25. Na jātu kāmaḥ kāmānām upabhogenaṣā myati; haviṣā kṛṣṇavartmeva bhūya evābhivardhate. *Viṣṇu Purāṇa* IV.10.9, Bombay: Oriental Press, 1811; *Bhāgavata Purāṇa* IX.19.14, Bombay: Veṇkaṭeśvara Press, 1830, 1908; *Liṅga Purāṇa* I.67.16 and I.8.25,

Gurumandala Series 16, Calcutta: Manasukharāya. Mora, 1960; *Matsya Purāṇa* 34.10, Gurumandala Series 13; *Brahmāṇḍa Purāṇa* 2.3.68.70b.

CHAPTER ONE

1. *Śiva Purāna,* Veṇkaṭeśvara Press, 1906. Rudrasamhitā, II Satīkhaṇḍa, 2.18–42.

2. *Kālikā Purāna,* Veṇkaṭeśvara Press, 1907. I.1.44–50, 53, 57–60.

3. *Sandhyā* means a time of union or conjunction, but more specifically the three times (dawn, noon, and twilight) when night meets day, when the first half of day meets the second half, and when day meets night. A reference to three times for Vedic prayer, *sandhyā* also offers a double entendre referring to the union of men and women.

4. The makara is a mythical water creature most like a crocodile. See chapter seven.

5. The editors of the Shastri translation series note the five flower arrows as: arabinda (white lotus), aśoka (Jonesia Aśoka), a red flower, āmra (mango root), and nīlotpala (blue lotus).

6. *Śiva Purāṇa,* Rudrasamhitā, II Satīkhaṇḍa, 2.18–42; See J. L. Shastri, "AITM series vol. 1, "The Śiva Purāṇa" Part I, pp. 279–281.

7. Although the Sanskrit text uses the word for navel, this "navel" most probably refers to her vagina. The vagina, not the navel, would be surrounded by plum red skin and deep like a river's eddy.

8. Henna designs are applied to the hands and feet of brides for their wedding rituals.

9. Although the verse certainly describes the beauty of her arms, the exact meaning of "coral splendour" is not clear.

10. This is a reference to a story in which Śiva agrees to allow the River Gaṅgā to flow through his hair as she descends to Earth.

11. *Śiva Purāṇa,* Rudrasamhitā, II Satīkhaṇḍa, 7.37–42, 45.

12. *Śiva Purāṇa,* Rudrasamhitā, II Satīkhaṇḍa, 7.33–35, 42–46.

13. A full translation of this text from the *Skanda Purāna* is included at the end of this chapter.

14. In this text, the Goddess is known as Devī (Goddess), Gaurī (the Golden-Skinned), Girijā (Born of the Mountain), and Pārvatī (Daughter of Parvata, the Mountain Himālaya).

15. Literally, "you will be joined to youthfulness."

16. The Vāsudeva nakṣatra is a specific phase of the moon.

CHAPTER TWO

1. *Śiva Purāṇa,* Bombay: Śrī Veṇkaṭeśvara Press, 1906. Rudrasaṃhitā, Pārvatīkhaṇḍa 17.1–43, 18.1–45, 19.1–52, 20.1–23; *Śiva Purāṇa,* Kasi: Panditapustakalaya, 1963. Rudrasaṃhitā (II). Pārvatīkhaṇḍa (3) 17.1–43, 18.1–45, 19.1–52, 20.1–23; *Liṅga Purāṇa,* Veṇkaṭeśvara edition I.101.1–46; *Matsya Purāṇa,* edited by Kṛṣṇadvaipāyana

Maharṣi Śrīvedavyāsa, Calcutta, 1812, 1890. 154.212–286; *Padma Purāṇa,* Gurumandal Series no. 18, edited by Srhiman Maharshi Krishna Dwaipayan Vyasdeva, Sṛṣṭikhaṇḍa (I).45.204–286; Anandāśrama Series, 1816, 1894, Sṛṣṭikhaṇḍa (5).40.203–281; *Skanda Purāṇa,* Veṇkaṭeśvara edition. I (Māheśvarakhaṇḍa). 1 (Kedārakhaṇḍa).21.48–99; (Kumārikākhaṇḍa) 2.24.17–20, 42–49; *Brahmāṇḍa Purāṇa,* edited by J. L. Shastri, Delhi: Motilal Banarsidass, 1973. Lalitopākhyānam: III.4. 11.7–38, 12.1–75, 29.141–148, 30.1–93; *Vāmana Purāṇa,* edited by Anand Swarup Gupta, Varanasi: All India Kashiraj Trust, 1968. 6.1–107; *Saura Purāṇa,* Calcutta, 1816. Chapters 54 and 55; *Kālikā Purāṇa,* Veṇkaṭeśvara edition, Chapter 44; *Brahmavaivarta Purāṇa* Kṛṣṇajanmakhaṇḍa (IV).39.40–59; *Brahma Purāṇa,* Calcutta, 1954. 38.1–13.

2. It is difficult to date the stories in the purāṇas not only because these written versions are retellings of tales from a long and diverse oral tradition, but also because the purāṇas themselves were copied and recopied over the centuries. The *Matsya/Padma* variant recounts the major components of the story.

3. *Matsya Purāṇa,* edited by Kṛṣṇadvaipayāna Maharṣi Śrīvedavyāsa, Calcutta, 1812, 1890. 154.207–288. And Sarasvatī Press, 1876, 154.208–290; *Padma Purāṇa,* Gurumandal Series no. XVIII, 1957, Sṛṣṭīkhaṇḍa (1).45.204–286 and Anandāśrama Press, 1816, 1894, Sṛṣṭīkhaṇḍa (4).40.203–281. These two accounts are virtually identical narratives.

4. Ludo Rocher, *The Purāṇas,* pp.199–208. The *Matsya* has been placed in different time periods but all beginning quite early: Kane (200–400 CE), R. Dikshitar (400 BCE to 300 CE), and Kantawala (400 BCE to 1250 CE).

5. Both the *Matsya* and the *Padma* give the same verse: Sandaṃśena vināṣ aktir ayaskārasya neśyate. (*Padma,* Anandāśrama edition 5.40.212b; Matsya, Calcutta edition 154.218b). N. A. Deshpande, translating *Padma* I.43.210b in the AITM series, suggests: "The ironsmith has no power other than to make weapons."

6. According to Indian philosophical texts, hatred, anger, and envy are all rooted in desire, making each of these complex emotions a good seed for Kāma to plant in the mind of Śiva.

7. See chapter seven for discussion of the makara.

8. *Atharva Veda* VI.130.1–3, 131.1, 132.1–5. The *Atharva Veda* is difficult to date and contains material written during different time periods, but was composed roughly between the tenth and fifth centuries BCE.

9. Barbara Stoler Miller, "Kālidāsa's World and His Plays," *Theater of Memory,* Columbia University Press, 1984, p. 39–40.

10. Ananda Coomaraswamy, "Recollection, Indian and Platonic," *Journal of the American Oriental Society,* vol. 64, suppl. no. 3, 1944.

11. In the story of Indra and Ahalyā, Indra is cursed with 1000 female sexual organs, but ultimately has them changed to 1000 eyes. *Brahmā Purāṇa,* Poona: Anandāśrama edition, 1895, 87.59

12. See the story of Kaṇḍu in the *Brahmā Purāṇa,* Bombay: Veṇkaṭeśvara edition, 1906, 1.69.7–28; 43–101. See the story of Agastya and Vasiṣtha in the *Matsya Purāṇa,* Calcutta: Sarasvatī Press, 1876, 60.21–31.

13. Apsarases are seductive, celestial nymphs associated with the waters and Indra's heaven. See chapter seven for a discussion of apsarases.

14. *Brahmavaivarta Purāṇa,* Anandāśrama Sanskrit Series, 1937, 4.47.100–160.

15. See translations by Barbara Stoler Miller, Toronto: Bantam Books, 1986; and Kees Bolle, Berkeley: University of California, 1979.

16. Hatred (dveṣa) and desire are understood to be flip sides of the same mental state, producing either attraction or repulsion depending on circumstance.

17. *Padma Purāṇa* I.43.228.

18. See Chandradhar Sharma, *A Critical Survey of Indian Philosophy,* Delhi: Motilal Banarsidas, 1976. pp. 149–317.; Sarvepalli Radhakrishnan and Charles A. Moore, *A Sourcebook in Indian Philosophy,* pp. 349–574.

19. The most compelling description of this transformation occurs in the *Vāmana Purāṇa* 6.1–107, and the *Kālikā Purāṇa* ch. 44, in accounts of Śiva's infatuation with Satī, Pārvatī's previous incarnation. Though Satī also performed asceticism to win the great god, her efforts were rewarded only when Śiva was pierced by Kāma's arrow.

20. See Wendy Doniger O'Flaherty's discussion "The Partial Identity of Śiva and Kāma," pp. 169–171 in *Śiva, the Erotic Ascetic,* Oxford University Press, 1973.

21. Wendy Doniger O'Flaherty. *Śiva, the Erotic Ascetic,* p. 143.

22. *Śiva Purāṇa,* Veṇkaṭeśvara edition, Rudrasaṃhitā (II), Pārvatīkhaṇḍa (3); 17.1–43; 18.1–45; 19.1–52.

23. R. C. Hazra, "The Problems Relating to the Śiva Purāṇa," *Our Heritage,* vol. 1, 1953, p. 67. See also Ludo Rocher, *The Purāṇas,* pp. 222–228, for discussion of the difficulty of dating the different sections of this purāṇa. In this section, Rocher notes that much of the Rudrasaṃhitā is found in the *Kālikā Purāṇa,* and indeed the narratives of the burning story in the two purāṇas are quite close. This may indicate that this version of the story has origins in Assam, i.e. Kāmarūpa, or that part of Bengal which is closest to Assam (p. 182), but the evidence for such a conclusion is far from definitive.

24. This passage seems to mix two reasons for Indra's decision to disturb Śiva's penance: 1) Śiva's tapas is getting so intense that the world, including Indra's throne, may burn up; that is, Indra may lose his own power. 2) The gods need Śiva to produce a son to kill the powerful demon, Tāraka. Śiva's rigorous asceticism is thwarting the gods' need to have Śiva spill his seed and produce this son.

25. This is a reference to the Vaiṣṇava story of Pradyumna. See chapter three for discussion of Kāma as Pradyumna.

26. Attendant, member of a body of troops or of a class of inferior deities.

27. *Śiva Purāṇa* (Paṇḍita Pustakalaya and Veṇkaṭeśvara editions) Rudrasaṃhitā (II). Pārvatīkhaṇḍa (3).19.48.

28. *Vāmana Purāṇa* critical edition, edited by Anand Swarup Gupta and translated by S. M. Mukhopadhyaya, A. Bhattacharya, N. C. Nath, and V. K. Verma, Varanasi: All India Kashiraj Trust, 1968, 6.25–107.

29. R. C. Hazra, *Studies in the Purāṇic Records on Hindu Rites and Customs,* Dacca University, 1940, p. 91 (Reprint Delhi: Motilal Banarsidas, 1975); Haraprasad Shastri, *A Catalogue of Palm-Leaf and Selected Manuscripts in the Government Collection under the*

care of the Asiatic Society of Bengal, Calcutta: ASB, vol.V, 1928, p. clxxxii–clxxxiii; The *Vāmana Purāṇa* edited by Ananda Swarup Gupta, translated by S. M. Mukhopadhyaya, et al, Varanasi: All India Kashiraj Trust, 1968, p. xxxv.

30. The Campaka blooms with a fragrant yellow flower. The Kesara, also known as a Bukula or Mimusops Elengi tree, is "said to put forth blossoms when sprinkled with nectar from the mouths of lovely women." The Pāṭala, Bignonia Suaveolens, bears a pale red or pink trumpet-flower. The Mallika is Jasminum Zambac. Monier-Williams, *Sanskrit-English Dictionary,* Oxford: Clarendon Press, 1899.

31. The rituals include dancing, noise-making, playing musical instruments, and laughing as part of the worship of Kāmadeva. See chapter five for descriptions of rituals to Kāmadeva.

32. Wendy Doniger O'Flaherty, *Śiva, the Erotic Ascetic.* See also Stella Kramrisch, *The Presence of Śiva,* Princeton University Press, 1981.

33. *Vamana Purāṇa* 6.86–92.

34. *Brahmāṇḍa Purāṇa,* Upasaṃhārapāda (IV).11.7–38, 12.1–75. 30.1–107. Translated and annotated by G. V. Tagare, AITM series, vol. 26, Delhi: Motilal Banarsidass, 1984.

35. See Rocher, *The Purāṇas,* p. 157; P. V. Kane, *History of Dharmaśāstra,* vol. 5, part 2, "Origin and Development of Purāṇa Literature," Poona: BORI, 1962. pp. 895–896; S. N. Roy, "On the Date of the Brahmāṇḍa Purāṇa," *Purāṇa,* vol. 5, 1963. pp. 305–319.

36. *Brahmāṇḍa Purāṇa,* Upasaṃhārapāda (4), chapters 5–44.

37. Kāma is already invisible in this variant. Storytellers combine elements of earlier narratives in different ways to make their own points.

38. Kāma's banner displays the makara, probably a type of crocodile. For discussion of this epithet see chapter seven.

39. Tagare conjectures that "bhaṇḍ" is from the root meaning "to be fortunate," and that "bhaṇḍiti" was likely a blessing. *Brahmāṇḍa Purāṇa,* AITM series, vol. 26, 1984, p. 1077.

40. Dānavas/daityas are demons, celestial powers who oppose the gods.

41. In this passage, Rudra is an epithet of Śiva. Rudra is a Vedic god associated with thunder, lightning, and the rage of monsoon floods.

42. "Three worlds" indicate the universe, traditionally heaven, earth, and nether regions.

43. All of the following references are epithets of the Great Goddess, here known as Lalitā: Supporter of the Universe [Jagaddhātrī], Mother of the Universe [Jagadambikā], the Great Goddess [Paramā Śaktī], Honored Goddess [Śrīdevī], Conqueror of Desire [Kāmeśvarī], and Mother Lalitā [Lalitāmbikā].

44. Sacrifice of human flesh.

45. Kāmeśvara is one of Śiva's traditional epithets, meaning Ruler of the God Kāma and Conqueror of Desire. The epithet communicates the image of one who controls desire and one who wields desire, i.e., another Kāmadeva.

46. This is a common way to perform austerity: to stand in water for a given period, usually through many seasons, reciting prayers, performing yoga, and meditating. This

austerity is understood to discipline the body, mind, and emotions, while propitiating the gods. In this case, Pārvatī is performing penance to gain Śiva's attention.

47. *Brahmāṇḍa Purāṇa* 12.71–73.

48. Thomas J. Hopkins, *The Hindu Religious Tradition,* Encino California: Dickenson Publishers, 1971, p. 129.

CHAPTER THREE

1. This story or some reference to it is found in at least six of the major purāṇas, the *Liṅga, Śiva, Viṣṇu, Bhagavata, Brahma, and Brahmavaivarta,* as well as in the *Harivamśa. Harivamśa* 99.1–49, edited by P. L. Vaidya, Poona: Bhandarkar Oriental Institute, 1969. *Viṣṇu Purāṇa* Bombay: Oriental Press, 18ll, 5.27.1–31. Also, Cornelia Dimmitt & J. A. B. van Buitenen, editors and translators of *Classical Hindu Mythology,* Philadelphia: Temple University Press, 1978. pp. 141–142. *Bhāgavata Purāṇa,* Bombay: Veṇkaṭeśvara Press, 1830, 1908. "Harivaradā Skandha" X, chapter 55. *Brahma Purāṇa* Bombay: Veṇkaṭeśvara Press, 1906, 1963. 91.13–42; *Śiva Purāṇa,* Bombay: Veṇkaṭeśvara Press, 1906. Rudrasamhitā (II). Pārvatīkhaṇḍa (3).19.38–44; *Brahmavaivarta Purāṇa* Bombay: Veṇkaṭeśvara Press, 1908. Kṛṣṇajanmakhaṇḍa 112.11–32a.

2. *Liṇga Purāṇa,* Bombay: Veṇkaṭeśvara Press, 1924, 1966. I.101.44–45a.

3. *Śiva Purāṇa,* Bombay: Veṇkaṭeśvara Press, 1906, Rudrasamhitā (II). Pārvatīkhaṇḍa (3).19.38–44.

4. *Bhāgavata Purāna,* tenth skandha, chapters 103–108.

5. The episode recounted in the *Viṣṇu Purāṇa* is virtually identical to that in the *Brahma Purāṇa.*

6. *The Harivamśa* critically edited by P. L. Vaidya, vol. II, Appendix I, Poona: BORI, 1971, no. 30, lines 1–419, pp. 364–379.

7. *Viṣṇu Purāṇa* 27.3: sughore makarālaye.

8. See Joel Chandler Harris's "The Wonderful Tar Baby Story," *Uncle Remus, His Songs and His Sayings,* New York: Appleton and Co., 1895.

9. The Indian philosophical tradition speaks of six sense organs: sight, smell, hearing, taste, touch, and mind. The mind is understood to process the information sent by the other five sense organs.

10. *Harivamśa* Appendix 1, no. 30, lines 267–274, p. 374.

11. Rocher, *The Purāṇas,* p. 163. "The *Brahmavaivarta Purāṇa* is generally recognized as one of the more recent puranas. Both the 15th and the 16th centuries have been proposed for the transformation into its present form, from an older version belonging to the 10th century."

12. This detail is not included in the *Harivamśa* version but is fully narrated in the *Bhāgavata* and *Viṣṇu Purāṇas.*

13. *Bhāgavata Purāṇa* X.55.8a.

14. *Brahmavaivarta Purāṇa* Kṛṣṇajanmakhaṇḍa 112.9

15. The clear parallel here is to the situation of Sitā in the *Rāmāyaṇa* after living with the demon Rāvaṇa for fourteen years. Sitā has to prove her purity before Rāma can

accept her again as his wife. Just as Rāma can accept her as his wife only if she has not been polluted by the touch of another man, so Kāmadeva can be reunited with Rati only if she has not been polluted by sleeping with Śambara.

16. *Harivamśa* 99.44a.

17. In the bhakti tradition of devotion to Kṛṣṇa, the god is portrayed as the divine lover who manifests himself to all who are devoted to him.

CHAPTER FOUR

1. *Skanda Purāṇa,* Bombay: Veṇkaṭeśvara edition, 1867, 1910, 6.134.1–80. The story of Khaṇḍaśilā is found in a section of the purāṇa called the "Śrīhāṭakeśvarakṣetra Māhātmya" or "In praise of the Hāṭakeśvara Tīrtha," a Śaivite shrine on the banks of the Godāvarī River. Māhātmyas are devotional texts written to explain why a particular location is associated with the sacred. The Hāṭakeśvara tīrtha is known both for its Kāmeśvara Liṅgam and the Saubhāgya Kūpikā (Auspicious Well) of Khaṇḍaśilā.

2. Rocher in *The Purāṇas,* p. 233–34, notes that the Hāṭakeśvarakṣetra Māhātmya demonstrates some Gujarati influence and seems to date from the seventeenth century.

3. *Pūrṇakalā* means she who is full of digits or time periods, an epithet of the moon.

4. *Khaṇḍaśilā* is a name meaning "broken rock" or "broken wifely conduct," an intentional play on words. *Śilā* (f) means "rock" while *śīla* (n) means "proper conduct," but both meanings are applicable.

5. A translation of the Sanskrit text is appended to the end of this chapter.

6. Guru dakṣiṇā is the fee given to a spiritual preceptor or teacher.

7. She was no longer mindful or conscious of her dharma as a wife.

8. The intended sexual symbolism is evident, as the man offers the blossoms and the woman the filaments of the red kumkum flower. The filament or stamen of the flower is the pollen-bearing organ of the flower. The origin of the word *stamen* is the Latin verb *stare,* meaning "to stand," cognate with the Sanskrit verb "to stand." Clearly the stamens are meant to represent male sexual arousal in this ritual.

9. *Brahmāṇḍa Purāṇa* 2.27; *Śiva Purāṇa* Dharmasamhitā II.1–12; *Padma Purāṇa* I.56.15–53; *Mahābhārata* XII 329.14; *Rāmāyaṇa* Bālakhaṇḍa 47–48.

10. Narayan, R. K. *The Rāmāyaṇa,* New York: Penguin Books, 1972.

11. According to the Valmiki *Rāmāyaṇa,* I.47.19, Ahalyā responded out of her lust for Indra.

12. *Yoni* is the female generative organ, often depicted with the lingam to represent divine procreative energy. But here the yoni is simply the female sexual organ. Indra is cursed to exhibit female genitalia so that no others will mistake his thoughts and intentions.

13. *Sāmba Purāṇa* 3.6–55. See R. C. Hazra, *Studies in the Upapurāṇas,* vol. I, pp. 36–41.

14. In the *Rāmāyaṇa* (63.11), a story is recounted of the apsaras Rambhā, who is cursed by the great sage Viśvāmitra. On Indra's orders, Rambhā has attempted to

seduce the sage. For this act, Viśvāmitra ultimately curses her to become a stone for 10,000 years.

15. A tīrtha is a shrine or sacred place of pilgrimage, often situated near a body of water such as a stream or river. Tīrthas may also be designated by a tree, particular stone, or location associated with gods or saints. Bathing in a tīrtha purifies and offers blessing.

16. *Matsya Purāṇa* 190.86–89; *Kūrma Purāṇa* 2.39.42–44.

17. The bright half of the lunar month is when the moon is waxing.

18. Apsarases are seductive celestial water nymphs who can assume different forms. Apsarases often seduce ascetics attempting to overcome desire. See chapter seven.

19. In this context, *dharma* is one's sacred duty, based on station and stage of life. For example, doing one's dharma as a wife or husband means upholding all the social and religious responsibilities of this relationship.

20. This stone motif parallels the image of Nandin, Śiva's bull, who is not fully aware while guarding Śiva's door. As a result, Nandin is cursed by Gaurī to be born from a mother who is lifeless [jaḍa], a rock. *Skanda Purāṇa* 1.2.27–58, 73a, 74–84; 1.2.28.1–14; 1.2.19.1–69a, 72b–81. Recounted by Wendy Doniger O'Flaherty in *Hindu Myths,* Baltimore: Penguin Books, 1975, pp. 258–260.

21. Wendy Doniger O'Flaherty, *Dreams, Illusion and Other Realities,* University of Chicago, 1984, pp. 234–237.

22. Wendy Doniger O'Flaherty, *Śiva, the Erotic Ascetic,* pp. 172–209.

23. Wendy Doniger O'Flaherty, *Hindu Myths,* pp. 143 and 144.

24. *Brahmāṇḍa Purāṇa* 1.2.27.1–64a, 91b–97, 101–23.

25. Interestingly, an epithet of Kubera as a marriage deity is Kāmeśvara, Lord of Desire, who is also three-legged like the Greek fertility god, Priapus. (E. Washburn Hokpkins in *Epic Mythology,* p. 148.) Kubera is further associated with Kāmadeva in a character called Naravāhanadatta, "given by Kubera," in the *Kathāsaritsāgara* who is said to be an incarnation of Kāmadeva.

26. *Śiva Purāṇa* Śatarudrasaṃhitā (III).8.36–66 and III.9.1–72. Summarized from translation by Wendy Doniger O'Flaherty in *The Origins of Evil in Hindu Mythology,* p. 281; and from the translation edited by J. L. Shastri, *Śiva Purāṇa,* pp. 1097–1110.

27. *Śiva Purāṇa* III.9.61–62.

28. Bruno Bettelheim, *The Uses of Enchantment,* New York: Alfred A. Knopf, 1976; William R. Bascom, "Four Functions of Folklore," *Journal of American Folklore,* vol. 67, 1954, pp. 333–349.

29. This place is the Haṭakeśvara Tīrtha, shrine of the Kāmeśvara Liṅgam.

30. "Body hair standing on end" is a stock description in classical Sanskrit literature of a person filled with uncontrollable emotion.

31. This is a reference to the *ardhanarīśvara* image, which is one body split vertically, half male, half female. *Ardhanarīśvara* is a popular form of Śiva and his consort.

32. Her name should be Ahalyā.

33. The use of the word *dharma* here conveys that even though Kāma is clearly seducing her for his own pleasure, he is also following his sacred duty. Kāma's dharma is to always instill desire in all beings.

34. The *dharmaśāstra* texts describe proper behavior, how to uphold one's dharma.

35. According to tradition, beings were understood to be generated in different ways, e.g., air-born, water-born, and sweat-born. The sweat-born are the very smallest insects.

36. The double entendre rests on Sanskrit word play. The word *śīla* with a long *i* means good conduct; while the word *śilā* with a short *i* and long *a* means rock.

37. Appropriately in the *Skanda Purāṇa,* the narrator is Kārtikeya-Skanda.

CHAPTER FIVE

1. A tīrtha, literally "crossing," is typically a sacred area near a body of water where people make offerings and perform devotional rituals.

2. *Matsya Purāṇa* 191.86 ff. and *Kūrma Purāṇa* II.41.43–45.

3. *Agni Purāṇa,* Vratakhaṇḍa,188.1 ff.

4. Ibid., 191.1–2; 178.1 ff.

5. A late-thirteenth-century CE text.

6. Hemadri, Caturvargacintāmaṇi volume I, II.2.S.834 ff, and III.2.S.63ff and III.2.S.618. Hemādri includes such rituals as the Kāmadevavrata from the *Viṣṇudharmottara Purāṇa,* the Madanamahotsava from the *Bhaviṣyottara Purāṇa,* the Kāmavrata from the *Padma Purāṇa,* and the Kāmatrayodaśi from the *Bhaviṣya Purāṇa.*

7. Two Marathi works, *Bhāratiya Saṃskriti Koṣa* and *Vrataśiromaṇi,* present descriptions of vratas and pūjās found in the purāṇas.

8. *Vrataśiromaṇi; Agni Purāṇa* 188.1; *Matsya Purāṇa* 7.1–29.

9. *Vrataśiromaṇi; Bhāratiya Samskriti Koṣa.*

10. *Matsya Purāṇa* 70.32 ff, and *Padma Purāṇa* I.23.73 ff.

11. *Matsya Purāṇa* 191.86 ff.

12. Six of twenty rituals substituted Viṣṇu for Kāmadeva, although Kāmadeva remained the primary deity of the pūjā.

13. Artemisia Indica; related to the mugwort. In Maharashtra when the damanaka, or davana in Marathi, blooms in Caitra, women wear the flower in their hair or place it in bath water, to enjoy its strong perfume. Such references to Kāma's flower continue to carry the connotations of the god's seductive charm, even in twenty-first-century India.

14. Four of twenty rituals substituted a damanaka plant for Kāmadeva.

15. *Padma Purāṇa* Uttarakhaṇḍa 86.1–35. Anandāśrama edition, edited by Mahadev Cimanaji Apte, 1894. Complete translation of the passage appears at the end of this chapter.

16. *Padma Purāṇa* Uttarakhaṇḍa 86.5–6.

17. Damanakotsava described in *Bhāratiya Samskriti Koṣa* and *Veṇkaṭācala Māhātmya* 9.23.24.; Kāma trayodaśi described in the *Vrataśiromaṇi.*

18. A female Sanskrit professor in India explained to me that no one (man or woman) would offer a pūjā to Kāma these days. Such worship would be in very poor taste. (Discussions in Pune, summer 1988).

19. A vrata is a vow to perform certain rituals or fasts to receive help from the deity.

20. *Padma Purāṇa* I.23.73ff, Guru Mandal edition; translation by N. A. Deshpande,; *Matsya Purāṇa* Kṛṣṇadvaipayanam edition, 1812, Ch. 70; translation by a Taluqdar of Oudh.

21. Jaggery is unrefined sugar, very dark in color with a strong flavor.

22. *Padma Purāṇa* I.24.126–127; *Matsya Purāṇa* 70.52. yathāntaram na paśyāmi kāmakeśavayoh sadā.

23. This mantra, well known through its recitation in many wedding rituals, suggests that the vrata creates a type of marriage between the prostitute and the brahmin.

24. This instruction for the brahmin to recite this mantra is found in the *Matsya* recension (70.54), but not in the *Padma.* Also *Atharva Veda* III.29.7.

25. Double entendre in Sanskrit alludes to *kāma* as deity and desire. Translation based on Whitney, *Atharva Veda Samhitā,* p.137.

26. *Padma Purāṇa* I.23.141–142.

27. *Bhaviṣya Purāṇa* Uttarakhaṇḍa 135.1ff, as cited in Sadashiv A. Dange, *Encyclopaedia of Puranic Beliefs and Practices,* New Delhi: Navrang Publishers, 1987, vol.II. p. 494.

28. Dange, vol. II, p. 495, referring to *Bhaviṣya Purāṇa* Uttarakhaṇḍa 135.30–32.

29. Frederique Apffel Marglin in *Wives of the God-King,* p. 113, notes that devadasis "like [the king], are intimately associated with auspiciousness in the form of good rains and crops." Though devadasis have a higher status than common prostitutes, this connection with fertility is interesting given that they do not produce heirs for the king.

30. R. C. Hazra, *Studies in the Upapurāṇas* vol. I, pp. 36–41. Summary of the story from *Sāmba Purāṇa* chapters 3–26. Wendy Doniger O'Flaherty in *The Origins of Evil,* p. 268, translates the story from *Samba Purāṇa* 3.6–55 and *Bhaviṣya Purāṇa* 1.72–73.

31. Hazra, *Studies in the Upapurāṇas,* vol. I, p. 38.

32. *Skanda Purāṇa* VI.127.1–20. Veṇkaṭeśvara edition.

33. Wendy Doniger O'Flaherty, *The Rig Veda,* London: Penguin Books, 1981, pp. 256–257.

34. *Śatapatha Brāhmaṇa* IV.1.5.1 ff. Margaret and James Stutley, *Harper's Dictionary of Hinduism,* p. 63; Wendy Doniger O'Flaherty, *Śiva, the Erotic Ascetic,* pp. 57–61.

35. For the full tale of Karṇotpalā, see translation and discussion in chapter one.

36. *Skanda Purāṇa* 1.2.27.58–73a, 74–84; 1.2.28.1–14; 1.2.19.1–69a, 72b–81. Doniger O'Flaherty, *Hindu Myths,* pp. 252–261.

37. *Skanda Purāṇa* 2.3.3.1–12. This section of the purāṇa is the māhātmya of present-day Badrinath, in the Himālayas, so the couples' tīrtha would be located in this area.

38. In Chicago, an Indian devotee of Lord Bālaji (Śrī Veṇkaṭeśvaramswamy) compiled a booklet of the "mantras that are common to all the Gṛhya Sūtras" for use during a proper wedding ritual. Using two English commentaries on marriage, a Tamil text called "Vivāha Mantrārtha Bhodini" by N. Gupta, and the Sanskrit *Apastamba Gṛhya Sūtra* edited by A. C. Sastri, Mr. R. Raghavan collected these mantras for use in marriage ceremonies performed in the United States. without a priest. One of the best known is *Atharva Veda* III.29.7, cited earlier in the description of the prostitute vrat.

39. P. V. Kane, *History of Dharmaśāstra,* vol. V, Part I, "Vratas, Utsavas and Kala etc.," p. 55.

40. Caitra is the spring month of March–April and is particularly associated with Kāmadeva.

41. The twelfth day of the bright half of the lunar month, as in other editions of the *Padma Purāṇa.*

42. Damanaka plant is Artemisia Indica, related to mugwort. The word *damanaka,* literally meaning "one who subdues or tames," can refer to a tamer of horses or a charioteer, but may also indicate one who is self-controlled, according to Monier-Williams. The *Skanda Purāṇa* mentions a demon called Damanaka killed by Viṣṇu in his Matsyāvatāra. This sea-demon was thrown on the earth, where he became a fragrant plant/flower through Viṣṇu's touch. Vettam Mani, *Purānic Encyclopaedia,* p. 195.

43. Commentaries and references to the damanakotsava in other texts refer to the damanaka as a symbol of both Kāmadeva and Viṣṇu. Emphasizing the Vaiṣṇava association, davana is also said to be offered to the god Rāma on Rāmnomi.

44. This prayer is written in the gāyatrī meter, common to many mantras recited in pūjās. Devoted to different deities, verses in gāyatrī meter have 24 syllables, eight in each foot. Dange, *Encyclopaedia of Purānic Beliefs and Practices,* vol. II, pp. 604–615.

45. Many of the epithets in verses 17 through 21 are traditional names of Viṣṇu, but here refer to Kāmadeva. Conversely, several of Kāmadeva's epithets may refer to Viṣṇu here, e.g., *viṣva mandana,* Confuser of All, and *sarva-bīja,* Seed/Source of All. Conflating the identities of Kāma and Viṣṇu is intentional here. In a Vaiṣṇava text, devotion to the god of desire appears more acceptable when he is presented as a multiform of Viṣṇu.

46. The madhuka is a mellifluous species of tree, probably Bassia Latifolia or Jonesia Asoka. Monier-Williams, *Sanskrit-English Dictionary,* p. 781.

47. Becoming more like a god, or more specifically like Viṣṇu.

48. A reference to the three puruṣārthas or aims of life: dharma, artha, and kāma.

CHAPTER SIX

1. In *History of the Upapurāṇas,* pp. 194–259, R. C. Hazra discusses the date of the *Kālikā Purāṇa.* Hazra postulates the existence of an earlier *Kālikā Purāṇa* composed in

the seventh century CE without Tantric influence, and a later one composed during the tenth or eleventh century. This later text is identified as the present *Kālikā Purāṇa.* But because the Kāma stories contain no Tantric content, they likely date from the seventh century CE. For location, see Hazra p. 232; van Kooij, p.3, note 4.

2. *Kālikā Purāṇa* Veṇkaṭeśvara Press, 1907. I.1.44–50, 53, 57–60.

3. *Ṛg Veda* 10.129.3–4. *The Rig Veda, an Anthology,* Wendy Doniger O'Flaherty, p. 25.

4. Franklin Edgerton, *Beginnings of Indian Philosophy,* p. 21.

5. The term "blind darknesses" [andhā tamānsi] indicates a particular division of hell.

6. *Atharva Veda Samhitā,* IX.2, translated by W. D. Whitney, pp. 521–525.

7. *Atharva Veda Samhitā* XIX.52, translated by W. D. Whitney, pp. 985–987.

8. *Hymns of the Atharva-Veda,* translated by Bloomfield, p. 102.

9. The word *uttuda* may reflect Kāma's association with male sexual arousal.

10. *Atharva Veda* III.25, translated by W. D. Whitney, vol. VII, pp. 130–131.

11. Arthur Berriedale Keith, *The Religion and Philosophy of the Veda and Upanishads,* Westport, Conn.: Greenwood Press, 1971, p. 18.

12. Keith, p. 19.

13. *Śatapatha Brāhmaṇa* in the Mādhyandina-Śākhā of the Śukla-Yajur-Veda I.6.2.7, New Delhi: Gurugangeśvara Granthamālā, 1972.

14. *Śatapatha Brāhmaṇa* 1.9.3.16.

15. *Śatapatha Brāhmaṇa* IV.3.4.32, translated by Whitney: ko'dā kasmā adāt kāmo'dāt kāmāyādāt; kāmodātā kāmaḥ pratigrahītā kāmai tat te iti

16. *Atharva Veda* III.29.7 reads: ka idam kasmā adāt kāmaḥ kāmāyādāt; kāmo dātā kāmaḥ pratigrahītā kāmaḥ samudramā viveśa; kāmena tvā prati gṛhnāmi kāmai tat te. See chapter five for reference to this verse in Hindu wedding rituals.

17. *Jaiminīya Brāhmaṇa* I.22–25. *Jaiminiya Brāhmaṇa* I, 1–65, translation and commentary by H. W. Bodewitz, Leiden: E. J. Brill, 1973, pp. 72–77.

18. *Jaiminīya Upaniṣad Brāhmaṇa* I.54. *Jaiminīya or Talavakāra Upaniṣad Brāhmaṇa,* Text, Translation and Notes, Hanns Oertel, *Journal of the American Oriental Society,* vol. XVI, New Haven: Tuttle, Morehouse & Taylor, 1896, pp.130–132.

19. Wendy Doniger O'Flaherty, *Tales of Sex and Violence, Folklore, Sacrifice, and Danger in the Jaiminīya Brāhmaṇa,* University of Chicago Press, 1985.

20. *Chāndogya Upaniṣad,* 1.1.7, Sanskrit text in *The Twenty-eight Upanishads,* edited by Vasudev Laxman Shastri Phansikar, Bombay: Tukaram Javaji, 1906.

21. *Bṛhadāranyaka Upaniṣad,* 1.3.28. Translation by Olivelle, *Upaniṣads,* p.13.

22. *Chāndogya Upaniṣad,* 1.7.8–9. Olivelle, *Upaniṣads,* pp. 103–104.

23. *Chāndogya Upaniṣad* 8.7.1. Olivelle, *Upaniṣads,* p. 171.

24. *Bṛhadāranyaka Upaniṣad,* 4.4.6. Olivelle, *Upaniṣads,* p. 65.

25. *Muṇḍaka Upaniṣad* 3.2.1. Olivelle, *Upaniṣads,* p. 275.

26. *Muṇḍaka Upaniṣad,* 3.1.10. Olivelle, *Upaniṣads,* p. 275.

27. Hume, *The Thirteen Principal Upanishads,* pp. 60–61.

28. Often portraying overzealous religious characters who follow the letter rather than the spirit of religious teachings, the novelist R. K. Narayan reflects this later Upaniṣadic attitude toward desire. Those who use religious practices for selfish purposes always seem to fall. See *Mr. Sampath,* which incorporates the story of Kāma into the framework of the novel.

29. *Mahābhārata* XII.161.2ff.

30. *Mahābhārata* XII.161.28 and XII.161.38a

31. *Mahābhārata,* I.164.5. Adi Parvan, edited by V. S. Sukthankar, Poona: BORI, 1933.

32. *Mahābhārata* I.61.66–67.

33. K. M. Ganguli says that verse 12.192.110 is obscure, but probably means that the situation has forced the king into accepting the gift, a position which should be that of the Brahmin. But the king then makes a gift of his own merits to the Brahmin, making both acts equal. *Mahābhārata,* translated by P. C. Roy (K. M. Ganguli), vol. IX, (part II), p. 67.

34. *Mahābhārata* 12.192.1–127 and 193.1–10.

35. *Mahābhārata* V.109.7 edited by Sushil Kumar De, Poona: BORI, 1940, p. 417.

36. *Mahābhārata.* This chapter was not included in the text of the critical edition but is found in Appendix I, no. 18, vv. 85–86a, p. 1040. *The Anuśāsana Parvan,* edited by R. N. Dandekar, Poona: BORI, 1966.

37. *Mahābhārata* XIII.84.11a, edited by V. S. Sukthankar, Poona: BORI, 1963.

38. *Manavadharmaśāstra* II.2–5. Wendy Doniger O'Flaherty and Brian K. Smith, *The Laws of Manu,* p. 17.

39. The same Kṛṣṇa is Arjuna's charioteer and spiritual teacher in the *Bhagavad Gītā.*

40. *Mahābhārata* 14.12.11–13. āśvamedhikaparvan, R. D. Karmarkar, Poona: BORI, 1960.

41. *Mahābhārata* 14.13.12–17

42. Elisabeth Benard, *Chinnamastā, the Aweful Buddhist and Hindu Tantric Goddess,* Delhi: Motilal Banarsidass, 1994, p. 106.

43. These are the *pañca tattva* or *five makāras* (acts beginning with *m*): *madya* (wine), *māmsa* (meat), *matsya* (fish), *mudrā* (parched grain), and *maithuna* (sexual union). Benard, *Chinnamastā,* p. 31; Kinsley, *Tantric Visions of the Divine Feminine,* p. 46.

44. See analysis of goddesses as "social anti-models" in Kinsley, *Tantric Visions,* University of California Press, 1997, pp. 233–252.

45. Kinsley, *Tantric Visions,* p. 251.

46. Ibid. p. 155.

47. Ibid. pp. 243–244.

48. See Benard, *Chinnamastā,* p. 29, for complete translation of the pīthapūjā section of the *Śākta Pramoda* quoted here.

49. J. A. B. van Buitenen, *The Mahābhārata,* pp. xxiii–xxv; Moriz Winternitz, *A History of Indian Literature,* pp. 396, 422–425. Didactic sections include Śānti and Anuśāsana Parvans, as well as large parts of the Adi, Vana, Udyoga, Strī, and āśvamedhika Parvans.

50. Goldman, *The Rāmāyaṇa of Vālmīki* vol. I: Bālakāṇḍa, Princeton University Press, 1984, pp. 14–23. Goldman traces the composition of the central *Rāmāyaṇa* to 750 to 500 BCE, with Books I and VII much later. Hopkins, *The Great Epic of India,* pp. 58–84, dates Books I and VII to the late second century CE.

51. "Cupid and Psyche," in Lucius Apuleius of Madaura, *The Metamorphoses or Golden Ass.*

CHAPTER SEVEN

1. Gopinatha Rao, *Elements of Hindu Iconography,* vol. I, part 1, p. 277.

2. Ibid.

3. The Sanskrit plural of the singular *apsaras* is *apsarās.* However, for the sake of English readers who find this form confusing, I use the anglicized plural *apsarases.*

4. *Ṛg Veda* X.123, 5.

5. *Manavadharmaśāstra* I.37. Cited in Stutley, p.16.

6. *Ṛg Veda* X.95.

7. In the story of Indra and Ahalyā recounted in the *Rāmāyaṇa,* Indra goes to great lengths to seduce another man's wife, a woman he finds irresistibly beautiful. When Ahalyā's husband catches him in bed with his wife (who has been tricked), he curses Indra to display his true nature for all to see: displaying a thousand vaginas on his body.

8. Stutley, p. 17.

9. *Viṣṇu Purāṇa* I.9.

10. *Viṣṇu Purāṇa* I.5.

11. *Taittirīya Samhitā* III.4, 8. Cited in Stutley, p. 16.

12. *Atharva Veda* XIV. 2, 9.

13. *Atharva Veda* IV. 38.1–4.

14. Though educated Indians today do not subscribe to the idea that widows are inauspicious, traditionally a widow was feared to bring ill fortune to any who came within her sight.

15. *Atharva Veda* XIV.2.35–36.

16. James G. Lochtefeld, *The Illustrated Encyclopedia of Hinduism,* New York: The Rosen Publishing Group, Inc. 2002, p. 427.

17. A contemporary novel addresses the painful choices suffered by a couple from different religious communities. Rohinton Mistry, *Family Matters,* New York: Knopf, 2002.

18. *Ṛg Veda,* X.86, 36; VIII.66, 5. Cited in Stutley, p. 90.

19. *Atharva Veda* IV.4.1.

20. *Taittirīya Samhitā* III.4, 8. Cited in Stutley, p. 90.

21. *Atharva Veda* III.25.6; VI.132.5.

22. Gopinatha Rao, vol. I, part 2, p. 529.

23. "Psittaciform," *Encyclopaedia Brittannica,* 2003. Encyclopaedia Britannica Online, accessed 17 June 2003. http://www.search.eb.com/eb/article?eu=108278

24. Conversation in India with Professor Brahmanand Deshpande of Marathwada University in Ellora, Maharashtra, January 2003.

25. Justin E. Abbott, translator, Dasopant Digambar: Translation of the *Dasopant Charitra, Poet Saints of Maharashtra* Series, no. 4. Pune: Scottish Mission Industries, 1927. pp. 58–59.

26. S. K. Ramachandra Rao, *Pratima Kosha,* vol. V, pp. 4–5.

27. Gopinatha Rao, vol. I, part 2, pp. 529–530.

28. The sea is called "the abode of makaras": *makarāvāsa, makarālaya, makarākara.*

29. Stephen Leatherwood, *Sierra Club Handbook of Whales and Dolphins,* San Francisco: Sierra Club Books, 1983, p. 282. http://www.geocities.com/darthdusan/river_dolphins.htm

30. Brian D. Smith, "1990 Status and Conservation of the Ganges River Dolphin, Platanista gangetica, in the Karnali River, Nepal," *Biological Conservation,* 66 (1993), pp. 159–169.

31. Alison Smith, "River Dolphins: The Road to Extinction," in *The Conservation of Whales and Dolphins, Science and Practice,* edited by Mark P. Simmonds and Judith D. Hutchinson. New York: John Wiley & Sons, 1996, ch. 14. http://www.geocities.com/darthdusan/river_dolphins.htm

32. Alison Smith, "River Dolphins: The Road to Extinction," p. 376.

33. R. K. Sinha and Samir Kumar Sinha, "Time Running Out for Ganga Dolphins?" July 2002, Clean Ganga Campaign. www.cleanganga.com

34. J. Ph. Vogel, "Errors in Sanskrit Dictionaries," *Bulletin of the School of Oriental and African Studies,* University of London, Volume 20, Issue1/3, 1957. *Studies in Honour of Sir Ralph Turner,* Director of the School of Oriental and African Studies, 1937–1957, pp. 561–567.

35. Pāli variants are the following Jātakas: *Vānarinda* (no. 57), *Sumsumāra* (208), Kumbhīla (224), and *Vānara* (342). The Buddhist Hybrid Sanskrit text is found in the *Mahāvastu Avadāna* II, 246–250. See reference and description in Sadhan Chandra Sarkar, *Studies in the Common Jātaka and Avadāna Tales,* pp. 102–103.

36. The Pāli word *sumsumāra* (baby-killer) is cognate with the Sanskrit *śiśumāra* (baby-killer) which usually connotes the Gangetic dolphin, the susu. However, the Pāli "baby-killer," *sumsumāra,* indicates a crocodile. The Rhys-Davids Pāli dictionary notes this discrepancy between the Sanskrit and Pāli "baby-killers," but maintains that the Pāli baby-killer is a crocodile rather than a river dolphin because crocodiles are much more likely to kill babies than river dolphins are. Though several Sanskrit-English dictionaries list *śiśumāra* as the Gangetic dolphin, Monier Williams includes *alligator* as one possible referent. Interestingly, the Pāli variants present a protagonist that never leaves the river

or becomes friends with the monkey, details more consistent with the exclusively aquatic nature of a river dolphin.

37. ZooGoer 31(6) 2002. Smithsonian National Zoological Park, November/December 2002. http://natzoo.si.edu/Publications/ZooGoer/2002/6/gharials.cfm

38. Indian wildlife website: http:www.india4u.com/wildlife/Crocodile.asp

39. "Makara-vaktra-damshtrān," meaning "from the tusk or tooth of/on the snout of a makara."

40. J. Ph. Vogel p. 563. Cited by Vogel as verse 4 of Bhartrihari's *Nītiśataka*. Barbara Miller, *Bhartrihari: Poems,* lists this poem as number 8 on p. 8.

41. See carved makara images at the Bhārhut stupa and Rāmeśvaram temple in S. K. Ramachandra Rao's *Pratima Kosha,* p. 4 (1).

42. Although gharials may be subject to this belief because of their unique narrow snout and ghara, crocodile species in other countries, including Venezuela, Colombia, Cuba, Australia, Japan, and the Philippines, are also hunted and sold for body parts thought to enhance sexual attractiveness or performance. Eating crocodile meat or drinking alcohol in which a crocodile penis has been soaked is believed to improve one's libido.

43. www.nationalgeographic.com/wildworld/profile/terrestrial/im/im0162.html; article by Adam Britton www.flmnh.ufl.edu/natsci/herpetology/brittoncroc/csp_ggan.htm

44. Personal e-mail, Mumbai, 5 July 2003.

CHAPTER EIGHT

1. Other āsravas are: bhava, "existence, continual rebirth"; avidyā, "ignorance" and dṛṣṭī, metaphysical speculation. Har Dayal, *The Bodhisattva Doctrine,* pp. 116–121.

2. *Dīgha-nikāya,* edited by T. W. Rhys Davids and J. E. Carpenter, vol I, p.156; *Majjhima-nikāya,* edited by V. Trenckner and R. Chalmers, vol.II, p. 39; *The Bodhisattva Doctrine,* translated by Har Dayal, pp. 121–2.

3. *Divyāvadāna,* edited by E. B. Cowell and R. A. Neil, Cambridge (England): The University Press, 1886, 37.29 ff.

4. *The Buddha-karita of Aśvaghoṣa,* edited from three mss. by E. B. Cowell, Oxford: Clarendon Press, 1893. Canto XI, vv. 35, 41–42.

5. The *Saundarananda,* edited and translated by E. H. Johnston, London: Oxford University Press, 1928; Edward Conze, *Buddhist Scriptures,* pp. 222–224.

6. *Jātaka* II, 92, no. 182. *The Jātaka,* edited by E. B. Cowell, vol. I, translated by Robert Chalmers, pp. 63–65; Henry Clarke Warren, *Buddhism in Translation,* pp. 269–274.

7. *Dhammapadāṭṭhakathā* I.9, commentary on *Dhammapada* 13 and 14. Eugene W. Burlingame, *Buddhist Legends,* Harvard Oriental Series, vol. 28, pp. 217–225.

8. *The Saundarananda of Aśvaghoṣa,* edited and translated by E. H. Johnston, pp. 20ff. Passages from the *Saundarananda* are from Johnston's edition and translation.

9. *Sneha* means "affection" or "friendship," but is derived from the verb *snih,* which also means "oily" or "adhesive like oil"—that is, love is like oil, not easily rinsed from skin.

10. *Jātaka* II. no. 182. *The Jātaka,* translated by Robert Chalmers, pp. 63–65.

11. E. W. Burlingame, *Buddhist Legends,* Harvard Oriental Series vol. 28, p. 225.

12. *Samyutta-nikāya, Majjhima-nikāya, Buddhacarita, Lālitavistara,* and *Mahāvastu.*

13. In early texts, *the bodhisattva* refers to Gautama before gaining enlightenment.

14. *Samyutta-nikāya* vol. I, pp. 115–116; translated. by J. W. Boyd, *Satan and Māra,* pp. 81–2.

15. *Mahāvastu,* vol. II, pp. 237–238; translated by J. W. Boyd, *Satan and Māra,* p. 83.

16. *Lālitavistara* 378.4; *Samyutta-nikāya* I, 124, calls the daughters "Tanhā" [craving], "Arati" [pleasure], and "Rāga" [passion]; Aśvaghoṣa names them "Rati," "Tṛṣṇā," and "Priti" [Love, Attachment] in the *Buddhacarita;* See also Etienne Lamotte, *Le Traité de la grande vertu de sagesse de Nagārjuna,* vol. II, pp. 880–881, notes 1 and 2.

17. *Samyutta-nikāya,* vol. II, pp. 226–227; reference in J. W. Boyd in *Satan and Māra,* p. 83.

18. *Mahāvastu,* vol. II, p. 410; *Lālitavistara,* 305; *Buddhacarita,* Canto XIII, v. 19; *Bodhisattvāvadāna-kalpalatā,* edited by S. C. Das and H. M. Vidyābhūṣaṇa, vol. I, p. 729.

19. Har Dayal, *The Bodhisattva Doctrine,* p. 313.

20. *Mahāvastu,* II, 283.4

21. *Lālitavistara* 130.8; Aśvaghoṣa's *Buddhacarita,* Canto XIII, v. 2; *Kṣemendra's Bodhisattvāvadāna-kalpalatā,* II, 583.61.

22. Alex Wayman, "Studies in Yama and Mara," *Indo-Iranian Journal,* III (1959), pp. 44 ff. and 112 ff.

23. J. W. Boyd, *Satan and Māra,* p. 75. See also "Mara Kills and Destroys," pp. 96–99.

24. *Mahāvastu,* vol. II, p. 407.

25. J. W. Boyd, *Satan and Māra,* p. 83.

26. T. S. Eliot associates death, memory and desire in *The Waste Land:* April is the cruelest month, breeding—Lilacs out of the dead land, mixing—Memory and desire, stirring—Dull roots with spring rain. ("Burial of the Dead")

27. *Aśokāvadāna,* edited by Sujitkumar Mukhopadhyaya, New Delhi: 1963, pp. 14–27; *Divyāvadāna,* edited by E. B. Cowell and R. A. Neil, pp. 356–364. For list of texts, see John S. Strong, *The Legend and Cult of Upagupta,* ch. 5.

28. *Aśokāvadāna,* edited by Sujitkumar Mukhopadhyaya, pp. 14–27. Although I have consulted the Sanskrit text for clarification of nuance, this translation is primarily from John S. Strong, *The Legend of King Asoka, A Study and Translation of the Aśokāvadāna,* Princeton University Press, 1983, pp. 184–197.

29. Strong, *Legend of King Asoka,* p. 186.

30. Ibid., pp. 188–189.

31. Ibid., pp. 190–91.

32. In a story from the *Śiva Purāṇa,* Rudrasamhita, Yuddhakhaṇḍa, 19.30–50, the King of the Daityas, Jalandhara, sends his messenger Rāhu to ask Śiva for the hand of Pārvatī. When Śiva hears the request, his rage becomes a monster who begins to devour Rāhu. As Rāhu runs in fear, he takes refuge in Śiva, who does indeed protect him from the wrathful monster.

33. Wendy Doniger O'Flaherty, *The Origins of Evil in Hindu Mythology,* p. 103.

34. John S. Strong, *The Legend and Cult of Upagupta,* pp. 102–104.

35. In the Indian tradition, dead bodies of humans and animals are understood to be polluting.

36. John S. Strong, *The Legend of King Aśoka,* pp. 195–196.

37. Ibid., p. 187.

38. John S. Strong, *The Legend and Cult of Upagupta,* p. 107.

39. Ibid., p. 116.

40. Cited in Strong, *The Legend and Cult of Upagupta,* p. 113; *Sīhaḷavatthuppakaraṇa,* p. 21 (French translation, Ver Eecke 1980:23).

41. Robert A. F. Thurman, *The Holy Teaching of Vimalakīrti,* pp. 37–39.

42. Ibid., pp. 54–55.

43. R. S. Gupte, *Iconography of the Hindus, Buddhists, and Jains,* pp. 127–28. These figures are: Dharmadhātu Vāgiśvara, Vajrānaṅga, Mañjuvara, Mañjuvajra, Mañjukumāra, Arapacana, Sthiracakra, Vādirāt, and possibly Nāmasamgiti Mañjuśrī.

44. A compound of *vajra* and *anaṅga. Anaṅga,* epithet of Kāmadeva, means "bodiless" or "invisible"; *vajra* means "thunderbolt," "diamond," or "impenetrable." In Vajrayana Buddhism, the vajra represents the adamantine state of emptiness, and insight.

45. B. Bhattacharyya, *Indian Buddhist Iconography,* pp. 114–115.

46. Pander, *Pantheon des Tschangtscha Hutuktu,* p. 61. Retold by Alice Getty in *Gods of Northern Buddhism,* pp. 152–53.

47. *Bhāgavata Purāṇa* 12.8–10; T. A. Gopinatha Rao, *Elements of Hindu Iconography,* vol. II, part 1, pp. 156–158; Wendy Doniger O'Flaherty, *Origins of Evil in Hindu Mythology,* pp. 231–237.

48. *Sādhana Māla* 59 and 60.

49. *Sādhana Māla* 59 and 60; Bhattacharyya, *Indian Buddhist Iconography,* p. 115.

50. *Practices of the Noble Tara Kurukullā,* translated by Ts'utr'im jewa, a disciple of Atiṣa; *ārya-tāra-kukukulle-kalpa,* p. 76, vol. 3, 148.2.5–154.2.2, Rgyud CA 30a–45b.

51. Stephen Beyer, *The Cult of Tara,* University of California Press, 1973, pp. 303–304 and p. 496, note 80.

52. *Jewel Ornament of Liberation,* translated by Herbert V. Guenther, pp. xiii–xiv.

53. C. Trungpa and H. V. Guenther, The *Dawn of Tantra,* pp. 28–30.

54. *Ratnamegha Sutra, Śikṣāsamuccaya, The Buddhist Tradition,* W. T. deBary, ed., p. 100.

CHAPTER NINE

1. *Śiva Purāṇa,* Veṇkaṭeśvara edition, Rudrasamhitā (II). Satīkhaṇḍa (2).2.19–78.

2. Reference to male sexual arousal.

3. In modern Marathi, *vikṛta* indicates a man who is said to be sexually perverted.

4. Ananda Coomaraswamy, "Recollection, Indian and Platonic"; Karl Potter, ed., *Indian Metaphysics and Epistemology,* pp. 172–73, 219, 258, 297–98, 312–13.

5. Barbara Stoler Miller, *Theater of Memory,* p. 40; Raniero Gnoli, *The Aesthetic Experience According to Abhinavagupta,* text pp. 16 ff; trans. pp. 74 ff.

6. Barbara Stoler Miller, *ibid.*, pp. 39–40.

7. *Vāmana Purāṇa* 6.45.

8. *Brahmavaivarta Purāṇa,* Anandāśrama edition, Poona: 1935, Sṛṣṭikhaṇḍa 4.11.

9. S. A. Dange, *Encyclopaedia of Purānic Beliefs and Practices,* vol. II, pp. 672–673.

10. *Śiva Purāṇa* II.2.3.12.

11. *Matsya Purāṇa* 154.251–252.

12. *Śiva Purāṇa* II.3.20.1–23.

13. *Śiva Purāṇa* II.2.2.37–39.

14. *Śiva Purāṇa* II.2.3.40.

15. T. N. Madan, *Non-Renunciation, Themes and Interpretations of Hindu Culture,* pp. 72–100. Passages quoted are from pp. 90 and 94.

16. The three novels discussed are *Chitralekha* by B. Varma, *Samskara* by U. R. Anantha Murthy, and *Yayati* by V. S. Khandekar.

17. Madan, *Non-renunciation,* p. 98.

18. *Bhagavad Gītā* II.62–63.

19. Madan, *Non-Renunciation,* p. 98.

Bibliography of Sanskrit Texts

Āryamañjuśrīmūlakalpa, edited by Ganapati Śāstri, Trivandrum Sanskrit Series, in three volumes, (nos. 70, 74, 86), 1920–1925.

Aśokāvadāna, Sanskrit text compared with Chinese versions, edited, annotated, and partly translated by Sujitkumar Mukhopadhyaya, New Delhi: Sahitya Akademi, 1963.

Aśvaghoṣa's Saundarananda-kāvya, edited by E. H. Johnston, London, 1928.

Atharva Veda Saṃhitā, edited by W. D. Whitney, Varanasi: Chowkhamba Sanskrit Studies, vol. 20, second edition, 1962 (original 1856).

Bhāgavata Purāṇa, Bombay, Veṇkaṭeśvara Press, 1830, 1908.

Bhaviṣyapurāṇam, edited by Srirama Sarma, Bareli: Sanskrit Institute, 1968–1969.

Bodhisattvāvadāna-kalpalatā of Kṣemendra, edited by S. C. Das and H. M. Vidyābhūṣana, 2 volumes, Calcutta: Bibliotheca Indica, 1888.

Brahma Purāṇa, Bombay: Veṇkaṭeśvara Press, 1906, 1963.

Brahma Purāṇa, Gurumandala Series no. 11, Calcutta: Manasukharāya Mora, 2 volumes, 1954.

Brahmāṇḍa Purāṇa, edited by J. L. Shastri, Delhi: Motilal Banarsidas, 1973.

Brahmavaivarta Purāṇa, Bombay: Veṇkaṭeśvara Press, 1908.

Bṛhadāranyaka Upaniṣad with commentary of Śankarācārya, Sanskrit text by Swami Madhavananda, Mayavati, Almora: Advaita Ashrama, 1934.

Buddha-karita of Aśvaghoṣa, edited from three mss. by E. B. Cowell, Oxford: Clarendon Press, 1893.

Chāndogya Upaniṣad, in *The Twenty-eight Upaniṣads,* edited by Vasudev Laxman Shastri Phansikar, Bombay: Tukaram Javaji, 1906.

Devī-Bhāgavata Purāṇa, Bombay: Veṇkaṭeśvara Press, 1919.

Dīgha-nikāya, edited by T. W. Rhys Davids and J. E. Carpenter, 3 vol., London: Pali Text Society, 1890–1911.

Divyāvadāna, edited by E. B. Cowell and R. A. Neil, Cambridge (England): The University Press, 1886.

Guhyasamāja Tantra, critically edited by B. Bhattacharyya, published as Gaekwad Sanskrit series, no. 53, Baroda: Oriental Institute, 1931.

Harivamśa, critically edited by Parashuram Lakshman Vaidya, Poona: Bhandarkar Oriental Institute, 1969.

Harivanshaparvan, edited by Ramachandrasastri Kinjawadekar, Poona: Chitrasala Press, 1936.

Jaiminīya Upaniṣad Brāhmaṇa, Text, Translation and Notes, Hanns Oertel, *Journal of the American Oriental Society,* vol. XVI, New Haven: Tuttle, Morehouse, & Taylor, 1896.

Kālikā Purāṇa, Bombay: Veṇkaṭeśvara Press, 1907.

Kālikā Purāṇam, edited by Sri Biswanārāyana Śāstri, Varanasi: Chowkhamba Sanskrit Series, 1972.

Kūrma Purāṇa, edited by Sri Anand Swarup Gupta, Varanasi: All-India Kashi Raj Trust, 1972.

Lālitavistara, edited by S. Lefmann, Halle: Waisenhauses, 1902–1908.

Liṅga Purāṇa, Gurumandala Series 16, Calcutta: Manasukharaya Mora, 1960.

Liṅga Purāṇa, Bombay: Veṇkaṭeśvara Press, 1924, 1966.

Mahābhārata, edited by Vishnu S. Sukthankar, 19 vol., Poona: Bhandarkar Oriental Institute, 1933–1959.

Mahāvastu, edited by E. Senart, Paris: Société Asiatique, Collection d'ouvrages orientaux, 1882–1897.

Majjhima-nikāya, edited by V. Trenckner and R. Chalmers, 3 vol., London: Pali Text Society, 1888–1899.

Mārkaṇḍeya Purāṇam, K. M. Banerjea, Calcutta: Bibliotheca Indica, no. 29, 1862.

Matsya Purāṇa, edited by Kṛṣṇadvapāyana Maharṣi Śrīvedavyāsa. Calcutta: 1812, 1890.

Matsya Purāṇa, Gurumandala Series 13, Calcutta: Manasukharaya Mora, 1954.

Muṇḍaka Upanisad, in *Eight Upanisads with the commentary of Śankarācārya,* by Swami Gambhirananda, Calcutta: Advaita Ashrama, 1966.

Padma Purāṇa, Gurumandala Series no. 18, edited by Shriman Maharshi Krishna Dwaipayan, Calcutta: Manasukharaya Mora, 1957.

Padma Purāṇa, Ānandāśrama edition, edited by Mahadev Cimanaji Apte, 1894.

Ramayuna of Valmeeki in the Original Sungskrit, edited by William Carey and Joshua Marshman, Serampore, 1806.

Rig-veda Samitā, Wilson, H. H., London: N. Trubner & Co., 1866.

Sāmba Purāṇa, Bombay: Veṇkaṭeśvara Press, 1885, 1942.

Samyutta-nikāya, edited by Leon Feer, 5 vol., London: Pali Text Society, 1884–1898.

Śatapatha Brāhmaṇa in the Mādhyandina-Śākhā of the Śukla-Yajur-Veda, New Delhi: Gurugangesvara Granthamala, 1972.

Saundarananda of Aśvaghoṣa, edited by E. H. Johnston, London; Oxford University Press, 1928. [Reprint of the 1928 text, Delhi: Motilal Banarsidass, 1975.]

Saura Purāṇa, Calcutta: 1816.

Śiva Mahā Purāṇam of Kṛṣṇadvaipāyana, Kasi: Paṇḍita Pustakalaya, 1963.

Śiva Purāṇa, Bombay: Veṇkaṭeśvara Press, 1906, 1965.

Skanda Purāṇa, Bombay: Veṇkaṭeśvara Press, 1867, 1910.

Skanda Purāṇam, Calcutta: Gurumandala Granthamalaya. Calcutta: Mansukharaya Mora, 1960.

Valmiki-Rāmāyaṇa, critically edited by G. H. Bhatt, Baroda: Baroda Oriental Institute, 1960.

Vāmana Purāṇa, edited by Sri Anand Swarup Gupta, Varanasi: All-India Kashi Raj Trust, 1968.

Viṣṇu Purāṇa, Bombay: Oriental Press, 1811.

Bibliography of Sanskrit Translations

[*Aśokāvadāna*] *The Legend of King Aśoka,* A Study and Translation of the *Aśokāvadāna,* by John S. Strong, Princeton University Press, 1983.

Atharva Veda Samhitā, translated by William D. Whitney, Harvard Oriental Series, Harvard University Press, 1905.

Bhāgavata Purāṇa, translated and annotated by Ganesh Vasudeo Tagare, Ancient Indian Tradition and Mythology Series, Delhi: Motilal Banarsidass, 1977.

Bṛhadāranyaka Upaniṣad with the Commentary of Śankarācārya, Sanskrit text and translation by Swami Madhavananda, Mayavati, Almora: Advaita Ashrama, 1934.

Bṛhadāranyaka Upaniṣad, in *The Thirteen Principal Upanishads,* translation by Robert Ernest Hume, Delhi: Oxford University Press, 1877, 1983.

Buddha-Carita of Aṣvaghoṣa, translated from the Sanskrit by E. B. Cowell, Oxford: Sacred Books of the East, vol. 14, 1894; reprinted New York: Dover Publications, 1969.

Buddhacarita or Acts of the Buddha, edited and translated by E. H. Johnston, Cantos I–XIV, two vol., Calcutta, 1935 and 1936.

Buddhist Legends, translated from the original Pali text of the *Dhammapada Commentary (Dhammapadaṭṭhakathā)* by Eugene Watson Burlingame, Harvard Oriental Series vol. 28, Harvard University Press, 1921.

Cāraka Samhitā, vol. I and II, translated by Ram Karan Sharma and Vaidya Bhagwan Dash, Varanasi: Chowkhamba Sanskrit Series, vol. XCIV, 1976.

Chāndogya Upaniṣad, in *The Thirteen Principal Upanishads,* translation by Robert Ernest Hume, Delhi: Oxford University Press, 1877, 1983.

Dhammapadaṭṭhakathā, translated from the Pali by Eugene Watson Burlingame, Harvard University Press, 1921 (Harvard Oriental Series, vol. 28).

Dimmitt, Cornelia and van Buitenen, A. B., editors and translators. *Classical Hindu Mythology,* Philadelphia: Temple University Press, 1978.

Enchanted Parrot, The: Selection from the "Śuka Saptati," translated by B. Hale Wortham, London: Luzac & Co., 1911.

Gaṇḍavyūha, translated by Jan Fontein in *The Pilgrimage of Sudhana,* Hague: Mouton & Co., 1967.

Hymns of the Atharva-Veda, translated by Maurice Bloomfield, Delhi: Motilal Banarsidass, 1964 (original 1897).

Jaiminīya Brāhmaṇa, translation and commentary by H. W. Bodewitz, Leiden: E. J. Brill, 1973.

Jaiminīya Upaniṣad Brāhmaṇa, Text, Trans. and Notes, Hanns Oertel, *Journal of the American Oriental Society,* vol. XVI, New Haven: Tuttle, Morehouse, & Taylor, 1896.

Jātaka, The, edited by E. B. Cowell, vol. I, translated by Robert Chalmers, London: Pali Text Society (reprinted London: Luzac & Co., Ltd., 1969).

Kālikā Purāṇa, part I in *Worship of the Goddess According to the Kālikāpurāṇa,* Leiden: E. J. Brill, 1972.

Kūrma Purāṇa, edited by Sri Anand Swarup Gupta, translated by Sri Ahibhushan Bhattacharya, et al., Varanasi: All-India Kashi Raj Trust, 1972.

Mahābhārata, The, An English version based on Selected Verses, Chakravarthi V. Narasimhan, Columbia University Press, 1965.

Mahābhārata, trans, P. C. Roy (K. M. Ganguli), Calcutta: Oriental Publishing Co., 1927–1932.

Mahābhārata, The, translated and edited by J. A. B. van Buitenen et al., University of Chicago Press, 1973–1978.

Mahāprajñāpāramitāśāstrā, called *Le Traité de la grande vertu de sagesse de Nagārjuna,* translated by Etienne Lamotte, 5 vol., Louvain, 1944, 1949, 1970, 1976, 1980.

Mahāvastu, translation into English by J. J. Jones, London: Routledge and Kegan Paul (Pali Text Society), 1973. [Sacred Books of the Buddhists, v. 16.]

Majjhima-nikāya, as *Further Dialogues of the Buddha,* Sacred Books of the Buddhists, vol. 5–6, London, 1926–1927.

Mañjuśrī-nāma Saṃgīti as *The Litany of the Names of Mañjuśrī: Text and Translation of the Mañjuśrī-nāma Saṃgīti,* translated by Ronald M. Davidson, in *Tantric and Taoist Studies,* edited by Michel Strickmann, Melanges Chinios et Bouddhiques, vol, 20, Bruxelles: Institut Belge des Hautes Études Chinoises, 1981, pp. 1–69.

Mārkaṇḍeya Purāṇa, translated by F. Eden Pargiter, Delhi: Indological Book House, 1969. (original Calcutta: Bibliotheca Indica, 1904).

Mārkaṇḍeya Purāṇa, translated by Manmath Nath Dutt, Calcutta: H.C. Dass, 1896.

Padma Purāṇa, Guru Mandal edition, and translation by N. A. Deshpande, Delhi: Motilal Banarsidass, 1988.

Pancatantra, translated by Patrick Olivelle, Oxford University Press, 1997.

Panchatantra, The, translated from the Sanskrit by Arthur W. Ryder, University of Chicago Press, 1956 (original 1925).

Rāmāyaṇa of Vālmiki, The, translated by Robert P. Goldman (vol. 1) and Sheldon I. Pollock (vol. 2) et al., Princeton University Press, 1984–1986.

Rigveda Brahmanas, edited by Charles R. Lanman, and translated by Arthur B. Keith, vol. 25, Harvard University Press, 1920.

Sādhanamālā, translated by B. Bhattacharyya for the Gaekwad's Oriental Series Series, no. 26 and 41, Baroda: Oriental Institute, 1925–1928.

Samyutta-nikāya as *The Book of Kindred Sayings,* 5 vol., London: Pali Text Society, 1918–1930.

Samyutta-nikāya, translation by J. W. Boyd in *Satan and Mara,* Leiden: E. J. Brill, 1974.

Śāntideva. *Śikṣasamuccaya,* translated by Cecil Bendall and W. H. D. Rousse, London: John Murray, 1922.

Śatapatha Brāhmaṇa, The, translated by Julius Eggeling, Sacred Books of the East, vol. 12, Oxford: Clarendon Press, 1882.

Saundarananda of Aṣvaghoṣa, translated by E. H. Johnston, London: Oxford University Press, 1932. [Reprint of the 1932 translation, Delhi: Motilal Banarsidass, 1975.]

Shuka Saptati, translated by A. N. D. Haksar, New Delhi: HarperCollins, 2002.

Vāmana Purāṇa, edited by Sri Anand Swarup Gupta, translated by Satyamsu Mohan Mukhopadhyaya et al., Varanasi: All-India Kashi Raj Trust, 1968.

Vatsyayana Mallanaga. *Kamasutra,* translated by Wendy Doniger and Sudhir Kakar, Oxford: Oxford University Press, 2002.

Vimalakīrtinirdeśasūtra, The Holy Teaching of Vimalakīrti, translated by Robert A. F. Thurman, University Park: Pennsylvania State University Press, 1976.

Worterbuch Zum Rig-Veda, trans, Hermann Grassmann, Wiesbaden: Otto Harrassowitz, 1955.

Bibliography of General Sources

Agrawala, P. K. *Skanda-Kārttikeya, a study in origin and development,* Varanasi: Banaras Hindu University, 1967.

Agrawala, Vasudeva S. *Matsya Purāṇa, A Study,* Ramnagar, Varanasi: All India Kashiraj Trust, 1963.

Agrawala, Vasudeva S. "The Meaning of Mahādeva," *Purāṇa,* vol. VII, no. 2, July 1965, pp. 291–299.

Agrawala, Vasudeva S. *Vāmaṇa Purāṇa, A Study,* Varanasi: Prithivi Prakashan, 1964.

Apuleius of Madaura. "Cupid and Psyche," Books 4, 5, and 6 from *The Metamorphoses or Golden Ass,* translated by H. E. Butle, Oxford: Clarendon Press, 1910.

Archer, William G. *The Loves of Krishna,* London: George Allen & Unwin Ltd., 1957.

Artola, George T. *The Banner of Kamadeva,* Bombay: Popular Prakashan, 1977.

Banerjea, J. N. *Development of Hindu Iconography,* Calcutta: University of Calcutta, 1956.

Banerjea, J. N. *Pauranic and Tantric Religion,* Calcutta: University of Calcutta, 1966.

Bascom, William R. "Four Functions of Folklore," *Journal of American Folklore,* vol. 67, 1954.

Basham, A. L. *The Origins and Development of Classical Hinduism,* edited by Kenneth G. Zysk, Boston: Beacon Press, 1989.

Basham, A. L., edited by Kenneth G. Zysk. *The Origins and Development of Classical Hinduism,* Boston: Beacon Press, 1989.

Basham, A. L. *The Wonder That Was India,* New York: Grove Press, Inc., 1954.

Bedekar, V. M. "The Story of Suda in the Mahābhārata and the Purāṇas: A Comparative Study," *Purana,* vol. VII no. 1, February 6, 1965, pp. 87–127.

Benard, Elisabeth Anne. *Chinnamastā, the Aweful Buddhist and Hindu Tantric Goddess,* Delhi: Motilal Banarsidass Publishers, 1994.

Bettelheim, Bruno. *The Uses of Enchantment, the Meaning and Importance of Fairy Tales,* New York: Alfred A. Knopf, 1976.

Beyer, Stephen. *The Cult of Tārā,* University of California Press, 1973.

Bharati, Agehananda. *The Tantric Tradition,* New York: Samuel Weiser, Inc., 1975.

Bhartrihari: Poems, translated by Barbara Stoler Miller, Columbia University Press, 1967.

Bhattacharyya, Benoytosh. *An Introduction to Buddhist Esoterism,* Varanasi: Chowkhamba Sanskrit Series Office, 1964. (Chowkhamba Sanskrit Studies, vol. XLVI).

Bhattacharyya, Benoytosh. *Indian Buddhist Iconography mainly based on the Sādhanamāla and other cognate Tantric texts of rituals,* London: Oxford University Press, 1924.

Bhattacharyya, Narendra Nath. *History of the Śakta Religion,* New Delhi: Munshiram Manoharlal, 1974.

Bhattasali, Nalini Kanta. *Buddhist and Brahmanical Sculptures in the Dacca Museum,* Dacca: Rai S. N. Bhadra Bahadur, 1929.

Blackburn, Stuart H. "Hanging in the Balance: Rama in the Shadow Puppet Theater of Kerala," in *Gender, Genre, and Power in South Asian Expressive Traditions,* edited by Appadurai, Korom, and Mills, Philadelphia: University of Pennsylvania, 1991.

Bloomfield, Maurice. *A Vedic Concordance (to lines),* Harvard Oriental Series, vol. X, Harvard University Press, 1906 (second edition 1964).

Bloomfield, Maurice. *The Religion of the Veda,* New York: G. P. Putnam's Sons, 1908.

Bloss, Lowell W. "The Taming of Māra: Witnessing to the Buddha's Virtues," *History of Religions,* vol. 18, no. 2, November 1978, pp. 156–176.

Blurton, T. Richard. *Hindu Art,* Harvard University Press, 1993.

Bonazzoli, Giorgio. "Seduction Stories in the Brahmavaivarta Purāṇa," *Purana,* vol. XIX, no. 2, July 1977, pp. 321–341.

Boyd, James. *Satan and Māra, Christian and Buddhist Symbols of Evil, Studies in The History of Religions,* vol. 27, Leiden: E. J. Brill, 1975.

Brown, W. Norman. *India and Indology,* selected articles, edited by Rosane Rocher, Delhi: Motilal Banarsidass, 1978.

Burlingame, Eugene Watson. *Buddhist Parables,* New Haven: Yale University Press, 1922.

Chakladar, H. C. *Social Life in Ancient India, a Study in Vatsyāyana's Kāmasūtra,* Calcutta: Susil Gupta, 1954.

Champakalakshmi, R. *Vaiṣṇava Iconography in the Tamil Country,* New Delhi: Orient Longman, 1981.

Chatterjee, Asim Kumar. *The Cult of Skanda-Kārttikeya in Ancient India,* Calcutta: Punthi Pustak, 1970.

Chatterjee, Dipankar. "Towards a Better Understanding of Indian Ethics," in S. S. Rama Rao Pappu and R. Puligandla, *Indian Philosophy Past and Future,* Delhi: Motilal Banarsidass, 1982. pp. 165–166.

Clothey, Fred W. *The Many Faces of Murukan, the History and Meaning of a South Indian God,* Hague: Mouton Publishers, 1978.

Conio, Caterina. "Relationship Between Symbols and Myths in the Cosmogonies of Mahāpurāṇa," *Purāṇa,* vol. XIX, no. 2, July 1977, pp. 257–282.

Conze, Edward. *Buddhist Scriptures,* New York: Penguin Books, 1979.

Coomaraswamy, Ananda. "Recollection, Indian and Platonic," *Journal of the American Oriental Society,* vol. 64, suppl. no. 3, 1944.

Coomaraswamy, Ananda. *Yakṣas, Essays in the Water Cosmology,* new edition edited by Paul Schroeder, Delhi: Oxford University Press, 1993.

Courtright, Paul. *Ganeṣa, Lord of Obstacles, Lord of Beginnings,* New York: Oxford University Press, 1985.

Cousins, L., ed. *Buddhist Studies in Honour of I. B. Hormer,* Dordresht, Holland: D. Reidel Publishing Co., 1974.

Dange, Sadashiv A. *Encyclopaedia of Purāṇic Beliefs and Practices,* New Delhi: Navrang Publishers, 1987.

Danielou, Alain. *Hindu Polytheism,* New York: Pantheon Books, Bollingen Series XIII, 1964.

Dasopant Digambar: Translation of the Dasopant Charitra, Justin E. Abbott, translator, *Poet Saints of Maharashtra* Series, no. 4. Pune: Scottish Mission Industries, 1927.

Dayal, Har. *The Bodhisattva Doctrine in Buddhist Sanskrit Literature,* London: Kegan Paul, Trench Trubner Co., Ltd., 1932.

deBary, William Theodore, ed. *Sources of Indian Tradition,* vol. I and II, Columbia University Press, 1958.

deBary, William Theodore, ed. *The Buddhist Tradition,* New York: Vintage Books, 1969.

Dehejia, Vidya. *Indian Art,* London: Phaidon Press Ltd., 1997.

de Mallmann, Marie Thèrése. *Étude Iconographique sur Mañjuśrī,* Paris: École Française de'Extrême Orient, 1964.

Desai, Devangana. *Erotic Sculpture of India,* Delhi: Tata McGraw-Hill Publishing Co., 1975.

De, Sushil Kumar. *Ancient Indian Erotics and Erotic Literature,* Calcutta: Firma K. L. Mukhopadhyay, 1969.

de Vries, Jan. *Heroic Song and Heroic Legend,* London: Oxford University Press, 1963 (original 1959).

Dictionary of Classical Mythology, The, edited by Pierre Grimal, translated by A. R. Maxwell-Hyslop, London: Basil Blackwell, Ltd., 1986.

Dimmit, Cornelia and J. A. B. van Buitenen. *Classical Hindu Mythology,* University of Chicago Press, 1979.

Dimock, Edward C. *The Place of the Hidden Moon,* University of Chicago Press, 1966.

Dimock, Edward C. *The Thief of Love,* University of Chicago Press, 1956.

Dodds, E. R. *The Greeks and the Irrational,* University of California Press, 1956.

Doniger, Wendy. *The Bedtrick, Tales of Sex and Masquerade,* University of Chicago Press, 2000.

Doniger, Wendy. Introduction to the *Kamasutra,* New York: Oxford University Press, 2002.

Doniger, Wendy. *Splitting the Difference: Gender and Myth in Ancient Greece and India,* University of Chicago Press, 1999.

Doniger O'Flaherty, Wendy. "The Symbolism of the Third Eye of Śiva in the Purāṇas," *Purāṇa,* vol. XI, no. 2, July 1969, pp. 273–284.

Doniger O'Flaherty, Wendy. "The Symbolism of Ashes in the Mythology of Siva," *Purāṇa,* vol. XIII, no. 1, January 1971, pp. 26–35.

Doniger O'Flaherty, Wendy. *Asceticism and Sexuality in the Mythology of Śiva,* Harvard University Thesis, 1968.

Doniger O'Flaherty, Wendy. *Dreams, Illusion and Other Realities,* University of Chicago Press, 1984.

Doniger O'Flaherty, Wendy. *Hindu Myths,* Baltimore: Penguin Books, 1975.

Doniger O'Flaherty, Wendy . *Śiva, the Erotic Ascetic,* Oxford University Press, 1973.

Doniger O'Flaherty, Wendy. *Orgins of Evil in Hindu Mythology,* University of California Press, 1976.

Doniger O'Flaherty, Wendy. *Other Peoples' Myths,* New York: Macmillan Publishers, 1989.

Doniger O'Flaherty, Wendy. *Tales of Sex and Violence,* University of Chicago Press, 1985.

Doniger O'Flaherty, Wendy. *The Rig Veda,* London: Penguin Books, 1981.

Dorson, Richard M. *Folklore: Selected Essays,* Indiana University Press, 1972.

Dubois, Abbe J. A. *Hindu Manners, Customs, and Ceremonies,* Oxford: Clarendon Press, 1924 (original 1897).

Dumezil, Georges. *Destiny of a King,* University of Chicago Press, 1973.

Dumont, Louis. *Religion/Politics and History of India,* Paris: Mouton Publishers, 1970.

Dundes, Alan. *Analytic Essays in Folklore,* The Hague: Mouton & Co., 1975.

Dundes, Alan. *Cinderella: A Folklore Casebook,* New York: Garland Publishing, Inc., 1982.

Dundes, Alan. *Interpreting Folklore,* Indiana University Press, 1980.

Dundes, Alan. *The Study of Folklore,* Englewood Cliffs: Prentice-Hall, 1965.

Dundes, Alan and Edmunds, Lowell. *Oedipus: A Folklore Casebook,* New York: Garland Publishing, 1983.

Eck, Diana. *Banaras, City of Light,* New York: Alfred A. Knopf, 1982.

Edgerton, Franklin. *Beginnings of Indian Philosophy,* Harvard University Press, 1965.

Edgerton, Franklin. *The Panchatantra,* London: George Allen & Unwin, Ltd., 1965.

Edgerton, Franklin. *The Panchatantra Reconstructed,* New Haven: American Oriental Society, vol. 2, 1924.

Eliot, Charles. *Hinduism and Buddhism, an Historical Sketch,* in three vol., London: Edward Arnold & Co., 1921.

Elwin, Verrier. *Tribal Myths of Orissa,* Oxford University Press, 1954.

Emmerick, R. E. *Tibetan Texts Concerning Khotan,* "Prophecy of the Li Country," London: Oxford University Press, 1967.

Epic Poems and Puranas, the Ramayana, the Mahabharata, the Vishnu Purana, Madras: Christian Literature Society for India, 1898.

Eschmann, Anncharlott et al. *The Cult of Jagannath and the Regional Tradition of Orissa,* Delhi: Manohar Books, 1978.

Fausboll, V. *Indian Mythology according to the Mahābhārata,* London: Luzac & Co., 1903.

Filliozat, Jean. *Political History of India, from the Earliest Times to the Seventh Century AD,* Calcutta: Susil Gupta, 1947.

Filliozat, Jean. *Un Texte de la Religion Kaumāra,* Le Tirumurukārrupatai, Pondichery: Institute Francais d'Indologie, 1973.

Fischer, Klaus. "Symbolism in Stupa Railing Reliefs: Coincidentia Oppositorum of Māra and Kāma," in *The Stūpa: Its Religious, Historical and Archaeological Significance,* edited by Anna Libera Dallapiccola in collaboration with Stephanie Zingel-Avé Lallemant, Wiesbaden: Franz Steiner Verlag, 1980.

Fontein, Jan. *The Pilgrimage of Sudhana,* Hague: Mouton & Co., 1967.

Foucher, Alfred. *Beginnings of Buddhist Art and Other Essays in Indian and Central Asian Archaeology,* translated by L. A. Thomas and F. W. Thomas, Paris: Paul Geuthner, 1917.

Foucher, Alfred. *Étude sur L'Iconographie Bouddhique de L'Inde d'apres des Textes Inédits,* vol. 1 and 2, Paris: Ernest Leroux, 1905.

Freud, Sigmund. *A General Introduction to Psychoanalysis,* New York: Pocket Books, 1953.

Gaster, T. H. "Myth and Story," *Numen,* vol. I, Fasc. 3, September 1954, pp. 184–212.

Geertz, Clifford. *Myth, Symbol, and Culture,* New York: W. W. Norton & Co., Inc., 1971.

Getty, Alice. *Gods of Northern Buddhism,* Oxford: Clarendon Press, 1928.

Ghosh, Juthika. *Epic Sources of Sanskrit Literature,* Calcutta: Sanskrit College, 1963.

Gokhale, B. G. *Indian Thought Through the Ages,* Bombay: Asia Publishing House, 1961.

Gold, Ann Grodzins. *Fruitful Journeys, the Ways of Rajasthani Pilgrims,* Prospect Heights, Ill: Waveland Press, 1988, 2000.

Goldman, Robert P. *The Rāmāyaṇa of Vālmīki* vol. I: Bālakāṇḍa, Princeton University Press, 1984.

Goldman, Robert P. "Fathers, Sons, and Gurus: Oedipal Conflict in the Sanskrit Epics," *Journal of Indian Philosophy,* Dordrecht, Holland: D. Reidel Publishing Co., vol. 6, no. 4, December 1978. pp. 325–392.

Gombrich, Richard F. and Margaret Cone. *The Perfect Generosity of Prince Vassantara, A Buddhist Epic,* Oxford: Clarendon Press, 1977.

Gonda, Jan. *Viṣṇuism and Śivaism, A Comparison,* University of London, Athlone Press, 1970.

Gordon, Antoinette. *The Iconography of Tibetan Lamaism,* Columbia University Press, 1939.

Gordon, Antoinette. *Tibetan Religious Art,* Columbia University Press, 1952.

Guenther, Herbert V. "The Indivisibility of Openness and Compassion," in *The Dawn of Tantra,* by H. V. Guenther and C. Trungpa, Berkeley: Shambhala, 1975.

Guenther, Herbert V. and Chogyam Trungpa. *The Dawn of Tantra,* Berkeley: Shambhala, 1975.

Guenther, Herbert V. *The Life and Teaching of Naropa,* Oxford: Clarendon Press, 1963.

Guenther, Herbert V. *The Tantric View of Life,* Boulder: Shambhala, 1976.

Guenther, Herbert V. translator and editor. *The Jewel Ornament of Liberation,* by S. Gam. Po. Pa., Berkeley: Shambhala, 1971.

Gupta, Dharmendra Kumar. "The Purāṇic Hindu Theological System in Seventh Century India," *Purāṇa,* vol. XX, no. 2, July 20, 1978, pp. 224–245.

Gupta, Shakti M. *Loves of Hindu Gods and Sages,* Bombay: Allied Publishers, 1973.

Gupte, R. S. *Iconography of the Hindus, Buddhists, and Jains,* Bombay: D. B. Taraporevala Sons & Co., Private Ltd., 1972.

Haberman, David L. *Journey Through the Twelve Forests, An Encounter with Krishna,* Oxford University Press, 1994.

Haldar, J. R. *Early Buddhist Mythology,* Delhi: Manohar Book Service, 1977.

Handelman, Don and David Shulman. *God Inside Out,* Oxford University Press, 1997.

Hawley, John Stratton and Donna Marie Wulff. *The Divine Consort,* Boston: Beacon Press, 1986.

Hazra, R. C. *History of the Upapurāṇas,* vol. 2, Calcutta: Sanskrit College, 1963.

Hazra, R. C. "The Problems Relating to the *Śiva Purāṇa,*" *Our Heritage,* vol. 1, 1953. p. 67. Hazra, R. C. *Studies in the Purāṇic Records on Hindu Rites and Customs,* Dacca University, 1940, p. 91 (Reprint Delhi: Motilal Banarsidas, 1975).

Hazra, R. C. *Studies in the Upapurāṇas,* Calcutta: Calcutta Sanskrit College Research Series, nos. 2 and 22, vol. 1, 1958; vol. 2, 1963.

Heifetz, Hank. *The Origin of the Young God: Kālidāsa's Kumārasambhava,* University of California Press, 1985.

Hiltebeitel, Alf. *The Ritual of Battle, Krishna in the Mahābhārata,* Cornell University Press, 1976.

Hodgson, Brian H. *Essays on the Languages, Literature and Religion of Nepal and Tibet* (1874), reprinted Varanasi: Bharat-Bharati, 1971.

Honti, Janas. *Studies in Oral Epic Tradition,* Budapest: Akademiai Kiado, 1975.

Hopkins, E. Washburn. *Epic Mythology,* New York: Biblo and Tannen, 1969 (original 1915).

Hopkins, E. Washburn. *The Great Epic of India,* New York: Charles Scribner's Sons, 1901.

Hopkins, Thomas. *The Hindu Religious Tradition,* Encino, California: Dickenson Publishers, 1971.

Ingalls, Daniel H. H. "Dharma and Mokṣa," *Philosophy East and West,* vol. VII, April–July 1957, pp. 41–49.

Jung, C. G. and C. Kerenyi. *Essays on a Science of Mythology,* Bollingen Series XXII, New York: Pantheon Books, 1949.

Jung, C. G. *Psyche and Symbol,* edited by Violet S. de Laszlo, Garden City, New York: Doubleday & Co., 1958.

Jung, C. G. *The Archetypes and the Collective Unconscious,* vol. 9.i of *The Collected Works of C. G. Jung,* Bollingen Series XX, Princeton University Press, 1959.

Kakar, Sudhir and John Munder Ross. *Tales of Love, Sex, and Danger,* New York: Basil Blackwell, 1987.

Kakar, Sudhir. "Aggression in Indian Society: An Analysis of Folk-Tales," *Indian Journal of Psychology,* vol. 49, part 2, January 1974, pp. 119–126.

Kakar, Sudhir. *The Ascetic of Desire, A Novel of the Kamasutra,* Woodstock, N.Y.: The Overlook Press, 2000.

Kakar, Sudhir. *Identity and Adulthood,* Delhi: Oxford University Press, 1979.

Kakar, Sudhir. *Shamans, Mystics, and Doctors,* New York: Alfred A. Knopf, 1982.

Kane, P. V. "Origin and Development of Purāṇa Literature," *History of Dharmaśāstra,* vol. 5, part 2, Poona: Bhandarkar Oriental Research Insititute, 1962, pp. 895–896.

Kane, P. V. *History of Dharmaśāstra,* nine volumes, Poona: Bhandarkar Oriental Research Institute, second edition, 1968.

Keith, Arthur Berriedale. "Indian Mythology," in *The Mythology of All Races (in 13 volumes),* vol. VI, edited by Louis Herbert Gray, Boston: Marshall Jones Co., 1917.

Keith, Arthur Berriedale. *The Religion and Philosophy of the Veda and Upanishads,* Westport, Conn.: Greenwood Press, 1971 (original Harvard University Press, 1925).

Kinsley, David. *Hindu Goddesses,* University of California Press, 1988.

Kinsley, David. *Tantric Visions of the Divine Feminine: The Ten Mahāvidyās,* University of California Press, 1997.

Kirk, G. S. *Myth, Its Meaning and Function in Ancient and Other Cultures,* Cambridge University Press, 1970.

Kirk, James A. *Stories of the Hindus,* New York: Macmillan Co., 1972.

Konow, Sten and Paul Tuxen. *The Religions of India,* Copenhagen: G. E. C. Gad Publishers, 1940.

Konow, Sten. "Ananga, the Bodiless Cupid," in *Antidoron, Festschrift Jacob Wackernagel,* Gottingen: Dandenhoed and Ruprecht, 1923, pp. 1–8.

Kramrisch, Stella. *Manifestations of Shiva,* Philadelphia Museum of Art, 1981.

Kramrisch, Stella. *The Presence of Śiva,* Princeton University Press, 1981.

Lalou, Marcelle. *Iconographie des Étoffes Peintes (Pata) dans le Mañjuśrī mūlakalpa,* Paris: Librarie Orientaliste Paul Geuthner, 1930.

LaMotte, Etienne. "Mañjuśrī," *T'oung Pao,* vol. XLVIII, Leiden: E. J. Brill, 1960, pp. 1–96.

LaMotte, Etienne. "Passions and Impregnations of the Passions in Buddhism," in *Buddhist Studies in Hounour of I. B. Horner,* edited by L. Cousins et. al., Dordrecht-Holland: D. Reidel Publishing Co., 1974, pp. 91–104.

Leach, Edmund R., ed. *Dialectic in Practical Religion,* Cambridge Papers in Social Anthropology, no. 5, Cambridge University Press, 1968.

Leatherwood, Stephen. *The Sierra Club Handbook of Whales and Dolphins,* San Francisco: Sierra Club Books, 1983.

Lochtefeld, James G. *The Illustrated Encyclopedia of Hinduism,* New York: The Rosen Publishing Group, Inc., 2002.

Macdonell, Arthur A. *Vedic Mythology,* Delhi: Motilal Banarsidass, 1898.

Madan, T. N. *Non-renunciation: Themes and interpretations of Hindu culture,* New York: Oxford University Press, 1987.

Magnusson, William E. "Crocodiles & Alligators," *Encyclopedia of Reptiles & Amphibians,* edited by Harold G. Cogger and Richard G. Zweifel, San Diego: Academic Press, 1998.

Maranda, Pierre and Elli Kongas Maranda, ed. *Structural Analysis of Oral Tradition,* Philadelphia: University of Pennsylvania Press, 1971.

Marglin, Frederique Apffel. *Wives of the God-King,* Delhi: Oxford University Press, 1985.

Martin, E. Osborn. *The Gods of India,* Delhi: Indological Book House, 1972 (original 1913).

Mehta, P. D. *Early Indian Religious Thought,* London: Luzac & Co., Ltd., 1956.

Mehta, R. N. "Purāṇic Archaeology," *Journal of the University of Baroda* 20–21, 1971–1972.

Meyer, Johann Jakob. *Sexual Life in Ancient India, a study in the comparative history of Indian culture,* New York: Barnes & Noble, Inc., 1953.

Michell, George. *Hindu Art and Architecture,* London: Thames & Hudson, 2000.

Miller, Barbara Stoler. "Kālidāsa's World and His Plays," in *Theater of Memory,* edited by Barbara Stoler Miller, Columbia University Press, 1984, p. 39.

Mistry, Rohinton. *Family Matters,* N.Y.: Knopf, 2002.

Monier-Williams, Monier. *A Sanskrit-English Dictionary,* Oxford: Clarendon Press, 1899, 1976.

Monier-Williams, Monier. *Religious Thought and Life in India,* London: John Murray, 1883.

Moor, Edward. *Hindu Pantheon,* Varanasi: Indological Book House, 1968 (original London: J. Johnson Publishers, 1864).

Mukhopadhyaya, Anjali. "Traditional Lore Regarding Mañjuśrī," *Adyar Library Bulletin,* vol. XVIII, parts 3–4, December 1954, pp. 27–36.

Nagaswamy, R. *Tantric Cult of South India,* Delhi: Agam Kala Prakashan, 1982.

Naravane, V. S. *Stories from the Indian Classics,* New York: Asia Publishing House, 1962.

Narayan, Kirin. *Mondays on the Dark Night of the Moon,* New York: Oxford University Press, 1997.

Narayan, R. K. *Mr. Sampath,* London: Eyre & Spottiswoode, 1949.

Narayan, R. K. *The Ramayana,* New York: Penguin Books, 1972.

Nyanatiloka. *Buddhist Dictionary: Manual of Buddhist Terms and Doctrines,* Third edition revised and enlarged by Nyanaponika, Colombo, Ceylon: Frewin & Co., Ltd., 1972.

Obeyesekere, Gananath. *The Cult of the Goddess Pattini,* University of Chicago Press, 1984.

Oman, John Campbell. *The Great Indian Epics,* London: George Bell & Sons, 1894.

Pargiter, F. E. *Purāṇic Texts of the dynasties of the Kali Age,* London: Oxford University Press, 1913.

Potter, Karl H. *Presuppositions of India's Philosophies,* Englewood Cliffs, N.J.: Prentice-Hall, Inc., 1963.

Preston, James J. *Cult of the Goddess, Social and Religious Change in a Hindu Temple,* New Delhi: Vikas Publishing House, 1980.

Pusalker, A. D. *Studies in the Epics and Purāṇas,* Chaupatty, Bombay: Bharatiya Vidya Bhavan, 1955.

Radhakrishnan, Sarvepalli and Charles A. Moore. *A Sourcebook in Indian Philosophy,* Princeton University Press, 1957.

Raghavan, V. "The Kālikā Purāṇa, Kālidāsa, and Magha," in the *Woolner Commemoration Volume,* edited by Mohammed Shafi, Lahore: Mehar Chand Lacchman Das, 1940, pp. 191–195.

Ramanujan, A. K. "The Indian Oedipus," Indian Literature, Proceedings of a Seminar, edited by Arabinda Poddar, Simla: Indian Institute of Advanced Study, 1972.

Rao, Gopinatha. *Elements of Hindu Iconography,* four vol., Madras: Law Printing House, 1916.

Rao, S. K. Ramachandra. *Pratima Kosha, Encyclopaedia of Indian Iconography,* Bangalore: Kalpatharu Research Academy, 1988.

Rawlinson, H. G. *India, A Short Cultural History,* New York: Frederick A. Praeger, 1952.

Rhys-Davids, T. W. and William Stede. *The Pali Text Society's Pali-English Dictrionary,* London: Luzac & Co. Ltd., 1966 (first published 1921–1925).

Robinson, Richard H. and Willard L. Johnson. *The Buddhist Religion, A Historical Introduction,* second edition, Encino, Calif.: Dickenson Publishing Co., 1977; third edition, Belmont, Calif.: Wadsworth Publishing Co., 1982.

Rocher, Ludo. *The Purāṇas,* vol. II of *A History of Indian Literature,* edited by Jan Gonda, Wiesbaden: Otto Harrassowitz, 1986.

Sahi, Jyoti. *The Child and the Serpent, Reflections on Popular Indian Symbols,* London: Routledge & Kegan Paul, 1980.

Sarkar, Sadhan Chandra. *Studies in the Common Jātaka and Avadāna Tales,* Calcutta Sanskrit College Research Series No. CXXXVII, studies no. 86, Calcutta: Sanskrit College, 1990.

Scholes, Robert and Robert Kellogg. *Nature of Narrative,* New York: Oxford University Press, 1966.

Sharma, Chandradhar. *A Critical Survey of Indian Philosophy,* Delhi: Motilal Banarsidas, 1976.

Shastri, Haraprasad. *A Catalogue of Palm-Leaf and Selected Manuscripts in the Government Collection under the care of the Asiatic Society of Bengal,* Calcutta: ASB, vol.V, 1928, pp. clxxxii–clxxxiii.

Shulman, David Dean. *Tamil Temple Myths, Sacrifice and Divine Marriage in the South Indian Śaiva Tradition,* Princeton University Press, 1980.

Siegel, Lee. *Fires of Love, Waters of Peace, Passion and Renunciation in Indian Culture,* University of Hawaii Press, 1983.

Singer, Milton, ed. *Krishna, Myths, Rites, and Attitudes,* University of Chicago Press, 1966.

Sircar, D. C. *Seminar on the Origin of the Śaktī Cult and Tārā,* April 1965, Calcutta University Press, 1967.

Slusser, Mary Shepherd. *Nepal Mandala,* Princeton University Press, 1982.

Smith, Alison. "The River Dolphins: The Road to Extinction," in *The Conservation of Whales and Dolphins, Science and Practice,* edited by Mark P. Simmonds and Judith D. Hutchinson. N.Y.: John Wiley & Sons, 1996.

Smith, Brian D. "1990 Status and Conservation of the Ganges River Dolphin, Platanista gangetica, in the Karnali River, Nepal," *Biological Conservation,* 66 (1993).

Smith, William. *A Dictionary of Greek and Roman Biography and Mythology,* vol. II, London: John Murray, 1876.

Snellgrove, David. *Indo-Tibetan Buddhism,* Boston: Shambhala Press, 1987.

Staal, Frits. *Agni: The Vedic Ritual of the Fire Altar,* Berkeley: Asian Humanities Press, 1983.

Steel, Flora Annie. *A Tale of Indian Heroes,* London: Hutchinson & Co., 1923.

Sternback, Ludwik. "The Katha Literature and the Purāṇas," *Purāṇa,* vol. VII, no. 1, February 6, 1965, pp. 19–86.

Strong, John S. *The Legend and Cult of Upagupta,* Princeton University Press, 1992.

Strong, John S. *The Legend of King Aśoka,* Princeton University Press, 1983.

Studies in Honor of Maurice Bloomfield, by a group of his pupils, Yale University Press, 1920.

Stutley, Margaret and James. *Harper's Dictionary of Hinduism,* San Francisco: Harper & Row, 1977, 1984.

Sukthankar, V. S. *Critical Studies in the Mahābhārata,* Bombay: Karnatak Publishing House, 1944.

Suryakanta. *Kālidāsa's Vision of Kumārasambhava,* Delhi: Mehar Chand Lacchman Das, 1963.

Sutherland, Gail Hinch. *The Disguises of the Demon, the development of the Yakṣa in Hinduism and Buddhism,* State University of New York Press, 1991.

Thomas, E. J. *Life of the Buddha as Legend and History,* London: Routledge & Kegan Paul, 1949, 1975.

Thomas, F. W. *Tibetan Literary Texts and Documents Concerning Chinese Turkestan,* "Annals of the Li Country," London, Royal Asiatic Society, new series vol. 32, 1935.

Thornton, Bruce S. *Eros, the Myth of Ancient Greek Sexuality,* Boulder: Westview Press, 1997.

van Buitenen, J. A. B. "Dharma and Mokṣa," *Philosophy East and West,* vol. VII, April–July 1957, pp. 33–40.

van Kooij, K. R. *Worship of the Goddess according to the Kālikāpurāṇa,* Leiden: E. J. Brill, 1972.

Vogel, J. Ph. "Errors in Sanskrit Dictionaries," *Bulletin of the School of Oriental and African Studies,* University of London, vol. 20, Issue1/3, 1957. *Studies in Honour of Sir Ralph Turner,* Director of the School of Oriental and African Studies, 1937–1957.

von Franz, Marie Louise. *Interpretation of Fairy Tales,* Irving, Texas: Spring Publishing, 1978.

Waddell, L. A. "The Buddhist Pictorial Wheel of Life," *Journal of the Asiatic Society of Bengal,* vol. 61, part 1, Calcutta: Asiatic Society, 1893, pp. 131–155.

Warren, Henry Clarke. *Buddhism in Translations,* New York: Atheneum, 1976.

Wayman, Alex. "Studies in Yama and Māra," *Indo-Iranian Journal,* volume III, 1959.

Wayman, Alex. *Chanting the Names of Mañjuśrī: The Mañjuśrī Nāma-Samgiti,* Boston: Shambhala, 1985.

Wayman, Alex. *The Buddhist Tantras,* New York: Samuel Weiser, 1973.

White, David Gordon. *The Alchemical Body: Siddha Traditions in Medieval India,* University of Chicago, 1996.

Winternitz, Moriz. *A History of Indian Literature,* Calcutta: University of Calcutta, 1927.

Zaehner, R. C. *Hindu Scriptures,* London: J. M. Dent & Sons, Ltd., 1966 (original 1938).

Zimmer, Heinrich. *Myths and Symbols in Indian Art and Civilization,* N.Y.: Harper & Row, 1962 (original 1946).

Zimmer, Heinrich. *Philosophies of India,* Princeton University Press, Bollingen Series XXVI, 1951.

Zvelebil, Kamil Veith. *Tamil Literature,* vol. X, fasc. 1 of *A History of Indian Literature,* edited by Jan Ganda, Wiesbaden: Otto Harrassowitz, 1974.

Index

The letter *f* following a page number denotes a figure.